Feast upon the Words of Christ

Feast upon the Words of Christ

New Testament (JST)
Book of Mormon

Kenneth and Lyndell Lutes

Previously published under the title:
Words of Christ
Restored for the Last Days
by Lutes International

Revised second edition

Published by Lutes Publishing

Distributed by:
Brigham Distributing
110 S 800 W
Brigham City, Utah 84302
435.723.6611

Cover Art by Liz Lemon Swindle, used with permission

Cover Design: Kenneth Lutes Jr.
Page Layout and Design: Lyndell Lutes
Editing: Kenneth Lutes Sr.

ISBN: 978-0-9891710-1-4

1st Printing, 2013
PRINTED IN THE UNITED STATES OF AMERICA

Feast upon the Words of Christ
also available at Amazon.com on Kindle
ISBN: 978-0-9891710-0-7

Other books by Kenneth and Lyndell Lutes:
Joseph Smith Translation
ISBN: 978-1-56684-633-2
Joseph Smith Translation on Kindle
ISBN: 978-0-9891710-2-1

Contents

New Testament

Book of Mormon

Sources

New Testament

The words of Christ and the background information were extracted from the following book, which contains all of the corrections made by the Prophet Joseph Smith to the King James Version of the Bible:

Joseph Smith Translation
(Formerly, *The Bible Corrected by Joseph Smith*)
by Kenneth and Lyndell Lutes
Printed edition (ISBN: 978-1-56684-633-2) distributed by:
Brigham Distributing, 110 S 800 W, Brigham City, Utah 84302
435.723.6611

Book of Mormon

The words that Christ spoke when He visited the ancient inhabitants of America have been extracted from the modern translation of ancient records known as the:

Book of Mormon
[The Church of Jesus Christ of Latter-day Saints] Liverpool: 1879

Preface

"Judge not, that ye be not judged" is often quoted from the New Testament (Matthew 7:1). But is it true? The correct translation is, "Judge not **unrighteously**, that ye be not judged**; but judge righteous judgment**" (Inspired Version, Matthew 7:**2**). This book shows hundreds of corrections, in this fashion, so you can see them. Omissions and mistranslation of the Bible that made many scriptures difficult to understand have been restored and corrected, adding much clarity to gospel doctrine.

The Prophet Joseph Smith was called by God in our day to translate the Bible and restore many of the "plain and precious things which have been taken away" (1 Nephi 13:40). During the years of 1830 to 1833 the Prophet went through the entire Bible making inspired corrections, which clarify many of the teachings of Jesus Christ.

Even before the Prophet made corrections to the Bible, he was chosen by the Lord to translate other ancient writings into English. The record of God's dealings with the people of ancient America is known as the Book of Mormon. It includes the words that Christ spoke when He visited them after His Resurrection.

The scriptures are replete with exhortations to "hear" His teachings. This book greatly simplifies access to the words of Christ, as restored and corrected in the New Testament, as well as those spoken in ancient America. Using an easy reading, paragraph style, this work focuses on what Our Savior said. Now, one can "hear," without commentary, what Jesus Christ really taught while He was on the earth, as recorded in the New Testament and the Book of Mormon.

We testify that Jesus is the Christ and that His words lead to eternal life.

Kenneth and Lyndell Lutes

Introduction

Text shown in italic type is condensed from the King James Version of the Holy Bible, as corrected, and the Book of Mormon. It contains background and context information.

Words in regular typeface are the words that Jesus spoke while on earth, as recorded in the New Testament and the Book of Mormon. Hundreds of translation errors have been corrected in the New Testament.

Bold typeface indicates **restored text** and **corrections**, while ~~strike-through~~ shows selected ~~deletions~~. A few minor publication errors have been corrected in later editions of the Book of Mormon; the latest revisions are included and are marked with an asterisk (*).

Modern capitalization and spelling are used throughout. Minor changes in punctuation have been made to accommodate the change from verse to paragraph style.

Words of Christ According to Saint Matthew

Matthew 3

Baptism of Jesus

Then cometh Jesus unto John to be baptized of him. John ~~forbad~~ ***refused****, I have need to be baptized of Thee, and* ***why*** *comest Thou to me?*

Suffer **me to be baptized of thee,** for thus it becometh us to fulfill all righteousness.

And John went down into the water and baptized Him.

Matthew 4

Temptation of Jesus

Then Jesus ***was*** *led up of the Spirit, into the wilderness, to be ~~tempted of the devil~~* ***with God****. And when He had fasted forty days and forty nights,* ***and had communed with God,*** *He was* ***afterwards*** *an hungered****, and was left to be tempted of the devil.*** *The tempter said, If Thou be the Son of God, command that these stones be made bread.* ***Jesus*** *answered,*

It is written, Man shall not live by bread alone, but by every word that proceedeth out of the mouth of God.

The Spirit *setteth Him on* ***the*** *pinnacle of the temple.* ***The devil came unto Him and said,*** *If Thou be the Son of God, cast Thyself down, for it is written, He shall give His angels charge concerning Thee, and in their hands they shall bear Thee up, lest at any time Thou dash Thy foot against a stone. Jesus said unto him,*

It is written again, Thou shalt not tempt the Lord thy God.

And *again, ~~the devil~~* ***Jesus was in the Spirit, and it*** *taketh Him up into an exceeding high mountain, and showeth Him all the kingdoms of the world and the glory of them.* ***The devil said,*** *All these things will I give* ***unto*** *Thee if Thou wilt fall down and worship me. Then* ***said*** *Jesus unto him,*

Get thee hence, Satan; for it is written, Thou shalt worship the Lord thy God, and Him only shalt thou serve.

Then the devil leaveth Him. Jesus departed into Galilee. From that time Jesus began to preach,

Repent: for the kingdom of heaven is at hand.

And Jesus, walking by the sea of Galilee, saw Simon called Peter, and Andrew his brother, casting a net into the sea: for they were fishers. And He ***said*** *unto them,*

I am He of whom it is written by the prophets; follow me, and I will make you fishers of men.

And they, ***believing on His words,*** *left their* ***net****, and* ***straightway*** *followed Him.*

Matthew 5

Sermon on the Mount

Jesus*, seeing the* ***multitude****, went up into a mountain. His disciples came unto Him, and He taught them, saying,*

Blessed are they who shall believe on me; and again, more blessed are they who shall believe on your words, when ye shall testify that ye have seen me and that I am. Yea, blessed are they who shall believe on your words, and come down into the depth of humility, and be baptized in my name; for they shall be visited with fire and the Holy Ghost, and shall receive a remission of their sins.

Yea, blessed are the poor in spirit, **who come unto me;** for theirs is the kingdom of heaven. **And again,** blessed are they that mourn; for they shall be comforted. **And** blessed are the meek; for they shall inherit the earth. **And** blessed are **all** they **that** do hunger and thirst after righteousness; for they shall be filled **with the Holy Ghost**. **And** blessed are the merciful; for they shall obtain mercy. **And** blessed are **all** the pure in heart; for they shall see God. **And** blessed are **all** the peacemakers; for they shall be called the children of God. Blessed are **all** they **that** are persecuted for ~~righteousness'~~ **my name's** sake; for theirs is the kingdom of heaven. **And** blessed are ye when men shall revile you, and persecute you, and shall say all manner of evil against you falsely, for my sake. **For ye shall have great joy**, and be exceeding glad; for great **shall be** your reward in heaven; for so persecuted they the prophets which were before you.

Verily, verily, I say unto you, I give unto you to be the salt of earth; but if the salt **shall lose its savor**, wherewith shall **the earth** be salted? **The salt shall** thenceforth **be** good for nothing, but to be cast out, and to be trodden under foot of men.

Verily, verily, I say unto you, I give unto you to be the light of the world; a city that is set on a hill cannot be hid. **Behold**, do men light a candle and put it under a bushel? **Nay**, but on a candlestick; and it giveth light **to** all that are in the house. **Therefore,** let your light so shine before ~~men~~ **this world**, that they may see your good works, and glorify your Father **who** is in heaven.

Think not that I am come to destroy the law, or the prophets: I am not come to destroy, but to fulfil. For verily I say unto you, Heaven and earth **must** pass **away**, **but** one jot or one tittle shall in no wise pass from the law, until all be fulfilled. Whosoever, therefore, shall break one of these least commandments, and shall teach men so **to do**, he shall ~~be called the least~~ **in no wise be saved** in the kingdom of heaven; but whosoever shall do and teach **these commandments of the law until it be fulfilled**, the same shall be called great**, and shall be saved** in the kingdom of heaven. For I say unto you, Except your righteousness shall exceed **that** of the scribes and Pharisees, ye shall in no case enter into the kingdom of heaven.

Ye have heard that it **hath been** said by them of old time **that**, Thou shalt not kill; and whosoever shall kill, shall be in danger of the judgment **of God**. But I say unto you, that whosoever is angry with his brother ~~without a cause~~, shall be in danger of **His** judgment; and whosoever shall say to his brother, Raca, **or Rabcah**, shall be in danger of the council; **and** whosoever shall say **to his brother**, Thou fool, shall be in danger of hell fire. Therefore, **if ye shall come unto me, or shall desire to come unto me, or** if thou bring thy gift to the altar, and there rememberest that thy brother hath **aught** against thee, leave **thou** thy gift before the altar, and go thy way **unto thy brother, and** first be reconciled to thy brother, and then come and offer thy gift.

Agree with thine adversary quickly, **while** thou art in the way with him; lest at any time **thine** adversary deliver thee to the judge, and the judge deliver thee to the officer, and thou be cast into prison. Verily I say unto thee, Thou shalt by no means come out thence, till thou hast paid the uttermost farthing.

Behold, it is written by them of old time, **that** thou shalt not commit adultery. But I say unto you, That whosoever looketh on a woman to lust after her hath committed adultery with her already in his heart. **Behold, I give unto you a commandment, that ye suffer none of these things to enter into your heart, for it is better that ye should deny yourselves of these things, wherein ye will take up your cross, than that ye should be cast into hell. Therefore,** if thy right eye offend thee, pluck it out and cast it from thee; for it is profitable for thee that one of thy members should perish, and not that thy whole body should be cast into hell. **Or** if thy right hand offend thee, cut it off and cast it from thee; for it is profitable for thee that one of thy members should perish, and not that thy whole body should be cast into hell. **And now this I speak, a parable concerning your sins; wherefore, cast them from you, that ye may not be hewn down and cast into the fire.**

It hath been **written that**, Whosoever shall put away his wife, let him give her a writing of divorcement. **Verily, verily,** I say unto you, that whosoever shall put away his wife, saving for the cause of fornication, causeth her to commit adultery; and whosoever shall marry her that is divorced, committeth adultery.

Again, it hath been **written** by them of old time, Thou shalt not forswear thyself, but shalt perform unto the Lord thine oaths. But I say unto you, Swear not at all; neither by heaven; for it is God's throne: nor by the earth; for it is His footstool: neither by Jerusalem; for it is the city of the great King. Neither shalt thou swear by thy head, because thou canst not make one hair white or black. But let your communication be, Yea, yea; Nay, nay: for whatsoever is more than these cometh of evil.

Ye have heard that it hath been said, An eye for an eye, and a tooth for a tooth: but I say unto you, That ye resist not evil: but whosoever shall smite thee on thy right cheek, turn to him the other also. And if any man will sue thee at the law, and take away thy coat, let him have **it; and if he sue thee again, let him have** thy **cloak** also. And whosoever shall compel thee to go a mile, go with him **a mile; and whosoever shall compel thee to go with him twain, thou shalt go with him** twain. Give to him that asketh **of** thee; and from him that would borrow of thee, turn not thou away.

Ye have heard that it hath been said, Thou shalt love thy neighbor, and hate thine enemy. But I say unto you, Love your enemies, bless them that curse you, do good to them that hate you, and pray for them which despitefully use you and persecute you; that ye may be the children of your Father **who** is in heaven; for He maketh His sun to rise on the evil and on the good, and sendeth rain on the just and on the unjust. For if ye love **only** them which love you, what reward have **you**? Do not even the publicans the same? And if ye salute your brethren only, what do ye more than others? Do not even the publicans **the same**? Ye **are** therefore **commanded to be** perfect, even as your Father **who** is in heaven is perfect.

MATTHEW 6

Sermon on the Mount—Lord's Prayer

Take heed that ye do not your alms before men, to be seen of them; otherwise ye have no reward of your Father **who** is in heaven. Therefore, when thou doest alms, do not sound a trumpet before thee, as the hypocrites do, in the synagogues and in the streets, that they may have glory of men. Verily I say unto you, They have their reward. But when thou doest alms, let **it be unto thee as** thy left hand **not knowing** what thy right hand doeth; that thine alms may be in secret; and thy Father **who** seeth in secret, Himself shall reward thee openly.

And when thou prayest, thou shalt not be as the hypocrites; for they love to pray standing in the synagogues and in the corners of the streets, that they may be seen of men; **for,** verily, I say unto you, They have their reward. But thou, when thou prayest, enter into thy closet, and when thou hast shut **the** door, pray to thy Father **who** is in secret; and thy Father **who** seeth in secret shall reward thee openly. But when ye pray, use not vain repetitions, as the ~~heathen~~ **hypocrites** do; for they think that they shall be heard for their much speaking. **Therefore,** be ye **not** like unto them; for your Father knoweth what things ye have need of, before ye ask Him.

Therefore, after this manner **shall** ye **pray, saying,** Our Father **who** art in heaven, hallowed be Thy name. Thy kingdom come. Thy will be done **on** earth, as it is **done** in heaven. Give us this day, our daily bread. And forgive us our ~~debts~~ **trespasses**, as we forgive ~~our debtors~~ **those who trespass against us**. And ~~lead us not~~ **suffer us not to be led** into temptation, but deliver us from evil. For Thine is the kingdom, and the power, and the glory, forever **and ever**, Amen. For if ye forgive men their trespasses, **who trespass against you,** your Heavenly Father will also forgive you; but if ye forgive not men their trespasses, neither will your **Heavenly** Father forgive **you** your trespasses.

Moreover when ye fast, be not, as the hypocrites, of a sad countenance: for they disfigure their faces, that they may appear unto men to fast. Verily I say unto you, They have their reward. But thou, when thou fastest, anoint **thy** head and wash thy face, that thou appear not unto men to fast, but unto thy Father **who** is in secret; and thy Father **who** seeth in secret, shall reward thee openly.

Lay not up for yourselves treasures upon earth, where moth and rust doth corrupt, and where thieves break through and steal: but lay up for yourselves treasures in heaven, where neither moth nor rust doth corrupt, and where thieves do not break through nor steal: for where your treasure is, there will your heart be also.

The light of the body is the eye; if therefore thine eye be single **to the glory of God**, thy whole body shall be full of light. But if thine eye be evil, thy whole body shall be full of darkness. If therefore the light **which** is in thee be darkness, how great **shall** that darkness **be**. No man can serve two masters: for either he will hate the one, and love the other; or else he will hold to the one, and despise the other. Ye cannot serve God and mammon.

And, again, I say unto you, go ye into the world, and care not for the world; for the world will hate you, and will persecute you, and will turn you out of their synagogues. Nevertheless, ye shall go forth from house to house, teaching the people; and I will go before you. And your Heavenly Father will provide for you, whatsoever things ye need for food, what you shall eat; and for raiment, what ye shall wear or put on. Therefore I say unto you, Take no thought for your life, what ye shall eat, or what ye shall drink; nor yet for your **bodies**, what ye shall put on. Is not the life more than meat, and the body than raiment?

Behold the fowls of the air, for they sow not, neither do they reap, nor gather into barns; yet your Heavenly Father feedeth them. Are ye not much better than they? **How much more will He not feed you? Wherefore take no thought for these things, but keep my commandments wherewith I have commanded you. For** which of you by taking thought can add one cubit unto his stature? And why take ye thought for raiment? Consider the lilies of the field, how they grow; they toil not, neither do they spin: and yet I say unto you, That even Solomon in all his glory was not arrayed like one of these. **Therefore,** if God so clothe the grass of the field, which today is, and tomorrow is cast into the oven, **how** much more **will He not provide for** you, **if** ye **are not** of little faith. Therefore, take no thought, saying, What shall we eat? or, What shall we drink? or, Wherewithal shall we be clothed?

Why is it that ye murmur among yourselves, saying, We cannot obey Thy word because ye have not all these things, and seek to excuse yourselves, saying that, After all these things do the Gentiles seek. **Behold, I say unto you, that** your Heavenly Father knoweth that ye have need of all these things. **Wherefore, seek not the things of this world;** but seek ye first **to build up** the kingdom of God, and **to establish** His righteousness, and all these things shall be added unto you. Take, therefore, no thought for the morrow; for the morrow shall take thought for the things of itself. Sufficient unto the day **shall be** the evil thereof.

MATTHEW 7
Sermon on the Mount

These are the words Jesus taught His disciples that they should say unto the people.

Judge not **unrighteously**, that ye be not judged**; but judge righteous judgment.** For with what judgment ye **shall** judge, ye shall be judged; and with what measure ye mete, it shall be measured to you again. And **again, ye shall say unto them,** Why **is it that thou** beholdest the mote that is in thy brother's eye, but considerest not the beam that is in thine own eye? Or how wilt thou say to thy brother, Let me pull out the mote out of thine eye; and **canst not** behold a beam in thine own eye?

Beholdest thou the scribes, and the Pharisees, and the Priests, and the Levites? They teach in their synagogues, but do not observe the law, nor the commandments; and all have gone out of the way, and are under sin. Go thou and say unto them, Why teach ye men the law and the commandments, when ye yourselves are the children of corruption? Say unto them, Ye hypocrites, first cast out the beam out of thine own **eyes**; and then shalt thou see clearly to cast out the mote out of thy brother's eye.

Go ye into the world, saying unto all, Repent, for the kingdom of heaven has come nigh unto you. And the mysteries of the kingdom ye shall keep within yourselves; for it is not meet to give that which is holy unto the dogs; neither cast ye your pearls **unto** swine, lest they trample them under their feet. **For the world cannot receive that which ye, yourselves, are not able to bear; wherefore ye shall not give your pearls unto them, lest they** turn again and rend you.

Say unto them, Ask of God; ask, and it shall be given you; seek, and ye shall find; knock, and it shall be opened unto you. For everyone that asketh receiveth; and he that seeketh findeth; and to him that knocketh it shall be opened.

Then said His disciples unto Him, They will say, We ourselves are righteous and need not that any man should teach us. Jesus answered,

Thus shall ye say unto them, What man among you, having a son, and he shall be standing out, and shall say, Father, open thy house that I may come in and sup with thee, will not say, Come in, my son; for mine is thine, and thine is mine? Or what man is there **among** you, **who**, if his son ask bread, will give him a stone? Or if he ask a fish, will he give him a serpent? If ye then, being evil, know how to give good gifts unto your children, how much more shall your Father **who** is in heaven give good things to them that ask Him? Therefore, all things whatsoever ye would that men should do **unto** you, do ye even so to them; for this is the law and the prophets.

Repent, therefore, and enter ye in at the strait gate; for wide is the gate, and broad is the way that leadeth to ~~destruction~~ **death**, and many there be **who** go in thereat. Because strait is the gate, and narrow is the way **that** leadeth unto life, and few there be that find it.

And, again, beware of false prophets, **who** come to you in sheep's clothing; but inwardly they are ravening wolves. Ye shall know them by their fruits; **for** do men gather grapes of thorns, or figs of thistles? Even so every good tree bringeth forth good fruit; but a corrupt tree bringeth forth evil fruit. A good tree cannot bring forth evil fruit; neither a corrupt tree bring forth good fruit. Every tree that bringeth not forth good fruit is hewn down, and cast into the fire. Wherefore by their fruits ye shall know them.

Verily I say unto you, it is not everyone that saith unto me, Lord, Lord, **that** shall enter into the kingdom of heaven; but he that doeth the will of my Father **who** is in heaven. **For the day soon cometh, that men shall come before me to judgment, to be judged according to their works. And** many will say **unto** me in that day, Lord, Lord, have we not prophesied in Thy name; and in Thy name cast out devils; and in Thy name done many wonderful works? And then will I **say**, ~~I~~ **Ye** never knew ~~you~~ **me**; depart from me ye that work iniquity.

Therefore, whosoever heareth these sayings of mine and doeth them,

I will liken him unto a wise man, **who** built his house upon a rock, and the **rains** descended, and the floods came, and the winds blew, and beat upon that house, and it fell not; for it was founded upon a rock. And everyone that heareth these sayings of mine, and doeth them not, shall be likened unto a foolish man, **who** built his house upon the sand; and the **rains** descended, and the floods came, and the winds blew, and beat upon that house, and it fell; and great was the fall of it.

MATTHEW 8

Heals—stills tempest—devils into swine

When ***Jesus*** *was come down from the mountain, there came a leper* ***worshiping*** *Him, saying, Lord, if Thou wilt, Thou canst make me clean. And Jesus put forth His hand, and touched him saying,*

I will; be thou clean.

And immediately his leprosy was cleansed.

See thou tell no man; but go thy way **and** show thyself to the priest, and offer the gift that Moses commanded, for a testimony unto them.

When Jesus was entered into Capernaum, there came unto Him a centurion, beseeching Him, saying, Lord, my servant lieth at home sick of the palsy, grievously tormented. Jesus saith unto him,

I will come and heal him.

The centurion answered and said, Speak the word only, and my servant shall be healed. Jesus said ***unto*** *them that followed,*

Verily I say unto you, I have not found so great faith, no, not in Israel. And I say unto you, that many shall come from the East, and **the** West, and shall sit down with Abraham, and Isaac, and Jacob, in the kingdom of heaven. But the children of the ~~kingdom~~ **wicked one** shall be cast out into outer darkness; there shall be weeping and gnashing of teeth.

Jesus said unto the centurion,

Go thy way; and as thou hast believed, so be it done unto thee.

And his servant was healed in the selfsame hour.

When Jesus saw great multitudes about Him, He gave commandment to depart unto the other side ***of the sea****. A scribe came unto Him* ***and said****, Master, I will follow Thee whithersoever Thou goest. And Jesus saith unto him,*

The foxes have holes, and the birds of the air have nests; but the Son of Man hath not where to lay His head.

Another of His disciples said unto Him, Lord, suffer me first to go and bury my father. But Jesus said unto him,

Follow me; and let the dead bury their dead.

When He was entered into a ship, there arose a great tempest in the sea, insomuch that the ship was covered with the waves: but He was asleep. His disciples awoke Him, saying, Lord, save us, ***else*** *we perish. He saith,*

Why are ye fearful, O ye of little faith?

Then He arose, and rebuked the winds and the sea: and there was great calm.

When He was come to the other side, into the country of the Gergesenes, there met Him ***a man*** *possessed with devils, saying, What have we to do with Thee, Jesus, Thou Son of God? Art Thou come hither to torment us before the time? So the devils besought Him, saying, If Thou cast us out, suffer us to go into the herd of swine. And He said unto them,*

Go.

They went into the herd of swine: and the whole herd ran violently down a steep place into the sea, and perished in the waters. The whole city came out to meet Jesus: and when they saw Him, they besought Him that He would depart out of their coasts.

MATTHEW 9

Heals—raises dead—new wine into old bottles

Jesus *entered into a ship, and passed over, and came into His own city. They brought to Him a man sick of the palsy, lying on a bed; and Jesus,* ~~*seeing*~~ ***knowing*** *their faith, said unto the sick of the palsy,*

Son, be of good cheer; thy sins be forgiven thee**; go thy way and sin no more.**

Certain of the scribes said within themselves, This man blasphemeth. Jesus, knowing their thoughts, said,

Wherefore **is it that** ye **think** evil in your hearts? For is **it not** easier to say, Thy sins be forgiven thee, **than** to say, Arise and walk. But **I said this** that ye may know that the Son of Man hath power on earth to forgive sins.

Jesus said unto *the sick of the palsy,*

Arise, take up thy bed, and go unto **thy** house.

He ***immediately*** *arose, and departed to his house.*

As Jesus passed forth from thence, He saw Matthew sitting at the ***place where they received tribute,*** *and He* ***said*** *unto him,*

Follow me.

And he arose and followed Him. And as Jesus sat at meat in the house, many publicans and sinners came and sat down with Him, and ***with*** *His disciples. The Pharisees said unto His disciples, Why eateth your Master with publicans and sinners? When Jesus heard* ***them,*** *He said,*

They that be whole need not a physician, but they that are sick. But go ye and learn what **this** meaneth, I will have mercy and not sacrifice; for I am not come to call the righteous, but sinners to repentance.

While He was thus teaching, there *came to Him the disciples of John, saying, Why do we and the Pharisees fast oft, but Thy disciples fast not? Jesus said,*

Can the children of the bridechamber mourn, as long as the bridegroom is with them? But the days will come, when the bridegroom shall be taken from them, and then shall they fast.

Then said the Pharisees unto Him, Why will ye not receive us with our baptism, seeing we keep the whole law? But Jesus said,

Ye keep not the law. If ye had kept the law, ye would have received me, for I am He who gave the law. I receive not you with your baptism, because it profiteth you nothing. For when that which is new is come, the old is ready to be put away. For no man putteth a piece of new cloth **on** an old garment; for that which is put in to fill it up, taketh from the garment, and the rent is made worse. Neither do men put new wine into old bottles: else the bottles break, and the wine runneth out, and the bottles perish: but they put new wine into new bottles, and both are preserved.

While He spake these things unto them, there came a certain ruler and worshiped Him, saying, My daughter is even now ~~dead~~ ***dying****; but come and lay Thy hand upon her and she shall live. And Jesus arose and followed him, and* ***also*** *His disciples****, and much people thronged Him****. And a woman with an issue of blood twelve years touched the hem of His garment. Jesus turned Him about and said,*

Daughter, be of good comfort; thy faith hath made thee whole.

And the woman was made whole from that hour.

When Jesus came into the ruler's house, and saw the minstrels and the people making a noise. He said,

Give place: for the maid is not dead, but sleepeth.

And they laughed Him to scorn. But when the people were put forth, He went in, and took her by the hand, and the maid arose.

When Jesus departed, two blind men followed Him, crying, ***Jesus****, have mercy on us. And when He was come into the house, Jesus saith unto them,*

Believe ye that I am able to do this?

Yea, Lord. Then touched He their eyes, saying,

According to your faith be it unto you. **Keep my commandments, and** see **ye tell no man in this place,** that no man know it.

When He saw the multitudes, He was moved with compassion, because they fainted, and were scattered abroad, as sheep having no shepherd. Then saith He unto His disciples,

The harvest truly is plenteous, but the laborers are few. Pray ye therefore the Lord of the Harvest, that He will send forth laborers into His harvest.

MATTHEW 10

Instructs Apostles—heals

He gave [His twelve disciples] power ***over*** *unclean spirits, to cast them out, and to heal all manner of sickness. These twelve Jesus sent forth, and commanded them,*

Go not into the way of the Gentiles, and **enter ye not** into any city of the Samaritans. But rather **go** to the lost sheep of the house of Israel. And as ye go, preach, saying, The kingdom of heaven is at hand. Heal the sick, cleanse the lepers, raise the dead, cast out devils: freely ye have received, freely give. Provide neither gold, nor silver, nor brass in your purses, nor scrip for your journey, neither two coats, neither shoes, nor yet staves: for the workman is worthy of his meat.

And into whatsoever town **or city** ye shall enter, inquire who in it is worthy, and there abide till ye go thence. And when ye come into a house, salute it. And if the house be worthy, let your peace come upon it: but if it be not worthy, let your peace return to you. And whosoever shall not receive you, nor hear your words, when ye depart out of that house, or city, shake off the dust of your feet **for a testimony against them. And,** verily, I say unto you, It shall be more tolerable for the land of Sodom and Gomorrah in the Day of Judgment than for that city.

Behold, I send you forth as sheep in the midst of wolves; be ye therefore wise ~~as serpents~~ **servants**, and **as** harmless as doves. But beware of men: for they will deliver you up to the councils, and they will scourge you in their synagogues; and ye shall be brought before governors and kings for my sake, for a testimony against them and the Gentiles. But when they deliver you up, take no thought how or what ye shall speak: for it shall be given you in that same hour what ye shall speak. For it is not ye that speak, but the Spirit of your Father which speaketh in you.

And the brother shall deliver up the brother to death, and the father the child: and the children shall rise up against their parents, and cause them to be put to death. And ye shall be hated of all ~~men~~ **the world** for my name's sake; but he that endureth to the end shall be saved. But when they persecute you in **one** city, flee ye into another; for verily, I say unto you, Ye shall not have gone over the cities of Israel, till the Son of Man be come.

Remember, the disciple is not above his master; nor the servant above his lord. It is enough **that** the disciple be as his master, and the servant as his lord. If they have called the master of the house Beelzebub, how much more shall they call them of his household? Fear them not therefore: for there is nothing covered, that shall not be revealed; and hid, that shall not be known. What I tell you in darkness, **preach** ye in light; and what ye hear in the ear, preach ye upon the housetops.

And fear not them **who are able to** kill the body, but are not able to kill the soul; but rather fear Him **who** is able to destroy both soul and body in hell. Are not two sparrows sold for a farthing? And one of them shall not fall **to** the ground without your Father **knoweth it**. **And** the very hairs of your head are all numbered. Fear ye not, therefore; ye are of more value than many sparrows. Whosoever, therefore, shall confess me before men, him will I confess also before my Father **who** is in heaven. But whosoever shall deny me before men, him will I also deny before my Father **who** is in heaven.

Think not that I am come to send peace on earth: I came not to send peace, but a sword. For I am come to set a man at variance against his father, and the daughter against her mother, and the daughter-in-law against her mother-in-law. And a man's foes shall be they of his own household. He **who** loveth father **and** mother more than me, is not worthy of me; and he **who** loveth son or daughter more than me, is not worthy of me. And he **who** taketh not his cross and followeth after me, is not worthy of me. He **who seeketh to save** his life shall lose it; and he **who** loseth his life for my sake shall find it.

He **who** receiveth you, receiveth me; and he **who** receiveth me, receiveth Him **who** sent me. He that receiveth a prophet in the name of a prophet shall receive a prophet's reward; he that receiveth a righteous man, in the name of a righteous man, shall receive a righteous man's reward. And whosoever shall give to drink unto one of these little ones a cup of cold water only in the name of a disciple, verily I say unto you, he shall in no wise lose his reward.

Matthew 11

John the Baptist—my yoke is easy

When Jesus had made an end of commanding His twelve disciples, He departed to teach and to preach in their cities. When John had heard in the prison the ~~works~~ ***words*** *of Christ, he sent two of his disciples, and* ***they*** *said, Art Thou He* ***of whom it is written in the prophets*** *that* ***He*** *should come, or do we look for another? Jesus answered,*

Go and ~~shew~~ **tell** John again **of** those things which ye do hear and see**; how that** the blind receive their sight, and the lame walk, **and** the lepers are cleansed, and the deaf hear, **and** the dead are raised up, and the poor have the gospel preached **unto** them. And blessed is **John, and** whosoever shall not be offended in me.

As they departed, Jesus began to say unto the multitudes concerning John,

What went ye out into the wilderness to see? **Was it** a reed shaken with the wind?

And they answered him, No.

But what went ye out for to see? **Was it** a man clothed in soft raiment? Behold they that wear soft **raiment** are in kings' houses. But what went ye out for to see? A prophet? Yea, I say unto you, and more than a prophet. For this is **the one** of whom it is written, Behold, I send my messenger before Thy face, which shall prepare Thy way before Thee.

Verily I say unto you, Among them that are born of women there hath not risen a greater than John the Baptist: notwithstanding he that is least in the kingdom of heaven is greater than he. And from the days of John the Baptist until now the kingdom of heaven suffereth violence, and the violent take it by force. **But the day will come, when the violent shall have no power;** for all the prophets and the law prophesied **that it should be thus** until John. **Yea, as many as have prophesied have foretold of these days.** And if ye will receive it, **verily, he was the** Elias, **who** was for to come **and prepare all things**. He that hath ears to hear, let him hear.

But whereunto shall I liken this generation? It is like unto children sitting in the markets, and calling unto their fellows, and saying, We have piped unto you, and ye have not danced; we have mourned **for** you, and ye have not lamented. For John came neither eating nor drinking, and they say, He hath a devil. The Son of Man came eating and drinking, and they say, Behold, a gluttonous **man** and a winebibber, a friend of publicans and sinners. But **I say unto you, Wisdom** is justified of her children.

Then began He to upbraid the cities wherein most of His mighty works were done, because they repented not:

Woe unto thee, Chorazin! Woe unto thee, Bethsaida! For if the mighty works which were done in you, had been done in Tyre and Sidon, they would have repented long **since** in sackcloth and ashes. But I say unto you, It shall be more tolerable for Tyre and Sidon at the Day of Judgment, than for you. And thou, Capernaum, which art exalted unto heaven, shalt be brought down to hell: for if the mighty works, which have been done in thee, had been done in Sodom, it would have remained until this day. But I say unto you, It shall be more tolerable for the land of Sodom in the Day of Judgment, than for thee.

And *at that time****, there came a voice out of heaven, and*** *Jesus said,*

I thank Thee, O Father, Lord of Heaven and Earth, because Thou hast hid these things from the wise and prudent, and hast revealed them unto babes. Even so, Father, for so it seemed good in Thy sight! All things are delivered unto me of my Father; and no man knoweth the Son, but the Father; neither knoweth any man the Father, save the Son, and **they** to **whom** the Son will reveal **Himself; they shall see the Father also.**

Then spake Jesus,

Come unto me, all ye that labor and are heavy laden, and I will give you rest. Take my yoke upon you, and learn of me; for I am meek and lowly in heart: and ye shall find rest unto your souls. For my yoke is easy, and my burden is light.

MATTHEW 12

Lord of Sabbath—blasphemy

At that time Jesus went on the Sabbath day through the corn; and His disciples were an hungered, and began to pluck the ears of corn, and to eat. When the Pharisees saw ***them,*** *they said, Behold, Thy disciples do that which is not lawful to do upon the Sabbath day. But He said,*

Have ye not read what David did, when he was an hungered, and they that were with him? How he entered into the house of God, and did eat the shewbread, which was not lawful for him to eat, neither for them which were with him; but only for the priests? Or have ye not read in the law, how that on the Sabbath days the priests in the temple profane the Sabbath, and **ye say they** are blameless? But I say unto you, That in this place is one greater than the temple. But if ye had known what this meaneth, I will have mercy and not sacrifice, ye would not have condemned the guiltless. For the Son of Man is Lord even of the **Sabbath**.

When He was departed, He went into their ***synagogues****. There was a man which had* ***a*** *withered* ***hand****. They asked, Is it lawful to heal on the Sabbath days? And He said,*

What man shall there be among you, that shall have one sheep, and if it fall into a pit on the Sabbath day, will he not lay hold on it, and lift it out? How much then is a man better than a sheep? Wherefore it is lawful to do well on the Sabbath days.

Then ***said*** *He to the man,*

Stretch forth **thy** hand.

And he stretched it forth, and it was restored whole like ***unto*** *the other. Then the Pharisees went out, and held a council against Him, how they might destroy Him. But Jesus knew* ***when they took counsel, and*** *He withdrew.*

Then was brought unto Him one possessed with a devil, blind, and dumb: and He healed him, insomuch that the blind and dumb both spake and saw. When the Pharisees heard ***that He had cast out the devil****, they said, This* ***man*** *doth not cast out devils, but by Beelzebub the prince of devils. Jesus knew their thoughts and said,*

Every kingdom divided against itself is brought to desolation; and every city or house divided against itself, shall not stand. And if Satan cast out Satan, he is divided against himself; how then **shall** his kingdom stand? And if I by Beelzebub cast out devils, by whom do your children cast out **devils**? Therefore they shall be your judges. But if I cast out devils by the Spirit of God, then the kingdom of God is come unto you. **For they also cast out devils by the Spirit of God, for unto them is given power over devils, that they may cast them out.** Or else how can one enter into a strong man's house, and spoil his goods, except he first bind the strong man? And then he will spoil his house. He that is not with me is against me; and he that gathereth not with me scattereth abroad.

Wherefore I say unto you, All manner of sin and blasphemy shall be forgiven unto men **who receive me and repent;** but the blasphemy against the Holy Ghost, **it** shall not be forgiven unto men. And whosoever speaketh a word against the Son of Man, it shall be forgiven him: but whosoever speaketh against the Holy Ghost, it shall not be forgiven him, neither in this world, neither in the world to come.

Either make the tree good and his fruit good; or else make the tree corrupt, and his fruit corrupt; for the tree is known by **the** fruit. O **ye** generation of vipers! How can ye, being evil, speak good things? For out of the abundance of the heart the mouth speaketh. A good man out of the good treasure of the heart bringeth forth good things: and an evil man out of the evil treasure bringeth forth evil things.

And again I say unto you, That every idle word that men shall speak, they shall give account thereof in the Day of Judgment. For by thy words thou shalt be justified, and by thy words thou shalt be condemned.

The scribes and Pharisees answered, Master, we would see a sign from Thee. But He answered,

An evil and adulterous generation seeketh after a sign; and there shall no sign be given to it, but the sign of the prophet Jonas: for as Jonas was three days and three nights in the whale's belly; so shall the Son of Man be three days and three nights in the heart of the earth.

The men of Nineveh shall rise **up** in judgment with this generation, and shall condemn it, because they repented at the preaching of Jonas; and **ye**, behold, a greater than Jonas is here. The queen of the south shall rise up in the **Day of** Judgment with this generation, and shall condemn it; for she came from the uttermost parts of the earth to hear the wisdom of Solomon; and **ye**, behold, a greater than Solomon is here.

Then came some of the scribes and said, Master, it is written that, Every sin shall be forgiven; but ye say, Whosoever speaketh against the Holy Ghost shall not be forgiven. How can these things be? And He said,

When the unclean spirit is gone out of a man, he walketh through dry places, seeking rest and findeth none**; but when a man speaketh against the Holy Ghost,** then he saith, I will return into my house from whence I came out; and when he is come, he findeth **him** empty, swept and garnished**; for the good spirit leaveth him unto himself.** Then goeth **the evil spirit**, and taketh with **him** seven other spirits more wicked than himself; and they enter in and dwell there; and the last ~~state~~ **end** of that man is worse than the first. Even so shall it be also unto this wicked generation.

While He yet talked to the people, one said, Thy mother and Thy brethren stand without, desiring to speak with Thee. But He answered and said unto ***the man*** *that told Him,*

Who is my mother? And who are my brethren?

He stretched forth His hand toward His disciples.

Behold my mother and my brethren!

And He gave them charge concerning her, saying,

I go my way, for my Father hath sent me. And whosoever shall do the will of my Father which is in heaven, the same is my brother, and sister, and mother.

MATTHEW 13

Parables of sower; wheat and tares; mustard seed; leaven; treasure in field; pearl of great price; gospel net; householder

The same day, Jesus ***went*** *out of the house, and sat by the seaside. Great multitudes were gathered together unto Him, so that He went into a ship and sat; and the whole multitude stood on the shore. And He spake many things unto them in parables, saying,*

Behold, a sower went forth to sow; and when he sowed, some seeds fell by the wayside, and the fowls came and devoured them up: some fell upon stony places, where they had not much earth; and forthwith they sprung up; and when the sun was up, they were scorched, **because they had no deepness of earth;** and because they had no root, they withered away. And some fell among thorns, and thorns, sprung up and choked them. But other fell into good ground, and brought forth fruit, some a hundredfold, some sixtyfold, some thirtyfold. Who hath ears to hear, let him hear.

Then *the disciples said unto Him, Why speakest Thou unto them in parables? He answered,*

Because it is given unto you to know the mysteries of the kingdom of heaven, but to them it is not given. For whosoever ~~hath~~ **receiveth**, to him shall be given, and he shall have more abundance; but whosoever ~~hath~~ **continueth** not **to receive**, from him shall be taken away even that he hath. Therefore speak I to them in parables: because they seeing see not; and hearing they hear not, neither do they understand. And in them is fulfilled the prophecy of Esaias **concerning them,** which saith, By hearing, ye shall hear and shall not understand; and seeing, ye shall see and shall not perceive. For this people's heart is waxed gross, and their ears are dull of hearing, and their eyes they have closed, lest at any time they should see with their eyes and hear with **their** ears, and should understand with **their hearts**, and should be converted, and I should heal them.

But blessed are your eyes, for they see; and your ears, for they hear. **And blessed are you because these things are come unto you, that you might understand them. And** verily, I say unto you, Many **righteous** prophets have desired to see **these days** which **you** see, and have not seen them; and to hear **that** which **you** hear, and have not heard.

Hear ye therefore the parable of the sower. When anyone heareth the word of the kingdom, and understandeth not, then cometh the wicked one, and ~~catcheth~~ **taketh** away that which was sown in his heart; this is he **who receiveth** seed by the wayside. But he that received the seed into stony places, the same is he that heareth the word and ~~anon~~ **readily** with joy receiveth it, yet **he** hath not root in himself, and **endureth but** for a while; for when tribulation or persecution ariseth because of the word, by and by he is offended. He also **who** received seed among the thorns, is he that heareth the word; and the care of this world and the deceitfulness of riches, choke the word, and he becometh unfruitful. But he **who** received seed into the good ground, is he **who** heareth the word and understandeth **and endureth**; which also beareth fruit, and bringeth forth, some a hundredfold, some sixty, **and** some thirty.

[Other parables] put He forth unto them, saying,

The kingdom of heaven is likened unto a man **who** sowed good seed in his field; but while ~~men~~ **he** slept, his enemy came and sowed tares among the wheat, and went his way. But when the blade sprung up, and brought forth fruit, then appeared the tares also. So the servants of the householder came and said unto him, Sir, didst not thou sow good seed in thy field? Whence then hath it tares? He said unto them, An enemy hath done this. **And** the servants said unto him, Wilt thou then that we go and gather them up? But he said, Nay; lest while ye gather up the tares, ye root up also the wheat with them. Let both grow together until the harvest, and in the time of harvest, I will say to the reapers, Gather ye together first the ~~tares~~ **wheat into my barn**; and **the tares are bound** in bundles to **be burned**.

The kingdom of heaven is like to a grain of mustard seed, which a man took and sowed in his field; which indeed is the least of all seeds:

but when it is grown, it is the greatest among herbs, and becometh a tree, so that the birds of the air come and lodge in the branches thereof. The kingdom of heaven is like unto leaven, which a woman took, and hid in three measures of meal, till the whole was leavened.

Jesus sent the multitude away, and went into the house. His disciples came unto Him, saying, Declare unto us the parable of the tares of the field. He answered,

He that soweth the good seed is the Son of Man; the field is the world; the good seed are the children of the kingdom; but the tares are the children of the wicked. The enemy that sowed them is the devil; the harvest is the end of the world**, or the destruction of the wicked.** The reapers are the angels**, or the messengers sent of heaven.** As, therefore, the tares are gathered and burned in the fire, so shall it be in the end of this world**, or the destruction of the wicked. For in that day, before** the Son of Man **shall come, He** shall send forth His angels **and messengers of heaven**. And they shall gather out of His kingdom all things that offend, and them which do iniquity, and shall cast them ~~into a furnace of fire~~ **out among the wicked; and** there shall be wailing and gnashing of teeth. **For the world shall be burned with fire.** Then shall the righteous shine forth as the sun in the kingdom of their Father. Who hath ears to hear, let him hear.

Again, the kingdom of heaven is like unto **a** treasure hid in a field. **And** when a man hath found **a treasure which is hid**, he **secureth it**, and, **straightway,** for joy thereof, goeth and selleth all that he hath, and buyeth that field. **And** again, the kingdom of heaven is like unto a **merchantman**, seeking goodly pearls, who, when he had found one pearl of great price, **he** went and sold all that he had and bought it.

Again, the kingdom of heaven is like unto a net, that was cast into the sea, and gathered of every kind: which, when it was full, they drew to shore, and sat down, and gathered the good into vessels, but cast the bad away. So shall it be at the end of the world: **and the world is the children of the wicked.** The angels shall come forth, and sever the wicked from among the just, and shall cast them **out** into the ~~furnace of fire~~ **world to be burned**. There shall be wailing and gnashing of teeth.

Have ye understood all these things? Every scribe **well** instructed **in the things of** the kingdom of heaven, is like unto a householder; **a**

man, therefore, which bringeth forth out of his treasure **that which is** new and old.

*When Jesus had finished these parables, He departed thence. And when He was come into His own country, He taught them in their **synagogues**. And they were offended **at** Him. But Jesus said unto them,*

A prophet is not without honor, save in his own country, and in his own house.

He did not many mighty works there because of their unbelief.

Matthew 14

Feeds five thousand—walks on sea

*When Jesus heard **that John** [the Baptist] **was beheaded**, He departed thence by ship into a desert place apart; and when the people had heard **of Him**, they followed Him on foot out of the cities. And Jesus went forth, and saw a great multitude, and was moved with compassion **towards** them, and He healed their sick. When it was evening, His disciples came to Him, saying, This is a desert place, and the time is now past; send the multitude away, that they may go into the villages and buy themselves victuals. But Jesus said unto them,*

They need not depart; give ye them to eat.

*And they **said**, We have here but five loaves and two fishes. He said,*

Bring them hither to me.

*And He commanded the multitude to sit down on the grass; and **He** took the five loaves and the two fishes, and looking up to heaven, He blessed and brake, and gave the loaves to ~~His~~ **the** disciples, and the disciples, to the multitude. And they did all eat, and were filled. And they took up of the fragments that remained, twelve baskets full. And they that had eaten were about five thousand men, **besides** women and children.*

And straightway Jesus constrained His disciples to get into a ship, and to go before Him unto the other side, while He sent the multitudes away. When evening was come, He was there alone. But the ship was now in the midst of the sea, tossed with the waves: for the wind was contrary. And in the fourth watch of the night Jesus went unto them, walking on the sea. When the disciples saw Him walking on the sea, they were troubled, saying, It is a spirit; and they cried out for fear. But straightway Jesus spake unto them, saying,

Be of good cheer; it is I; be not afraid.

Peter said, Lord, if it be Thou, bid me come unto Thee on the water. And He said,

Come.

Peter walked on the water, to go to Jesus. But when he saw the wind boisterous, he was afraid; and beginning to sink, he cried, Lord, save me. And immediately, Jesus stretched forth His hand, and caught him, and said,

O thou of little faith, wherefore didst thou doubt?

And when they were come into the ship, the wind ceased.

MATTHEW 15

Mouth defileth man—feeds four thousand

Then came to Jesus scribes and Pharisees, which were of Jerusalem, saying, Why do Thy disciples transgress the tradition of the elders? For they wash not their hands when they eat bread. He answered,

Why do ye also transgress the commandment of God by your tradition? For God commanded, saying, Honor thy father and mother; and, He that curseth father or mother, let him die the death **which Moses shall appoint**. But ye say, Whosoever shall say to father or mother, By whatsoever thou mightest be profited by me**, it is a gift from me** and honor not his father or mother, **it is well**. Thus have ye made the commandment of God of none effect by your **traditions**. **O** ye hypocrites! Well did Esaias prophesy of you, saying, This people draw nigh unto me with their mouth, and honoreth me with their lips; but their heart is far from me. But in vain do **they** worship me, teaching **the** doctrines **and** commandments of men.

He called the multitude, and said unto them,

Hear, and understand: not that which goeth into the mouth defileth a man; but that which cometh out of the mouth, this defileth **the** man.

Then came His disciples, and said unto Him, Knowest Thou that the Pharisees were offended, after they heard this saying? But He answered,

Every plant, which my Heavenly Father hath not planted, shall be rooted up. Let them alone: they be blind leaders of the blind. And if the blind lead the blind, both shall fall into the ditch.

Then answered Peter and said, Declare unto us this parable. Jesus said,

Are ye also yet without understanding? Do ye **not** yet understand, that whatsoever entereth in at the mouth goeth into the belly, and is cast into the draught? But those things which proceed out of the mouth come forth from the heart; and they defile the man. For out of the heart proceed evil thoughts, murders, adulteries, fornications, thefts, false witness, blasphemies: these are things which defile a man. But to eat with unwashen hands defileth not a man.

Then Jesus went thence and departed into the coasts of Tyre and Sidon. And a woman of Canaan came and cried, O Lord, Thou Son of David; my daughter is grievously vexed with a devil. But He answered her not a word. His disciples came and besought Him, Send her away; for she crieth after us. He answered,

I am not sent but unto the lost sheep of the house of Israel.

Then came she, saying, Lord, help me. He answered,

It is not meet to take the children's bread, and to cast it to dogs.

*She said, Truth, Lord; yet the dogs eat the crumbs **that** fall from **the master's** table. Jesus answered,*

O woman, great is thy faith: be it unto thee even as thou wilt.

And her daughter was made whole from that very hour.

*And Jesus departed from thence, and came nigh unto the sea of Galilee; and went up into a mountain, and sat down there. And great multitudes came unto Him, having with them **some** lame, blind, dumb, maimed, and many others, and cast them down at Jesus' feet; and He healed them; insomuch that the multitude wondered, when they saw the dumb to speak, the maimed to be whole, the lame to walk, and the blind to see. And they glorified the God of Israel.*

Then Jesus called His disciples and said,

I have compassion on the multitude, because they continue with me now three days, and have nothing to eat; and I will not send them away fasting, lest they faint in the way.

*His disciples say unto Him, Whence should we have so much bread in the wilderness, **so** as to fill so great a multitude? Jesus saith,*

How many loaves have ye?

*They said, Seven, and a few little fishes. He took the seven loaves and the fishes, and gave thanks, and brake **the bread**, and gave to His disciples, and the disciples to the multitude. And they did all eat, and were filled. And they took up of the broken meat seven baskets full. And they that did eat were four thousand men, **besides** women and children. And He sent away the multitude, and took ship, and came into the coasts of Magdala.*

MATTHEW 16

Jesus is the Christ—foretells Resurrection

*The Pharisees also, with the Sadducees, came, and tempting **Jesus**, desired Him that He would show them a sign from heaven. He answered,*

When it is evening ye say, **The** weather **is fair**, for the sky is red; and in the morning **ye say**, **The** weather **is foul** today; for the sky is red and **lowering**. O hypocrites! Ye can discern the face of the sky; but ye **cannot** ~~discern~~ **tell** the signs of the times. A wicked and adulterous generation seeketh after a sign; and there shall no sign be given unto it, but the sign of the prophet Jonas.

And He left them, and departed. And when His disciples were come to the other side, Jesus said,

Take heed and beware of the leaven of the Pharisees and of the Sadducees.

They reasoned among themselves, ***He said this*** *because we have taken no bread. Jesus perceived* ***it, and*** *said.*

O ye of little faith! Why reason ye among yourselves, because ye have brought no bread? Do ye not yet understand, neither remember the five loaves of the five thousand, and how many baskets ye took up? Neither the seven loaves of the four thousand, and how many baskets ye took up? How is it that ye do not understand, that I spake not **unto** you concerning bread, that ye should beware of the leaven of the Pharisees and of the Sadducees?

When Jesus came into the coasts of Caesarea Philippi, He asked His disciples,

Whom do men say that I, the Son of Man, am?

They said, Some say John the Baptist; some Elias; and others Jeremias; or one of the prophets.

But whom say ye that I am?

Simon Peter said, Thou art the Christ, the Son of the living God.

Blessed art thou, Simon Bar-jona; for flesh and blood hath not revealed **this** unto thee, but my Father **who** is in heaven. And I say also unto thee, That thou art Peter, and upon this rock I will build my church; and the gates of hell shall not prevail against it. And I will give unto thee the keys of the kingdom of heaven: and whatsoever thou shalt bind on earth shall be bound in heaven: and whatsoever thou shalt loose on earth shall be loosed in heaven.

Then charged He His disciples that they should tell no man that He was Jesus the Christ. From that time forth began Jesus to show unto His disciples that He must go ***to*** *Jerusalem, and suffer many things, and be killed, and be raised again the third day. Peter began to rebuke Him, This shall not be* ***done*** *unto Thee. But He said unto Peter,*

Get thee behind me, Satan: thou art an offense unto me; for thou savorest not the things that be of God, but those that be of men.

Then said Jesus unto His disciples,

If any man will come after me, let him deny himself, and take up his cross, and follow me. **And now for a man to take up his cross, is**

to deny himself all ungodliness, and every worldly lust, and keep my commandments. Break not my commandments for to save your lives; for whosoever will save his life **in this world,** shall lose it **in the world to come.** And whosoever will lose his life **in this world,** for my sake, shall find it **in the world to come**.

Therefore, forsake the world, and save your souls; for what is a man profited, if he shall gain the whole world, and lose his own soul? Or what shall a man give in exchange for his soul? For the Son of Man shall come in the glory of His Father with His angels; and then He shall reward every man according to his works. Verily I say unto you, There be some standing here, which shall not taste of death, till they see the Son of Man coming in His kingdom.

Matthew 17

Transfiguration—Elias—faith as grain of mustard seed

After six days, Jesus taketh Peter, James, and John up into a high mountain apart, and was transfigured before them: and His face did shine as the sun, and His raiment was white as the light. There appeared unto them Moses and Elias talking with Him. A bright cloud overshadowed them: and behold a voice out of the cloud said, This is my Beloved Son, in whom I am well pleased; hear ye Him. And when the disciples heard ***the voice****, they fell on their* ***faces****, and were sore afraid. Jesus touched them, and said,*

Arise, and be not afraid.

Jesus charged them, saying,

Tell the vision to no man, until the Son of Man be risen again from the dead.

His disciples asked, Why then say the scribes that Elias must first come? Jesus answered,

Elias truly shall first come, and restore all things**, as the prophets have written. And again** I say unto you that Elias **has** come already, **concerning whom it is written, Behold, I will send my messenger, and he shall prepare the way before me;** and they knew him not, **and** have done unto him, whatsoever they listed. Likewise shall the Son of Man suffer of them. **But I say unto you, Who is Elias? Behold, this is Elias, whom I sent to prepare the way before me.**

Then the disciples understood that He spake of John the Baptist, ***and also of another who should come and restore all things, as it is written by the prophets.***

When they were come to the multitude, there came to Him a man, saying, Lord, have mercy on my son; for he is lunatic, and sore vexed. And I brought him to Thy disciples, and they could not cure him. Jesus answered,

O faithless and perverse generation, how long shall I be with you? How long shall I suffer you? Bring him hither to me.

Jesus rebuked the devil; and the child was cured from that very hour. Then came the disciples to Jesus apart, and said, Why could not we cast him out? And Jesus said,

Because of your unbelief; for, verily, I say unto you, If ye have faith as a grain of mustard seed, ye shall say unto this mountain, Remove to yonder place, and it shall remove; and nothing shall be impossible unto you. Howbeit this kind goeth not out but by prayer and fasting.

While they abode in Galilee, Jesus said unto them,

The Son of Man shall be betrayed into the hands of men and they shall kill Him, and the third day He shall be raised again.

And they were exceeding sorry.

When they were come to Capernaum, they that received tribute came to Peter, and said, Doth not your Master pay tribute? He ***said, Yea****. And when he was come into the house, Jesus* ~~*prevented*~~ ***rebuked*** *him, saying,*

What thinkest thou, Simon? Of whom do the kings of the earth take custom or tribute? Of their own children, or of strangers?

Of strangers.

Then are the children free. Notwithstanding, lest we should offend them, go thou to the sea, and cast a hook, and take up the fish that first cometh up; and when thou hast opened his mouth, thou shalt find a piece of money: that take and give unto them for me and thee.

MATTHEW 18

Offenses—parables of lost sheep; unmerciful servant

At the same time came the disciples unto Jesus, saying, Who is the greatest in the kingdom of heaven? Jesus called a little child and set him in the midst of them, and said,

Verily I say unto you, Except ye be converted, and become as little children, ye shall not enter into the kingdom of heaven. Whosoever therefore shall humble himself as this little child, the same is greatest in the kingdom of heaven. And whoso shall receive one such little child in my name receiveth me. But whoso shall offend one of these little ones which believe in me, it were better for him that a millstone were hanged about his neck and he were drowned in the depth of the sea.

Woe unto the world because of offenses! For it must needs be that offenses come; but woe to that man by whom the offense cometh! Wherefore if thy hand or thy foot offend thee, cut **it** off and cast **it** from thee; **for** it is better for thee to enter into life halt or maimed, rather than having two hands or two feet to be cast into everlasting fire. And if thine eye offend thee, pluck it out, and cast it from thee: it is better for thee to enter into life with one eye, rather than having two eyes to be cast into hell fire. **And a man's hand is his friend, and his foot, also; and a man's eye, are they of his own household.**

Take heed that ye despise not one of these little ones; for I say unto you, that in heaven their angels do always behold the face of my Father **who** is in heaven. For the Son of Man is come to save that which was lost**, and to call sinners to repentance; but these little ones have no need of repentance, and I will save them.**

How think ye? If a man have a hundred sheep, and one of them be gone astray, doth he not leave the ninety and nine, and goeth into the mountains, and seeketh that which is gone astray? And if **it** so be that he find it, verily, I say unto you, he rejoiceth more **over** that **which was lost**, than **over** the ninety and nine which went not astray. Even so it is not the will of your Father which is in heaven, that one of these little ones should perish.

Moreover if thy brother shall trespass against thee, go and tell him his fault between thee and him alone: if he shall hear thee, thou hast gained thy brother. But if he will not hear thee, then take with thee one or two more, that in the mouth of two or three witnesses every word may be established. And if he shall neglect to hear them, tell it unto the Church: but if he neglect to hear the Church, let him be unto thee as a heathen man and a publican.

Verily I say unto you, Whatsoever ye shall bind on earth shall be bound in heaven: and whatsoever ye shall loose on earth shall be loosed in heaven. Again, I say unto you, that if two of you shall agree on earth as touching anything that they shall ask, **that they may not ask amiss,** it shall be done for them of my Father **who** is in heaven. For where two or three are gathered together in my name, there am I in the midst of them.

Then came Peter to Him, and said, Lord, how oft shall my brother sin against me, and I forgive him? Till seven times? Jesus saith,

I say not unto thee, Until seven times: but, Until seventy times seven. Therefore is the kingdom of heaven likened unto a certain king, which would take account of his servants. And when he had begun to reckon, one was brought unto him **who** owed him ten thousand talents. But forasmuch as he had not to pay, his lord commanded him to be sold, and his wife, and **his** children, and all that he had, and payment to be made. **And** the servant **besought** him, saying, Lord, have patience with me, and I will pay thee all. Then the lord of that servant was moved with compassion, and loosed him, and forgave him the debt. **The servant, therefore, fell down and worshiped him.**

But the same servant went out, and found one of his fellowservants, which owed him a hundred pence: and he laid hands on him, and took him by the throat, saying, Pay me that thou owest. And his fellowservant fell down at his feet, and besought him, saying, Have patience with me, and I will pay thee all. And he would not: but went and cast him into prison, till he should pay the debt.

So when his fellowservants saw what was done, they were very sorry, and came and told unto their lord all that was done. Then his lord, after that he had called him, said unto him, O thou wicked servant, I forgave thee all that debt, because thou desiredst me: shouldest not thou also have had compassion on thy fellowservant, even as I had pity on thee? And his lord was wroth, and delivered him to the tormentors, till he should pay all that was due unto him. So likewise shall my Heavenly Father do also unto you, if ye from your hearts forgive not everyone his brother their trespasses.

MATTHEW 19

Divorce—rich young man

Jesus came into Judea. The Pharisees came unto Him, tempting Him, saying, Is it lawful for a man to put away his wife for every cause? He answered,

Have ye not read, that He **who** made **man** at the beginning, made **him**, male and female, and said, For this cause shall a man leave father and mother, and shall cleave **unto** his wife; and they twain shall be one flesh? Wherefore they are no more twain, but one flesh. What therefore God hath joined together, let not man put asunder.

They say, Why did Moses then command to give a writing of divorcement, and to put her away? He saith,

Moses because of the hardness of your hearts suffered you to put away your wives: but from the beginning it was not so. And I say unto you, Whosoever shall put away his wife, except for fornication, and shall marry another, committeth adultery; and whoso marrieth her **that** is put away, doth commit adultery.

*His disciples say unto Him, If the case of the man be so with **a** wife, it is not good to marry. But He said unto them,*

All cannot receive this saying**; it is not for them** save to whom it is given. For there are some eunuchs, which were so born from their mother's womb; and there are some eunuchs which were made eunuchs of men; and there be eunuchs, which have made themselves eunuchs for the kingdom of heaven's sake. He that is able to receive, let him receive **my sayings**.

*Then were there brought unto Him little children, that He should put His hands on them and pray. The disciples rebuked them**, saying, There is no need, for Jesus hath said, Such shall be saved.** But Jesus said,*

Suffer little children **to come unto me**, and forbid them not, for of such is the kingdom of heaven.

And He laid hands on them, and departed thence.

And one came and said, Good Master, what good thing shall I do, that I may have eternal life? And He said,

Why callest thou me good? There is none good but one, that is, God: but if thou wilt enter into life, keep the commandments.

Which?

Thou shalt **not kill**. Thou shalt not commit adultery. Thou shalt not steal. Thou shalt not bear false witness. Honor thy father and mother. And, Thou shalt love thy neighbor as thyself.

All these things have I kept from my youth up: what lack I yet? Jesus said,

If thou wilt be perfect, go, sell that thou hast, and give to the poor, and thou shalt have treasure in heaven, and come and follow me.

But when the young man heard that saying, he went away sorrowful: for he had great possessions. Then said Jesus unto His disciples,

Verily I say unto you, That a rich man shall hardly enter into the kingdom of heaven. And again I say unto you, It is easier for a camel to go through the eye of a needle, than for a rich man to enter the kingdom of God.

*His disciples were amazed, saying, Who then can be saved? But Jesus beheld **their thoughts**, and said,*

With men this is impossible; but **if they will forsake all things for**

my sake, with God **whatsoever** things **I speak** are possible.

Then answered Peter and said unto Him, Behold, we have forsaken all, and followed Thee; what shall we have therefore?

Verily I say unto you, that ye **who** have followed me, **shall,** in the ~~regeneration~~ **Resurrection,** when the Son of Man shall **come sitting on** the throne of His glory, ye shall **also** sit upon twelve thrones, judging the twelve tribes of Israel. And everyone that hath forsaken houses, or brethren, or sisters, or father, or mother, or wife, or children, or lands, for my name's sake, shall receive a hundredfold, and shall inherit everlasting life. But many **of the** first shall be last, and the last first.

MATTHEW 20

Parable of laborers in vineyard—foretells Resurrection

For the kingdom of heaven is like unto a man, a householder, **who** went out early in the morning to hire laborers into his vineyard. And when he had agreed with the laborers for a penny a day, he sent them into his vineyard. And he went out about the third hour, and **found** others standing idle in the marketplace, and said unto them, Go ye also into the vineyard, and whatsoever is right I will give you. And they went their way. Again he went out about the sixth and ninth hour, and did likewise. And about the eleventh hour he went out, and found others standing idle, and saith unto them, Why stand ye here all the day idle? They **said** unto him, Because no man hath hired us. He **said** unto them, Go ye also into the vineyard; and whatsoever is right ye **shall** receive.

So when even was come, the lord of the vineyard saith unto his steward, Call the laborers and give them their hire, beginning from the last unto the first. And when they came that **began** about the eleventh hour, they received every man a penny. But when the first came, they supposed that they should have received more; and they likewise received every man a penny. And when they had received **a penny**, they murmured against the goodman of the house, saying, These last have wrought one hour **only** and thou hast made them equal unto us, **who** have borne the burden and heat of the day.

But he answered one of them, and said, Friend, I do thee no wrong: didst not thou agree with me for a penny? Take thine and go thy way; I will give unto this last even as unto thee. Is it not lawful for me to do what I will with mine own? Is thine eye evil, because I am good? So the last shall be first, and the first last; for many **are** called, but few chosen.

Jesus going up to Jerusalem took the twelve disciples apart in the way, and said,

Behold, we go up to Jerusalem, and the Son of Man shall be betrayed unto the chief priests, and unto the scribes, and they shall condemn Him to death; and shall deliver Him to the Gentiles to mock, and to scourge, and to crucify. And the third day He shall rise again.

Then came to Him the mother of Zebedee's children with her sons, worshiping ***Jesus****, and desiring a certain thing of Him. He said,*

What wilt thou **that I should do**?

Grant that these my two sons may sit, the one on Thy right hand, and the other on Thy left, in Thy kingdom. But Jesus answered,

Ye know not what ye ask. Are ye able to drink of the cup that I shall drink of, and to be baptized with the baptism that I am baptized with?

We are able.

Ye shall drink indeed of my cup, and be baptized with the baptism that I am baptized with; but to sit on my right hand, and on my left, is **for whom it is prepared of my Father, but** not mine to give.

When the ten heard ***this****, they were moved with indignation against the two brethren. But Jesus called them, and said,*

Ye know that the princes of the Gentiles exercise dominion over them, and they that are great exercise authority upon them; but it shall not be so among you. But whosoever will be great among you, let him be your minister; and whosoever will be chief among you, let him be your servant: even as the Son of Man came not to be ministered unto, but to minister, and to give His life a ransom for many.

As they departed from Jericho, two blind men sitting by the wayside, cried out, Have mercy on us, O Lord, Son of David. And Jesus called them, and said,

What will ye that I shall do unto you?

Lord, that our eyes may be opened. Jesus had compassion, and touched their eyes; and immediately their eyes received sight, and they followed Him.

MATTHEW 21

Casts out moneychangers—curses fig tree—
parables of two sons; wicked husbandmen

When ***Jesus*** *drew nigh unto Jerusalem, and* ***they*** *were come to Bethphage, unto the Mount of Olives, then sent Jesus two disciples,*

Go into the village over against you, and straightway ye shall find **a colt** tied; loose **it**, and bring **it** unto me; and if any **shall** say **aught** unto you, ye shall say, The Lord hath need of **it**; and straightway he will send **it**.

*The disciples did as Jesus commanded and brought the colt, and put on **it** their clothes; and **Jesus took the colt and sat** thereon**; and they followed Him.***

Jesus went into the temple of God, and cast out all them that sold and bought in the temple, and overthrew the tables of the moneychangers, and the seats of them that sold doves, and said unto them,

It is written, My house shall be called the house of prayer; but ye have made it a den of thieves.

And the blind and the lame came to Him in the temple; and He healed them.

*When the chief priests and scribes saw the wonderful things that He did, and the children **of the kingdom** crying in the temple, Hosanna to the Son of David! they were sore displeased, and said unto Him, Hearest Thou what these say?*

Yea; have ye never read **the scriptures which saith**, Out of the **mouths** of babes and sucklings, **O Lord,** Thou hast perfected praise?

*He left them, and went out of the city into Bethany; and He lodged there. In the morning as He returned into the city, He hungered. And when He saw a fig tree in the way, He came to it and **there was not any fruit on it**, but leaves only. **He** said unto it,*

Let no fruit grow on thee henceforward, forever.

*And presently the fig tree withered away. When the disciples saw **this**, they marveled **and said**, How soon is the fig tree withered away! Jesus answered,*

Verily I say unto you, If ye have faith, and doubt not, ye shall not only do this to the fig tree, but also, if ye shall say unto this mountain, Be thou removed, and be thou cast into the sea, it shall be done. And all things, whatsoever ye shall ask in prayer, **in faith** believing, ye shall receive.

When He was come into the temple, the chief priests and the elders of the people came unto Him as He was teaching, and said, By what authority doest Thou these things? And who gave Thee this authority? Jesus answered,

I also will ask you one thing, which if ye tell me, I, **likewise**, will tell you by what authority I do these things. The baptism of John, whence was it? From heaven, or of men?

We cannot tell.

Neither tell I you by what authority I do these things.

But what think ye? A man had two sons; and he came to the first, **saying**, Son, go work today in my vineyard. He answered and said, I will not: but afterward he repented, and went. And he came to the second, and said likewise. And he answered and said, I **will serve;** and went not. Whether of **these** twain did the will of **their** father?

The first.

Verily I say unto you, That the publicans and the harlots **shall** go into the kingdom of God before you. For John came unto you in the way of righteousness, **and bore record of me,** and ye believed him not; but the publicans and the harlots believed him; and ye, **afterward,** when ye had seen **me**, repented not, that ye might believe him. **For he that believed not John concerning me, cannot believe me, except he first repent. And except ye repent, the preaching of John shall condemn you at the Day of Judgment; for unto you that believe not, I speak in parables; that your unrighteousness may be rewarded unto you.**

And, again, hear another parable**; Behold,** there was a certain householder, **who** planted a vineyard, and hedged it round about, and digged a winepress in it; and built a tower, and let it out to husbandmen, and went into a far country. And when the time of the fruit drew near, he sent his servants to the husbandmen, that they might receive the fruits of it. And the husbandmen took his servants, and beat one, and killed another, and stoned another. Again, he sent other servants more than the first: and they did unto them likewise. But last of all he sent unto them his son, saying, They will reverence my son. But when the husbandmen saw the son, they said among themselves, This is the heir; come, let us kill him, and let us seize on his inheritance. And they caught him, and cast him out of the vineyard, and slew him. When the lord therefore of the vineyard cometh, what will he do unto those husbandmen?

They say, He will destroy those ***miserable****, wicked men, and will let out* ***the*** *vineyard unto other husbandmen,* ***who*** *shall render him the fruits in their seasons.*

Did ye never read in the scriptures, The stone which the builders rejected, the same is become the head of the corner; this is the Lord's **doings**, and it is marvelous in our eyes. Therefore say I unto you, The kingdom of God shall be taken from you, and given to a nation bringing forth the fruits thereof. **For** whosoever shall fall on this stone, shall be broken; but on whomsoever it shall fall, it will grind him to powder.

His disciples came to Him, and Jesus said,

Marvel ye at the words of the parable which I spake unto them?

Verily, I say unto you, I am the stone, and those wicked ones reject me. I am the head of the corner. These Jews shall fall upon me, and shall be broken. And the kingdom of God shall be taken from them, and shall be given to a nation bringing forth the fruits thereof *(meaning the Gentiles)*; wherefore, on whomsoever this stone shall fall, it shall grind him to powder. And when the Lord therefore of the vineyard cometh, He will destroy those miserable, wicked men, and will let again his vineyard unto other husbandmen, even in the last days, who shall render him the fruits in their seasons.

Then understood they the parable which He spake unto them, that the Gentiles should be destroyed also, when the Lord should descend out of heaven to reign in His vineyard, which is the earth and the inhabitants thereof.

MATTHEW 22

Parable of marriage of king's son—the great commandment

Jesus answered ***the people again****, and spake* **in** *parables,*

The kingdom of heaven is like unto a certain king, **who** made a marriage for his son. And **when the marriage was ready, he** sent forth his servants to call them **which** were bidden to the wedding; and they would not come. Again he sent forth other servants, saying, Tell them **that** are bidden, Behold, I have prepared my oxen, and my fatlings **have been** killed, **and my dinner is ready,** and all things are **prepared; therefore** come unto the marriage. But they made light of **the servants**, and went their ways; one to his farm, another to his merchandise; and the remnant took his servants, and entreated them spitefully, and slew them.

But when the king heard **that his servants were dead**, he was wroth; and he sent forth his armies, and destroyed those murderers, and burned up their city. Then said he to his servants, The wedding is ready; but they **who** were bidden were not worthy. Go ye therefore into the highways, and as many as ye shall find, bid to the marriage. So those servants went out into the highways, and gathered together all as many as they found, both bad and good: and the wedding was furnished with guests.

But when the king came in to see the guests, he saw there a man **who** had not a wedding garment. And he saith unto him, Friend, how camest thou in hither not having a wedding garment? And he was speechless. Then said the king **unto his** servants, Bind him hand and foot, and take **and cast** him away into outer darkness; there shall be weeping and gnashing of teeth. For many are called, but few chosen**; wherefore all do not have on the wedding garment.**

The Pharisees took counsel how they might entangle Him in talk. They sent unto Him their disciples, saying, Is it lawful to give tribute unto Caesar, or not? But Jesus perceived their wickedness, and said,

Ye hypocrites! Why tempt ye me? Show me the tribute money.

They brought Him a penny.

Whose image **is this,** and superscription?

*They **said**, Caesar's.*

Render therefore unto Caesar, the things which are Caesar's; and unto God the things which are God's.

*The same day the Sadducees asked, Master, Moses said, If a man die, having no children, his brother shall marry his wife, and raise up seed unto his brother. Now there were with us, seven brethren; and the first, when he had married a wife, deceased; and, having no issue, **he** left his wife unto his brother. Likewise the second also, and the third, and **even** unto the seventh. And last of all the woman died also. Therefore in the resurrection whose wife shall she be of the seven? For they all had her. Jesus answered,*

Ye do err, not knowing the scriptures, nor the power of God. For in the resurrection they neither marry, nor are given in marriage, but are as the angels of God in heaven. But as touching the resurrection of the dead, have ye not read that which was spoken unto you **of** God, saying, I am the God of Abraham, and the God of Isaac, and the God of Jacob? God is not the God of the dead, but of the living.

*Then a [Pharisee] lawyer, **tempting Him,** asked, saying, Master, which is the great commandment? Jesus said,*

Thou shalt love the Lord thy God with all thy heart, and with all thy soul, and with all thy mind. This is the first and great commandment. And the second is like unto it, Thou shalt love thy neighbor as thyself. On these two commandments hang all the law and the prophets.

While the Pharisees were gathered, Jesus asked them,

What think ye of Christ? Whose Son is He?

They say, The Son of David.

How then doth David in spirit call Him Lord, saying, The LORD said unto my Lord, Sit Thou on my right hand, till I make Thine enemies Thy footstool? If David then **called** Him Lord, how is He his Son?

Matthew 23

Hypocrites—weeps over Jerusalem

Then spake Jesus to the multitude and to His disciples,

The scribes and the Pharisees sit in Moses' seat: all, therefore, whatsoever they bid you observe, **they will make you** observe and do; **for they are ministers of the law, and they make themselves your judges.** But do not ye after their works; for they say, and do not. For they bind heavy burdens and lay on men's shoulders**, and they are grievous to be borne**; but they will not move them with one of their fingers. **And** all their works they do to be seen of men. They make broad their phylacteries, and enlarge the borders of their garments, and love the uppermost rooms at feasts, and the chief seats in the synagogues, and greetings in the markets, and to be called of men, Rabbi, Rabbi ***(which is master)***.

But be not ye called Rabbi; for one is your Master, **which is** Christ; and all ye are brethren. And call no **one** your Creator upon the earth, **or your Heavenly Father;** for one is your **Creator and Heavenly** Father, **even He who** is in heaven. Neither be ye called masters; for one is your Master, even **He whom your Heavenly Father sent, which is** Christ**; for He hath sent Him among you that ye might have life.** But he that is greatest among you shall be your servant. And whosoever shall exalt himself shall be abased **of Him**; and he that shall humble himself shall be exalted **of Him**.

But woe unto you, scribes and Pharisees, hypocrites! For ye shut up the kingdom of heaven against men: for ye neither go in yourselves, neither suffer ye them that are entering to go in. Woe unto you, scribes and Pharisees! **For ye are** hypocrites! Ye devour widows' houses, and for a pretense make long **prayers;** therefore ye shall receive the greater ~~damnation~~ **punishment**. Woe unto you, scribes and Pharisees, hypocrites! For ye compass sea and land to make one proselyte; and when he is made, ye make him twofold more the child of hell than **he was before, like unto** yourselves.

Woe unto you, blind guides, **who** say, Whosoever shall swear by the temple, it is nothing; but whosoever shall swear by the gold of the temple, he **committeth sin, and** is a debtor. **You are** fools and blind; for **which** is **the** greater, the gold, or the temple that sanctifieth the gold? And **ye say**, Whosoever **sweareth** by the altar, it is nothing; but whosoever sweareth by the gift that is upon it, he is guilty. **O** fools, and blind! **For which** is **the** greater, the gift, or the altar that sanctifieth the gift? **Verily I say unto you,** Whoso, therefore, **sweareth** by **it**, sweareth by **the altar**, and by all things thereon. And whoso shall swear by the temple, sweareth by it, and by Him **who** dwelleth therein. And he that shall swear by heaven, sweareth by the throne of God, and by Him **who** sitteth thereon.

Woe unto you, scribes and Pharisees, hypocrites! For **you** pay tithe of mint, and anise, and cummin; and have omitted the weightier **things** of the law; judgment, mercy, and faith; these ought ye to have done, and not to leave the other undone. You blind guides, **who** strain at a gnat, and swallow a camel**; who make yourselves appear unto men that ye would not commit the least sin, and yet you, yourselves, transgress the whole law.**

Woe unto you, scribes and Pharisees, hypocrites! For **you** make clean the outside of the cup, and of the platter; but within they are full of extortion and excess. **Ye** blind **Pharisees**! Cleanse first the cup and platter **within**, that the outside of them may be clean also. Woe unto you, scribes and Pharisees, hypocrites! For ye are like unto whited sepulchres, which indeed appear beautiful **outwardly**, but are within full of **the** bones **of the dead**, and of all uncleanness. Even so ye also outwardly appear righteous unto men, but within ye are full of hypocrisy and iniquity.

Woe unto you, scribes and Pharisees, hypocrites! Because **you** build the tombs of the prophets, and garnish the sepulchres of the righteous, and say, If we had been in the days of our fathers, we would not have been partakers with them in the blood of the prophets. Wherefore, ye **are** witnesses unto yourselves **of your own wickedness; and** ye are the children of them **who** killed the prophets**; and will** fill up the measure **then** of your fathers**; for ye, yourselves, kill the prophets like unto your fathers.** Ye serpents, **and** generation of vipers! How can ye escape the damnation of hell?

Wherefore, behold, I send unto you prophets, and wise men, and scribes; and of them ye shall kill and crucify; and of them **ye** shall scourge in your synagogues, and persecute from city to city; that upon you may come all the righteous blood shed upon the earth, from the blood of righteous Abel unto the blood of Zacharias son of Barachias, whom ye slew between the temple and the altar. Verily I say unto you,

All these things shall come upon this generation. **You bear testimony against your fathers, when ye, yourselves, are partakers of the same wickedness. Behold your fathers did it through ignorance, but ye do not; wherefore, their sins shall be upon your heads.**

Then Jesus began to weep over Jerusalem, saying,

O Jerusalem! Jerusalem! **Ye who will kill** the prophets, and **will stone** them **who** are sent unto **you**; how often would I have gathered **your** children together, even as a hen **gathers** her chickens under her wings, and ye would not. Behold, your house is left unto you desolate. For I say unto you, **that** ye shall not see me henceforth, **and know that I am He of whom it is written by the prophets,** until ye shall say, Blessed is He **who** cometh in the name of the Lord**, in the clouds of heaven, and all the holy angels with Him.**

Matthew 24

Second Coming—parable of fig tree

Jesus went out, and departed from the temple; and His disciples came to ***hear*** *Him****, saying, Master, show us concerning*** *the buildings of the temple****; as Thou hast said; They shall be thrown down and left unto you desolate.*** *Jesus said,*

See ye not all these things? **And do you not understand them?** Verily I say unto you, There shall not be left here **upon this temple,** one stone upon another, **which** shall not be thrown down.

Jesus left them and went upon the Mount of Olives. *The disciples came unto Him privately, saying, Tell us, when shall these things be* ***which Thou hast said concerning the destruction of the temple, and the Jews;*** *and what* ***is*** *the sign of Thy coming; and of the end of the world* ***(or the destruction of the wicked, which is the end of the world)****? Jesus answered,*

Take heed that no man deceive you. For many shall come in my name, saying, I am Christ; and shall deceive many. Then shall they deliver you up to be afflicted, and shall kill you: and ye shall be hated of all nations for my name's sake. And then shall many be offended, and shall betray one another, and shall hate one another. And many false prophets shall rise, and shall deceive many. And because iniquity shall abound, the love of many shall wax cold. But he that **remaineth steadfast, and is not overcome,** the same shall be saved.

When ye; therefore, shall see the abomination of desolation, spoken of by Daniel the prophet, **concerning the destruction of Jerusalem,**

then ye shall stand in the holy place. (Whoso readeth let him understand.) Then let them **who are** in Judea, flee into the mountains. Let him **who** is on the housetop**, flee, and** not **return** to take anything out of his house. Neither let him **who** is in the field, return back to take his clothes. And woe unto them that are with child, and **unto** them that give suck in those days!

Therefore, pray ye **the Lord,** that your flight be not in the winter, neither on the Sabbath day. For then**, in those days,** shall be great **tribulations on the Jews, and upon the inhabitants of Jerusalem;** such as was not **before sent upon Israel, of God,** since the beginning of **their kingdom until** this time; no, nor ever shall be **sent again upon Israel.** All **things which have befallen them,** are **only** the beginning of **the** sorrows **which shall come upon them;** and except those days should be shortened, there should **none of their** flesh be saved. But for the elect's sake, **according to the covenant,** those days shall be shortened.

Behold these things I have spoken unto you concerning the Jews. And again, after the tribulation of those days which shall come upon Jerusalem, if any man shall say unto you, Lo! here is Christ, or there; believe **him** not. For **in those days,** there shall **also** arise false Christs, and false prophets, and shall show great signs and wonders; insomuch that, if possible, they shall deceive the very elect**, who are the elect according to the covenant. Behold, I speak these things unto you for the elect's sake.**

And ye **also** shall hear of wars, and rumors of wars; see that ye be not troubled; for all **I have told you** must come to pass. But the end is not yet. Behold, I have told you before. Wherefore if they shall say unto you, Behold, He is in the desert; go not forth: behold, He is in the secret chambers; believe it not. For as the **light of the morning** cometh out of the East, and shineth even unto the West**, and covereth the whole earth**; so shall also the coming of the Son of Man be.

And now I show unto you a parable. Behold, wheresoever the **carcass** is, there will the eagles be gathered together**; so likewise shall mine elect be gathered from the four quarters of the earth. And they shall hear of wars, and rumors of wars. Behold, I speak for mine elect's sake.** For nation shall rise against nation, and kingdom against kingdom; there shall be **famine** and pestilences, and earthquakes in divers places. **And again, because iniquity shall abound, the love of**

men shall wax cold; but he that shall not be overcome, the same shall be saved.

And **again,** this gospel of the kingdom shall be preached in all the world, for a witness unto all nations, and then shall the end come**, or the destruction of the wicked. And again shall the abomination of desolation, spoken of by Daniel the prophet, be fulfilled. And** immediately after the tribulation of those days, the sun **shall** be darkened, and the moon shall not give her light, and the stars shall fall from heaven, and the powers of **heaven** shall be shaken.

Verily I say unto you, This generation**, in which these things shall be shown forth,** shall not pass **away** until all **I have told you shall** be fulfilled. **Although the days will come that** heaven and earth shall pass away, **yet** my **word** shall not pass away**; but all shall be fulfilled.** And **as I said before, after the tribulation of those days, and the powers of the heavens shall be shaken,** then shall appear the sign of the Son of Man in heaven; and then shall all the tribes of the earth mourn. And they shall see the Son of Man coming in the clouds of heaven with power and great glory. **And whoso treasureth up my words, shall not be deceived. For the Son of Man shall come,** and He shall send His angels **before Him** with **the** great sound of a trumpet, and they shall gather together **the remainder of** His elect from the four winds; from one end of heaven to the other.

Now learn a parable of the fig tree, When **its branches are** yet tender, and **it begins to put** forth leaves, **you** know that summer is nigh **at hand.** So likewise **mine elect**, when **they** shall see all these things, **they shall** know that **He** is near, even at the doors. But of that day and hour **no one** knoweth; no, not the angels of **God in** heaven, but my Father only.

But as **it was in** the days of **Noah**, so **it** shall **be** also **at** the coming of the Son of Man. For **it shall be with them** as **it was** in the days **which** were before the flood**; for until the day that Noah entered into the ark,** they were eating and drinking, marrying and giving in marriage, and knew not until the flood came and took them all away; so shall also the coming of the Son of Man be. **Then shall be fulfilled that which is written, that, In the last days, two** shall be in the field; the one shall be taken and the other left. Two shall be grinding at the mill; the one taken and the other left. **And what I say unto one, I say unto all men;** Watch, therefore, for **you** know not **at** what hour your Lord doth come.

But know this, if the goodman of the house had known in what watch the thief would come, he would have watched, and would not have suffered his house to **have been** broken up**; but would have been ready.** Therefore be ye also ready: for in such an hour as ye think not the Son of Man cometh. Who then is a faithful and wise servant, whom his lord hath made ruler over his household, to give them meat in due season? Blessed is that servant, whom his lord when he cometh shall find so doing. **And,** verily I say unto you, He shall make him ruler over all his goods.

But if that evil servant shall say in his heart, My lord delayeth his coming; and shall begin to smite his fellow servants, and to eat and drink with the drunken; the Lord of that servant shall come in a day when he looketh not for him, and in an hour that he is not aware of, and shall cut him asunder, and **shall** appoint him his portion with the hypocrites; there shall be weeping and gnashing of teeth. **And thus cometh the end of the wicked according to the prophecy of Moses, saying, They should be cut off from among the people. But the end of the earth is not yet; but by and by.**

Matthew 25

Parables of ten virgins; talents; sheep and goats

And then, at that day, before the Son of Man comes, the kingdom of heaven **shall** be likened unto ten virgins, **who** took their lamps, and went forth to meet the bridegroom. And five of them were wise, and five **of them** were foolish. They that were foolish took their lamps, and took no oil with them: but the wise took oil in their vessels with their lamps. While the bridegroom tarried, they all slumbered and slept. And at midnight there was a cry made, Behold, the bridegroom cometh; go ye out to meet him. Then all those virgins arose, and trimmed their lamps. And the foolish said unto the wise, Give us of your oil; for our lamps are gone out. But the wise answered, saying, Lest there be not enough for us and you, go ye rather to them that sell, and buy for yourselves. And while they went to buy, the bridegroom came; and they that were ready went in with him to the marriage: and the door was shut. Afterward came also the other virgins, saying, Lord, Lord, open **unto** us. But he answered and said, Verily I say unto you, ~~I~~ **Ye** know ~~you~~ **me** not. Watch therefore, for ye know neither the day nor the hour wherein the Son of Man cometh.

Now I will liken these things unto a parable. For ~~the kingdom of heaven~~ **it** is **like** as a man traveling into a far country, who called his own servants, and delivered unto them his goods. And unto one he gave five talents, to another two, and to another one; to every man according to his several ability; and straightway **went on** his journey. Then he that had received the five talents, went and traded with the same; and **gained** other five talents. And likewise he **who** received two **talents**, he also gained other two. But he **who** had received one, went and digged in the earth and hid his lord's money.

After a long time the lord of those servants cometh, and reckoneth with them. And so he that had received **the** five talents came, and brought other five talents, saying, Lord, thou deliveredst unto me five talents; behold, I have gained **besides** them, five talents more. His lord said unto him, Well done, good and faithful servant; thou hast been faithful over a few things, I will make thee ruler over many things; enter thou into the joy of thy lord. He also that had received two talents came and said, Lord, thou deliveredst unto me two talents; behold, I have gained two talents **besides** them. His lord said unto him, Well done, good and faithful servant; thou hast been faithful over a few things, I will make thee ruler over many things: enter thou into the joy of thy lord.

Then he **who** had received the one talent came, and said, Lord, I knew thee that thou art **a** hard man, reaping where thou hast not sown, and gathering where thou hast not ~~strawed~~ **scattered**. And I was afraid, and went and hid thy talent in the earth; **and** lo, **here is thy talent; take it from me as** thou hast **from thine other servants, for it** is thine. His lord answered and said unto him, **O** wicked and slothful servant! Thou knewest that I reap where I sowed not, and gather where I have not ~~strawed~~ **scattered**. **Having known this, therefore,** thou oughtest to have put my money to the exchangers, and at my coming I should have received mine own with usury. **I will** take, therefore, the talent from **you**, and give it unto him **who** hath ten talents. For unto everyone **who** hath **obtained other talents,** shall be given, and he shall have **in** abundance. But from him that hath not **obtained other talents,** shall be taken away even that which he hath **received**. And **his lord shall say unto his servants,** Cast ye the unprofitable servant into outer darkness; there shall be weeping and gnashing of teeth.

When the Son of Man shall come in His glory, and all the holy angels with Him, then **He** shall sit upon the throne of His glory; and before Him shall be gathered all nations; and He shall separate them one from another, as a shepherd divideth ~~his~~ sheep from the goats; the sheep on His right hand, but the goats on **His** left. **And He shall sit upon His throne, and the Twelve Apostles with Him.** Then shall the King say unto them on His right hand, Come, ye blessed of my Father, inherit the kingdom prepared for you from the foundation of the world: for I was an hungered, and ye gave me meat; I was thirsty, and ye gave me drink; I was a stranger, and ye took me in; naked, and ye clothed me; I was sick, and ye visited me: I was in prison, and ye came unto me. Then shall the righteous answer Him, saying, Lord, when saw we Thee an hungered, and fed Thee; or thirsty, and gave Thee drink? When saw we Thee a stranger, and took Thee in? Or naked, and clothed Thee? Or when saw we Thee sick, or in prison, and came unto Thee? And the King shall answer and say unto them, Verily I say unto you, Inasmuch as ye have done it unto one of the least of these my brethren, ye have done it unto me.

Then shall He say also unto them on the left hand, Depart from me, ye cursed, into everlasting fire, prepared for the devil and his angels: for I was an hungered, and ye gave me no meat; I was thirsty, and ye gave me no drink; I was a stranger, and ye took me not in: naked, and ye clothed me not: sick, and in prison, and ye visited me not. Then shall they also answer Him, saying, Lord, when saw we Thee an hungered, or athirst, or a stranger, or naked, or sick, or in prison, and did not minister unto Thee? Then shall He answer them, saying, Verily I say unto you, Inasmuch as ye did it not to one of the least of these **my brethren**, ye did it not unto me. And these shall go away into everlasting punishment: but the righteous into life eternal.

Matthew 26

Passover—Gethsemane

When Jesus had finished all these sayings, He said unto His disciples,

Ye know that after two days is the Passover, and **then** the Son of Man is betrayed to be crucified.

When Jesus was in Bethany, in the house of Simon the leper, there came unto Him a woman having an alabaster box of very precious ointment, and poured it on His head as He sat ***in the house****. But when* ***some*** *saw* ***this****, they had indignation, saying,* ***Unto*** *what purpose is this waste? For this ointment might have been sold for much, and given to the poor. Jesus said unto them,*

Why trouble ye the woman **and from whence is this evil in your hearts**? For **verily I say unto you** she hath wrought a good work upon me. For ye have the poor always with you; but me ye have not always. For she hath poured this ointment on my body, for my burial. **And in this thing that she hath done, she shall be blessed; for** verily I say unto you, Wheresoever this gospel shall be preached in the whole world, this **thing** that this woman hath done, **shall also** be told for a memorial of her **for in that she hath done for me she hath obtained a blessing of my Father**.

On *the first day of the Feast of Unleavened Bread, the disciples came* ***unto*** *Jesus, saying, Where wilt Thou that we prepare for Thee to eat the passover? He said,*

Go into the city to such a man, and say unto him, The Master saith, My time is at hand; I will keep the Passover at thy house with my disciples.

When the ***evening*** *was come, He sat down with the Twelve. And as they did eat, He said,*

Verily I say unto you, that one of you shall betray me.

And they were exceeding sorrowful, and began everyone of them to say unto Him, Lord, is it I? He answered,

He that dippeth his hand with me in the dish, the same shall betray me. **But** the Son of Man goeth as it is written of Him; but woe unto that man by whom the Son of Man is betrayed! It had been good for that man if he had not been born.

Then Judas, ***who*** *betrayed Him, answered and said, Master, is it I? He said unto him,*

Thou hast said.

As they were eating, Jesus took bread and ***brake*** *it and* ***blessed*** *it and gave to* ***His*** *disciples, and said,*

Take, eat; this is **in remembrance of** my body **which I give a ransom for you**.

And He took the cup, and gave thanks, and gave it to them, saying,

Drink ye all of it; for this is **in remembrance of** my blood of the new testament, which is shed for **as** many **as shall believe on my name,** for the remission of **their** sins. **And I give unto you a commandment, that ye shall observe to do the things which ye have seen me do, and**

bear record of me even unto the end. But I say unto you, I will not drink henceforth of this fruit of the vine, until that day when I **shall come and** drink it new with you in my Father's kingdom.

When they had sung a hymn, they went out into the Mount of Olives. Then ***said*** *Jesus,*

All ye shall be offended because of me this night; for it is written, I will smite the **Shepherd**, and the sheep of the flock shall be scattered abroad. But after I am risen again, I will go before you into Galilee.

Peter answered and said, Though all men shall be offended because of Thee, I ***will*** *never be offended. Jesus said,*

Verily I say unto thee, That this night, before the cock crow, thou shalt deny me thrice.

Then cometh Jesus with them unto a place called Gethsemane, and saith,

Sit ye here, while I go and pray yonder.

He took with Him Peter and the two sons of Zebedee, and began to be sorrowful and very heavy. Then saith He unto them,

My soul is exceeding sorrowful, even unto death: tarry ye here, and watch with me.

And He went a little farther, and fell on His face, and prayed,

O my Father, if it be possible, let this cup pass from me: nevertheless not as I will, but as Thou wilt.

He cometh unto the disciples, and findeth them asleep, and saith unto Peter,

What, could ye not watch with me one hour? Watch and pray, that ye enter not into temptation.

He went away again, and prayed,

O my Father, if this cup may not pass away from me, except I drink it, Thy will be done.

And He came and found them asleep again. He left them, and went away again, and prayed the third time, saying the same words. Then cometh He to His disciples, and saith,

Sleep on now and take rest. Behold, the hour is at hand, and the Son of Man is betrayed into the hands of sinners.

After they had slept, He said,

Arise, and let us be going. Behold, he is at hand that doth betray me.

Judas, and with him a great multitude, came to Jesus, and said, Hail Master! and kissed Him. Jesus said unto him,

Judas, wherefore art thou come **to betray me with a kiss**?

One of them which were with Jesus, stretched out his hand and drew his sword, and struck a servant of the high ***priest****, and smote off his ear. Then said Jesus unto him,*

Put up again thy sword into **its** place; for all they that take the sword shall perish with the sword. Thinkest thou that I cannot now pray to my Father, and He shall presently give me more than twelve legions of angels? But how then shall the scriptures be fulfilled, that thus it must be?

Said Jesus ***unto*** *the multitudes,*

Are ye come out as against a thief, with swords and staves, for to take me? I sat daily with you in the temple, **teaching,** and ye laid no hold on me. But all this was done, that the scriptures of the prophets might be fulfilled.

Then all the disciples forsook Him, and fled. And they that had laid hold on Jesus led Him away to Caiaphas the high priest. The high priest said unto Him, I adjure Thee by the living God, that Thou tell us whether Thou be the Christ, the Son of God.

Thou hast said: nevertheless I say unto you, Hereafter shall ye see the Son of Man sitting on the right hand of power, and coming in the clouds of heaven.

*The high priest rent his clothes, saying, He hath spoken blasphemy. What think ye? They answered, He is guilty****, and worthy*** *of death.*

MATTHEW 27

Trial—Crucifixion

When the morning was come, and when they had bound Him, they led Him away, and delivered Him to Pontius Pilate. The governor asked Him, Art Thou the King of the Jews? Jesus said,

Thou sayest **truly; for thus it is written of me.**

And when He was accused of the chief priests and elders, He answered nothing. Then said Pilate unto Him, Hearest Thou not how many things they witness against Thee? And He answered him ***not*** *to* ***his questions; yea,*** *never a word****,*** *insomuch that the governor marveled greatly.*

Now at ***the*** *feast the governor was wont to release unto the people a prisoner. And they had a notable prisoner, called Barabbas. When they were gathered together, Pilate said unto them, Whom will ye that I release unto you? Barabbas, or Jesus which is called Christ? For he knew that for envy they had delivered Him.*

*[Pilate's] wife sent unto him, saying, Have thou nothing to do with that just man****,*** *for I have suffered many things this day in a ~~dream~~* ***vision*** *because of Him.*

But the chief priests and elders persuaded the multitude that they should ask Barabbas, and destroy Jesus. ***And*** *the governor said, Whether of the twain will ye that I release unto you? They said, Barabbas. Pilate* ***said****, What shall I do with Jesus, which is called Christ?* ***And*** *all* ***said*** *unto him, Let Him be crucified. And the governor said, Why, what evil hath He done? But they cried out the more, saying, Let Him be crucified.*

When Pilate saw that he could prevail nothing, but rather ***that**** *a tulmult was made, he took water, and washed his hands before the multitude, saying, I am innocent of the blood of this just person****;*** *see ~~ye to it~~* ***that ye do nothing unto Him****. Then answered all the people, His blood ~~be on~~* ***come upon*** *us and our children. Then released he Barabbas unto them: and when he had scourged Jesus, he delivered Him to be crucified.*

Then the soldiers took Jesus and stripped Him, and put on Him a ~~scarlet~~ ***purple*** *robe. They put a [crown of thornes] upon His head, and a reed in His right hand: and they bowed the knee before Him, and mocked Him, saying, Hail, King of the Jews! And they spit upon Him, and took the reed, and smote Him on the head. And after they had mocked Him, they took the robe off Him, put His own raiment on Him, and led Him away to crucify Him.*

When they were come unto Golgotha (a place of ~~a skull~~ ***burial)****, they gave Him vinegar to drink mingled with gall****;*** *and when He had tasted* ***the vinegar****, He would not drink. And they crucified Him, and parted His garments, casting lots.*

Pilate wrote a title, and put it on the cross, and the writing was, *JESUS* **OF NAZARETH***, THE KING OF THE JEWS****, in letters of Greek, Latin, and Hebrew. And the chief priests said unto Pilate, It should be written and set up over His head, His accusation, This is He that said He was Jesus, the King of the Jews. But Pilate answered, What I have written, I have written; let it alone.***

Then were there two thieves crucified with Him, one on the right hand, and another on the left. And they that passed by reviled Him, wagging their heads, and saying, Thou that destroyest the temple, and buildest it ***again*** *in three days, save Thyself. If Thou be the Son of God come down from the cross. Likewise also the chief priests mocking with the scribes* and* ***the*** *elders, said, He saved others, Himself He cannot save. If He be the King of Israel, let Him now come down from the cross, and we will believe Him. He trusted in God; let Him deliver Him now****;*** *if He will* ***save*** *Him****; let Him save Him;*** *for He said, I am the Son of God.*

One of *the thieves also, which were crucified with Him, cast the same in his teeth.* ***But the other rebuked him, saying, Dost thou not fear God, seeing thou art under the same condemnation; and this man is just, and hath not sinned; and he cried unto the Lord that he would save him. And the Lord said unto him,***

This day thou shalt be with me in Paradise.

From the sixth hour there was darkness over all the land. And about the ninth hour Jesus cried with a loud voice,

Eli, Eli, lama sabachthani *(My God, my God, why hast Thou forsaken me)?*

Some of them that stood there, when they heard ***Him****, said, This man calleth for Elias. And straightway one of them ran, and took a* ***sponge****, and filled it with vinegar, and put it on a reed, and gave Him to drink. The rest said, Let* ***Him*** *be, let us see whether Elias will come to save Him.*

Jesus, when He had cried again with a loud voice, ***saying,***

Father, it is finished, thy will is done,

Yielded up the ghost.

Matthew28

Resurrection

As it began to dawn toward the first day of the week, ***early in the morning,*** *came Mary Magdalene, and the other Mary to see the sepulchre. There* ***had been*** *a great earthquake; for* ***two angels*** *of the Lord descended from heaven, and came and rolled back the stone from the door, and sat upon it. The* ***angels*** *said unto the women, Fear not ye; for* ***we*** *know that ye seek Jesus* ***who*** *was crucified. He is not here: for He is risen, as He said. Come, see the place where the Lord lay. And go quickly, and tell His disciples that He is risen from the dead; and, He goeth before you into Galilee; there shall ye see Him.*

They departed quickly from the sepulchre with fear and great joy; and did run to bring His disciples word. As they went to tell His disciples, Jesus met them, saying,

All hail.

And they came and held Him by the feet, and worshiped Him. Then said Jesus,

Be not afraid: go tell my brethren that they go into Galilee, and there shall they see me.

Then the eleven disciples went away into Galilee, into a mountain where Jesus had appointed them. And Jesus came and spake unto them, saying,

All power is given unto me in heaven and in earth. Go ye therefore, and teach all nations, baptizing them in the name of the Father, and of the Son, and of the Holy Ghost: teaching them to observe all things whatsoever I have commanded you; and, lo, I am with you **always,** unto the end of the world.

Words of Christ According to Saint Mark

MARK 1

Preaches the gospel—heals

After John was put in prison, Jesus came into Galilee, preaching the gospel of the kingdom of God, and saying,

The time is fulfilled, and the kingdom of God is at hand: repent ye, and believe the gospel.

As He walked by the sea of Galilee, He saw Simon and Andrew his brother, casting a net into the sea; for they were fishers. And Jesus said,

Come ye after me, and I will make you to become fishers of men.

And straightway they forsook their nets, and followed Him.

They went into Capernaum. And there was in their synagogue a man with an unclean spirit, saying, Let us alone; what have we to do with Thee, Thou Jesus of Nazareth? Art Thou come to destroy us? I know Thee, who Thou art, the Holy One of God. Jesus rebuked him,

Hold thy peace, and come out of him.

And he came out of him.

In the morning, rising up a great while before day, He went out, and departed into a solitary place, and there prayed. And Simon and they that were with Him followed after Him and said, All men seek for Thee. And He said,

Let us go into the next towns, that I may preach there also: for therefore came I forth.

And He preached throughout all Galilee.

There came a leper to Him, beseeching Him; and kneeling down to Him, ***said****, If Thou wilt, Thou canst make me clean. And Jesus touched him, and saith,*

I will; be thou clean.

Immediately the leprosy departed, and he was cleansed.

See thou say nothing to any man: but go thy way, show thyself to the priest, and offer for thy cleansing those things which Moses commanded, for a testimony unto them.

MARK 2

Forgives sins—heals—Lord of the Sabbath

He entered into Capernaum after ***many*** *days. And they* ***came*** *unto Him, bringing one sick of the palsy, which was borne of four* ***persons****. And when they* *could not come nigh unto Him for the press, they uncovered the roof where He was: and when they had broken it up, they let down the bed wherein the sick of the palsy lay. When Jesus saw their faith, He said,*

Son, thy sins be forgiven thee.

There were certain of the scribes sitting there, and reasoning in their hearts, Why doth this man thus speak blasphemies? Who can forgive sins but God only? And immediately, when Jesus perceived in His spirit, that they so reasoned within themselves, He said,

Why reason ye these things in your hearts? Is it **not** easier to say to the sick of the palsy, Thy sins be forgiven thee; **than** to say, Arise, and take up thy bed and walk? But that ye may know that the Son of Man hath power on earth to forgive sins, *(He **said** to the sick of the palsy)* I say unto thee, Arise, and take up thy bed, and go thy way into **thy** house.

Immediately he arose, took up the bed, and went forth.

*Jesus went forth again by the seaside; and as He passed by, He saw Levi the son of **Alpheus**, sitting at the **place where they receive tribute**, and said,*

Follow me.

And he arose and followed Him. As Jesus sat at meat in his house, the scribes and Pharisees said unto His disciples, How is it that He eateth and drinketh with publicans and sinners? When Jesus heard, He said unto them,

They that are whole have no need of the physician, but they that are sick. I came not to call the righteous, but sinners to repentance.

***They came and said,** Why do the disciples of John and of the Pharisees fast, but Thy disciples fast not? Jesus said,*

Can the children of the bridechamber fast, while the bridegroom is with them? As long as they have the bridegroom with them, they cannot fast. But the days will come, when the bridegroom shall be taken away from them, and then shall they fast in those days. No man also seweth a piece of new cloth on an old garment: else the new piece that filled it up taketh away from the old, and the rent is made worse. And no man putteth new wine into old bottles: else the new wine doth burst the bottles, and the wine is spilled, and the bottles will be marred: but new wine must be put into new bottles.

*He went through the corn fields on the Sabbath day; and His disciples began to pluck the ears of corn. The Pharisees said, Behold, why do **Thy disciples** on the Sabbath day that which is not lawful? And He said,*

Have ye never read what David did, when he had need, and was an hungered, he, and they that were with him? How he went into the house of God in the days of Abiathar the high priest, and did eat the shewbread, which is not lawful to eat but for the priests, and gave also to them which were with him? The Sabbath was made for man, and not man for the Sabbath: **wherefore the Sabbath was given unto man for a day of rest; and also that man should glorify God, and not that man should not eat; for the Son of Man made the Sabbath day,** therefore the Son of Man is Lord also of the Sabbath.

MARK 3

Heals on the Sabbath—house divided—blasphemies

He entered into the synagogue; and there was a man there which had a withered hand. And they watched Him ***to see*** *whether He would heal him on the Sabbath day; that they might accuse Him. And He* ***said*** *unto the man which had the withered hand,*

Stand forth.

And He saith unto them,

Is it lawful to do good on the Sabbath days, or to do evil? To save life, or to kill?

Being grieved for the hardness of their hearts, he ***said*** *unto the man,*

Stretch forth thine hand.

And he stretched out ***his hand****; and his hand was restored whole as the other. Jesus withdrew, with His disciples, to the sea.*

The scribes which came down from Jerusalem said, He hath Beelzebub, and by the prince of the devils casteth He out devils. ***Now Jesus knew this,*** *and He called them, and said unto them in parables,*

How can Satan cast out Satan? And if a kingdom be divided against itself, **how can** that kingdom stand? And if a house be divided against itself, that house cannot stand. And if Satan rise up against himself and be divided, he cannot stand; but **speedily** hath an end. No man can enter into a strong man's house, and spoil his goods, except he will first bind the strong man; and then he will spoil his house.

Then came certain men unto Him, accusing Him, Why do ye receive sinners, seeing Thou makest Thyself the Son of God? But He answered,

Verily I say unto you, All sins **which men have committed, when they repent,** shall be forgiven **them; for I came to preach repentance unto the sons of men**. And blasphemies, wherewith soever they shall blaspheme, **shall be forgiven them that come unto me, and do the**

works which they see me do. But **there is a sin which shall not be forgiven.** He that shall blaspheme against the Holy Ghost, hath never forgiveness; but is in danger of **being cut down out of the world. And they shall inherit** eternal damnation.

The multitude sat about Him, and they said unto Him, Behold, Thy mother and Thy brethren without seek Thee. He answered,

Who is my mother, or **who are** my brethren?

And He looked round about Him and said,

Behold my mother and my brethren! For whosoever shall do the will of God, the same is my brother, and my sister, and mother.

MARK 4

Parables of sower; candle under a bushel; seed growing by itself; mustard seed—tempest

He began again to teach by the seaside: and there was gathered unto Him a great multitude, so that He entered into a ship, and sat in the sea; and the whole multitude was by the sea on the land. He taught them many things by parables.

Hearken; Behold, there went out a sower to sow; And it came to pass, as he sowed, some fell by the wayside, and the fowls of the air came and devoured it up. And some fell on stony ground, where it had not much earth; and immediately it sprang up, because it had no depth of earth: but when the sun was up, it was scorched; and because it had no root, it withered away. And some fell among thorns, and the thorns grew up, and choked it, and it yielded no fruit. And other **seed** fell on good ground, and did yield fruit, that sprang up and increased, and brought forth, some **thirtyfold**, and some sixty, and some a hundred. He that hath ears to hear, let him hear.

*When He was alone **with the Twelve, and they that believed on Him**, they that were about Him with the Twelve, asked of Him the parable. He said,*

Unto you it is given to know the mystery of the kingdom of God: but unto them that are without, all these things are done in parables: that seeing they may see, and not perceive; and hearing they may hear, and not understand; lest at any time they should be converted, and their sins should be forgiven them. Know ye not this parable? And how then will ye know all parables?

The sower soweth the word. And these are they by the wayside, where the word is sown; but when they have heard, Satan cometh immediately, and taketh away the word that was sown in their hearts. And these are they likewise which ~~are sown~~ **receive the word** on stony ground; who, when they have heard the word, immediately receive it with gladness, and have no root in themselves, and so endure but for a time; **and** afterward, when affliction or persecution ariseth for the word's sake, immediately they are offended. And these are they **who** ~~are sown~~ **receive the word** among thorns; such as hear the word, and the cares of this world, and the deceitfulness of riches, and the **lust** of other things entering in, choke the word, and it becometh unfruitful. And these are they **who** ~~are sown~~ **receive the word** on good ground; such as hear the word, and receive it, and bring forth fruit; some thirtyfold, some sixty and some a hundred.

Is a candle brought to be put under a bushel, or under a bed, and not to be set on a candlestick? **I say unto you, Nay;** for there is nothing hid which shall not be manifested; neither was anything kept secret, but that it should **in due time** come abroad. If any man have ears to hear, let him hear. Take heed what **you** hear; **for** with what measure ye mete, it shall be measured to you; and unto you that ~~hear~~ **continue to receive**, shall more be given; for he that ~~hath~~ **receiveth**, to him shall be given; **but** he that ~~hath~~ **continueth** not **to receive**, from him shall be taken even that which he hath.

So is the kingdom of God, as if a man should cast seed into the ground; and should sleep, and rise night and day, and the seed should spring and grow up, he knoweth not how. For the earth bringeth forth fruit of herself; first the blade, then the ear, after that the full corn in the ear. But when the fruit is brought forth, immediately he putteth in the sickle, because the harvest is come.

Whereunto shall **I** liken the kingdom of God? Or with what comparison shall we compare it? It is like a grain of mustard seed, which, when it is sown in the earth, is less than all the seeds that be in the earth: But when it is sown, it groweth up, and becometh greater than all herbs, and shooteth out great branches; so that the fowls of the air may lodge under the shadow of it.

When the even was come, He saith unto [His disciples],

Let us pass over unto the other side.

When they had sent away the multitude, they took Him in the ship. And there arose a great storm, and the waves beat ***over*** *into the ship. He was in the hinder* *part of the ship asleep; and they* ***awoke*** *Him, and* ***said****, Master, carest Thou not that we perish? And He arose, and rebuked the wind, and said unto the sea,*

Peace, be still.

The wind ceased. And He said unto them,

Why are ye so fearful? How is it that ye have no faith?

MARK 5

Devils into swine—woman touches His garment—raises damsel

They came over unto the other side of the sea, into the country of the Gadarenes. And when He was come out of the ship, immediately there met Him out of the tombs, a man with an unclean spirit. He cried, What have I to do with Thee, Jesus, Thou Son of the Most High God? I adjure Thee by God, that Thou torment me not. For He said unto him,

Come out of the man, unclean spirit.

And He ***commanded*** *him* ***saying,***

Declare thy name.

And he answered, My name is Legion; for we are many. And all the devils besought Him, saying, Send us into the swine, that we may enter into them. And forthwith Jesus gave them leave. And the unclean spirits went out, and entered into the swine: and the herd ran violently down a steep place into the sea (they were about two thousand); and were choked in the sea. And ***the people*** *went out to see what it was that was done; and they were afraid. And they began to pray Him to depart out of their coasts.*

And when He was come into the ship, he that had been possessed with the devil, ***spoke to Jesus, and*** *prayed Him that he might be with Him. Howbeit Jesus suffered him not.*

Go home to thy friends, and tell them how great things the Lord hath done for thee, and hath had compassion on thee.

And when Jesus ***had*** *passed over again by ship unto the other side, one of the rulers of the synagogue, Jairus by name, fell at His feet and besought Him greatly, My little daughter lieth at the point of death; come lay Thy hands on her that she may be healed; and she shall live. And He went with him; and much people followed Him and thronged Him.*

And a woman which had an issue of blood twelve years touched His garment. And straightway the fountain of her blood was dried up; and she felt in her body that she was healed of that plague. And Jesus, immediately knowing in Himself that virtue had gone out of Him, turned Him about in the press and said,

Who touched my clothes?

The woman fearing and trembling, knowing what was done in her, came and fell down before Him, and told Him all the truth. He said,

Daughter, thy faith hath made thee whole; go in peace, and be whole of thy plague.

*While He yet spake, there came from the ruler of the synagogue's house, **a man who** said, Thy daughter is dead; why troublest thou the Master any further? As soon as **he spake,** Jesus heard the word that was spoken, **and said** unto the ruler of the synagogue,*

Be not afraid, only believe.

And He suffered no man to follow Him, save Peter, and James, and John. And He cometh to the house of the ruler of the synagogue, and seeth the tumult, and them that wept and wailed greatly. And when He was come in, He saith unto them,

Why make ye this ado, and weep? The damsel is not dead, but sleepeth.

And they laughed Him to scorn. But when He had put them all out, He taketh the father and the mother of the damsel, and them that were with Him, and entereth in where the damsel was lying. And He took the damsel by the hand, and said unto her,

Talitha cumi *(Damsel, I say unto thee, arise).*

And straightway the damsel arose and walked.

MARK 6

Sends Twelve—feeds five thousand—walks on sea

He went out from thence, and came into His own country; and His disciples follow Him. And when the Sabbath day was come, He began to teach in the synagogue; and many were offended at Him. Jesus said unto them,

A prophet is not without honor, **save** in his own country, and among his own kin, and in his own house.

*And He could do no mighty work **there**, save that He laid His hands upon a few sick folk and **they were** healed.*

*He called the Twelve, and began to send them forth by two and two; and gave them power over unclean spirits; and commanded them that they should take nothing for their journey, save a staff only; no scrip, **nor** bread, **nor** money in their purse; but **should** be shod with sandals, and not **take** two coats. He said unto them,*

In **whatsoever** place ye enter into **a** house, there abide till ye depart from that place. And whosoever shall not receive you, nor hear you;

when ye depart thence shake off the dust **of** your feet for a testimony against them. Verily I say unto you, It shall be more tolerable for Sodom and Gomorrah in the Day of Judgment, than for that city.

John the Baptist was beheaded and his corpse laid in a tomb. ***Now*** *the Apostles gathered themselves together unto Jesus, and told Him all things; both what they had done, and what they had taught. He said,*

Come ye yourselves apart into a ~~desert~~ **solitary** place, and rest awhile.

They departed by ship, privately. And the people saw them departing; and many knew ***Jesus****, and ran afoot thither out of all cities, and* **outran** *them, and came together unto Him. And Jesus, when He came out, saw much people, and was moved with compassion toward them, because they were as sheep not having a shepherd: and He began to teach them many things.*

And when the day was now far spent, His disciples came unto Him, and said, This is a ***solitary*** *place, and now the time* ***for departure*** *is* **come,** *send them away, that they may go into the country round about, and into the villages, and buy themselves bread: for they have nothing to eat. He answered,*

Give ye them to eat.

And they say, Shall we go buy two hundred pennyworth of bread, and give them to eat? He saith,

How many loaves have ye? Go and see.

They say, Five and two fishes.

He commanded them to make all sit down by companies upon the green grass. And when He had taken the five loaves and two fishes, He looked up to heaven, and blessed, and brake the loaves, and gave to His disciples to set before ***the multitude****; and the two fishes divided He among them all. And they did all eat, and were filled. And they took up twelve baskets full of the fragments, and of the fishes. And they that did eat of the loaves were about five thousand men.*

Straightway He constrained His disciples to get into the ship, and to go to the other side before ***Him****, unto Bethsaida, while He sent away the people. And when even was come, the ship was in the midst of the sea, and He alone on the land. And He saw them toiling in rowing; for the wind was contrary unto them. And about the fourth watch of the night He cometh unto them, walking upon the sea,* ***as if He*** *would have passed by them.* ***And*** *when they saw Him walking upon the sea, they supposed it had been a spirit, and cried out; for they all saw Him, and were troubled. And immediately He talked with them,*

Be of good cheer: it is I; be not afraid.

And He went up unto them into the ship; and the wind ceased.

MARK 7

Heart defileth—casts out devil—heals deaf

Then came together unto Him the Pharisees, and certain of the scribes, which came from Jerusalem, and asked, Why walk not Thy disciples according to the ***traditions*** *of the elders, but eat bread with unwashen hands? He answered,*

Well hath ~~Esaias~~ **Isaiah** prophesied of you hypocrites, as it is written, This people honoreth me with their lips, but their heart is far from me. Howbeit, in vain do they worship me, teaching **the** doctrines **and** commandments of men. For laying aside the commandment of God, ye hold the tradition of men; the washing of pots and **of** cups; and many other such like things ye do. **Yea, altogether** ye reject the commandment of God, that ye may keep your own tradition.

Full well is it written of you, by the prophets whom ye have rejected. They testified these things of a truth, and their blood shall be upon you. Ye have kept not the ordinances of God; for Moses said, Honor thy father and thy mother; and whoso curseth father or mother, let him die the death **of the transgressor, as it is written in your law; but ye keep not the law.** Ye say, If a man shall say to his father or mother, Corban, that is to say, a gift, by whatsoever thou mightest be profited by me, he ~~shall be free~~ **is of age**. And ye suffer him no more to do **aught** for his father or his mother; making the word of God of none effect through your tradition, which ye have delivered; and many such like things do ye.

When He had called all the people, He said unto them,

Hearken unto me everyone, and understand; there is nothing from without, that entering into **a man**, can defile him**, which is food;** but the things which come out of him; those are they that defile the man**, that proceedeth forth out of the heart.** If any man have ears to hear, let him hear.

When He was entered into the house from ***among*** *the people, the disciples asked Him concerning the parable.*

Are ye without understanding also? Do ye not perceive, that whatsoever thing from without entereth into the man, cannot defile him; because it entereth not into his heart, but into the belly, and goeth out into the draught, purging all meats? That which cometh out of **a** man, defileth the man. For from within, out of the heart of men, proceed evil thoughts, adulteries, fornications, murders, thefts, covetousness, wickedness, deceit, lasciviousness, an evil eye, blasphemy, pride, foolishness: All these evil things come from within, and defile the man.

A [Greek] woman besought Him that He would cast forth the devil out of her daughter. But Jesus said,

Let the children **of the kingdom** first be filled; for it is not meet to take the children's bread, and to cast it unto the dogs.

She said, Yes, Lord; ***Thou sayest truly,*** *yet the dogs under the table eat of the children's crumbs. And He said,*

For this saying go thy way; the devil is gone out of thy daughter.

When she was come to her house, she found ***that*** *the devil* ***had*** *gone out.*

Departing from the coasts of Tyre and Sidon, He came unto the sea of Galilee, through the midst of the coasts of Decapolis. And they ***brought*** *unto Him one that was deaf, and had an impediment in his speech; and they* ***besought*** *Him to put His hand upon him. And He took him aside from the multitude, and put His fingers into his ears, and He spit, and touched his tongue; and looking up to heaven, He sighed, and saith unto him,*

Ephphatha *(Be opened).*

And straightway his ears were opened, and the string of his tongue was loosed, and he spake plain.

MARK 8

Feeds four thousand—leaven—heals blind—Jesus is the Christ

In those days, the multitude being very great, and having nothing to eat, Jesus called His disciples, and ***said,***

I have compassion on the multitude, because they have now been with me three days, and have nothing to eat: and if I send them away fasting to their own houses, they will faint by the way: for divers of them came from far.

His disciples answered Him, From whence can a man satisfy these, ***so great a multitude,*** *with bread here in the wilderness?*

How many loaves have ye?

Seven.

He commanded the people to sit down on the ground; and He took the seven loaves, and gave thanks, and brake, and gave to His disciples to set before ***the people****; and they did set them before the people. And they had a few small fishes; and He blessed* ***them****, and commanded to set them also before* ***the people, that they should eat****. So they did eat, and were filled, and they took up of the broken* ~~*meat*~~ ***bread*** *that was left, seven baskets. And they that had eaten were about four thousand: and He sent them away.*

He entered into a ship with His disciples, and came into the parts of Dalmanutha. And the Pharisees came forth, and began to question with Him, seeking of Him a sign from heaven, tempting Him. He sighed deeply in His spirit, and saith,

Why doth this generation seek after a sign? Verily I say unto you, There shall no sign be given unto this generation**, save the sign of the prophet Jonah; for as Jonah was three days and three nights in the whale's belly, so likewise shall the Son of Man be buried in the bowels of the earth.**

He left them, and entering into the ship again departed to the other side. Now the ***multitude*** *had forgotten to take bread; neither had they in the ship with them, more than one loaf. And He charged them,*

Take heed**, and** beware of the leaven of the Pharisees, and the leaven of Herod.

They reasoned among themselves, ***He hath said this,*** *because we have no bread. And* ***when they said this among themselves,*** *Jesus knew it* ***and said****,*

Why reason ye because ye have no bread? Perceive ye not yet, neither understand **ye**? **Are** your **hearts** yet hardened? Having eyes, see ye not? And having ears, hear ye not? And do ye not remember? When I brake the five loaves among **the** five thousand, how many baskets full of fragments took ye up?

They say, Twelve.

And when the seven among **the** four thousand, how many baskets full of fragments took ye up?

Seven.

How is it that ye do not understand?

He cometh to Bethsaida; and they bring a blind man unto Him, and besought Him to touch him. And He took the blind man by the hand, and led him out of the town; and when He had spit on his eyes, and put His hands upon him, He asked him if he saw aught. And he looked up, and said, I see men as trees, walking. After that He put his hands again upon his eyes, and made him look up: and he was restored, and saw every man clearly. And He sent him away to his house,

Neither go into the town, nor tell **what is done**, to any in the town.

And Jesus went out, and His disciples, into the towns of Caesarea Philippi: and by the way He asked His disciples,

Whom do men say that I am?

They answered, John the Baptist: but some say, Elias; and others, One of the Prophets.

But whom say ye that I am?

Peter ***said,*** *Thou art the Christ****, the Son of the living God****. And He charged them that they should tell no man of Him. And He began to teach them, that the Son of Man must suffer many things, and be rejected of the elders, and the chief priests, and scribes, and be killed, and after three days rise again. And Peter began to rebuke Him. But when He had looked on His disciples, He rebuked Peter, saying,*

Get thee behind me, Satan: for thou savorest not the things that be of God, but the things that be of men.

When He had called the people, with His disciples also, He said,

Whosoever will come after me, let him deny himself, and take up his cross, and follow me. For whosoever will save his life, shall lose it; **or whosoever will save his life, shall be willing to lay it down for my sake; and if he is not willing to lay it down for my sake, he shall lose it.** But whosoever shall **be willing to** lose his life for my sake, and the gospel's, the same shall save it.

For what shall it profit a man, if he shall gain the whole world, and lose his own soul? Or what shall a man give in exchange for his soul? **Therefore deny yourselves of these, and be not ashamed of me.** Whosoever shall be ashamed of me, and of my words, in this adulterous and sinful generation, of him also shall the Son of Man be ashamed, when He cometh in the glory of His Father with the holy angels. **And they shall not have part in that Resurrection when He cometh. For verily I say unto you, That He shall come; and he that layeth down his life for my sake and the gospel's, shall come with Him, and shall be clothed with His glory in the cloud, on the right hand of the Son of Man.** Verily I say unto you, That there be some of them that stand here, which shall not taste of death, till they have seen the kingdom of God come with power.

MARK 9

Transfiguration—casts out dumb and deaf—offenses

After six days Jesus taketh Peter, James, and John, ***who asked Him many questions concerning His sayings;*** *and* ***Jesus*** *leadeth them up into* ***a*** *high mountain apart by themselves. And He was transfigured before them. And His raiment became shining, exceeding white, as snow; so* ***white*** *as no fuller on earth* ***could whiten*** *them. And there appeared unto them Elias with Moses****, or in other words, John the Baptist and Moses;*** *and they were talking with Jesus. And there was a cloud that overshadowed them: and a voice came out of the cloud,* *saying, This is my Beloved Son: hear Him. And suddenly, when they had looked round about* ***with great astonishment****, they saw no man anymore, save Jesus only, with themselves.* ***And immediately they departed.***

And as they came down from the mountain, they asked Him, Why say the scribes that Elias must first come? He told them,

Elias verily cometh first, and ~~restoreth~~ **prepareth** all things; **and teacheth you of the prophets;** how it is written of the Son of Man, that He must suffer many things, and be set at naught. **Again** I say unto you, That Elias is indeed come, **but** they have done unto him whatsoever they listed**; and even** as it is written of him**; and he bore record of me, and they received him not. Verily this was Elias.**

When He came to ***the*** *disciples, He saw a great multitude about them, and the scribes questioning with them.* ***Jesus*** *asked the scribes,*

What **questioned** ye with them?

One of the multitude answered, Master, I have brought unto Thee my son, ***who*** *hath a dumb spirit* ***that is a devil****; and I spake to Thy disciples that they* ***might*** *cast him out, and they could not.* ***Jesus spake unto*** *him,*

O faithless generation! How long shall I be with you? How long shall I suffer you? Bring him unto me.

Jesus *asked his father,*

How long **a time** is it since this came unto him?

His father *said,* ***When*** *a child; but if Thou canst,* ***I ask Thee to*** *have compassion on us, and help us. Jesus said,*

If thou **wilt** believe all things **I shall say unto you, this is** possible to him that believeth.

Immediately *the father cried out, and said, with tears, Lord, I believe; help Thou mine unbelief. When Jesus saw that the people came running together, He rebuked the foul spirit,*

I charge thee **to** come out of him, and enter no more into him.

Now *the* ***dumb and deaf*** *spirit cried, and rent him sore, and came out of him. When* ***Jesus*** *was come into the house, His disciples asked, Why could not we cast him out? He said,*

This kind can come forth by nothing, but by prayer and fasting.

They departed thence, and passed through Galilee ***privately; for*** *He would not that any man should know.* ***And*** *He taught His disciples,*

The Son of Man is delivered into the hands of men, and they shall kill Him; and after that He is killed, He shall rise the third day.

But they understood not, and were afraid to ask Him.

He came to Capernaum; and in the house, He asked,

Why was it that ye disputed among yourselves by the way?

But they held their peace, ***being afraid,*** *for by the way they had disputed among themselves, who* ***was*** *the greatest* ***among them. Now Jesus*** *called the Twelve and* ***said,***

If any man desire to be first, **he** shall be last of all, and servant of all.

He took a child, and ***sat*** *in the midst of them; and when He had taken* ***the child*** *in His arms, He said,*

Whosoever shall ~~receive~~ **humble himself like** one of **these** children, **and** receiveth me**, ye shall receive in my name**. And whosoever shall receive me, receiveth not me **only**, but Him that sent me**, even the Father**.

John ***spake,*** *saying, Master, we saw one casting out devils in Thy name, and he* ***followed*** *not us; and we forbade him, because he* ***followed*** *not us. But Jesus said,*

Forbid him not; for there is no man which shall do a miracle in my name, that can speak evil of me. For he that is not against us is on our part. **And** whosoever shall give you a cup of water to drink, in my name, because ye belong to Christ, verily I say unto you, He shall not lose his reward. And whosoever shall offend one of these little ones that believe in me, it is better for him that a millstone were hanged about his neck, and he were cast into the sea.

Therefore, if thy hand offend thee, cut it off**; or if thy brother offend thee and confess not and forsake not, he shall be cut off.** It is better for thee to enter into life maimed, than having two hands, to go into hell. **For it is better for thee to enter into life without thy brother, than for thee and thy brother to be cast into hell;** into the fire that never shall be quenched, where their worm dieth not, and the fire is not quenched. And **again,** if thy foot offend thee, cut it off**; for he that is thy standard, by whom thou walkest, if he become a transgressor, he shall be cut off.** It is better for thee to enter halt into life, than having two feet to be cast into hell, into the fire that never shall be quenched: **therefore, let every man stand or fall, by himself, and not for another; or not trusting another.**

Seek unto my Father, and it shall be done in that very moment what ye shall ask, if ye ask in faith, believing that ye shall receive. And if thine eye **which seeth for thee, him that is appointed to watch over thee to show thee light, become a transgressor and** offend thee, pluck ~~it~~ **him** out. It is better for thee to enter into the kingdom of God, with one eye, than having two eyes to be cast into hell fire. **For it is better that thyself should be saved, than to be cast into hell with thy brother,** where their worm dieth not, and **where** the fire is not quenched. For everyone shall be salted with fire; and every sacrifice shall be salted with salt**; but the** salt **must be** good. **For** if the salt have lost his saltness, wherewith will ye season it ***(the sacrifice)***? **Therefore it must needs be that ye** have salt in yourselves, and have peace one with another.

MARK 10

Divorce—little children—rich young man—riches—Resurrection—ministering

He arose from thence and cometh into the coasts of Judea by the farther side of Jordan; and the people resort to Him again; and as He was ***accustomed to teach,*** *He* ***also*** *taught them again. And the Pharisees came to Him and asked Him, Is it lawful for a man to put away his wife?* ***This they said, thinking to tempt*** *Him. He answered,*

What did Moses command you?

Moses suffered to write a bill of divorcement, and to put her away. Jesus answered,

For the hardness of your **hearts** he wrote you this precept; but from the beginning of the Creation God made them male and female. For this cause shall a man leave his father and mother, and cleave to his wife; and they twain shall be one flesh: so then they are no more twain, but one flesh. What therefore God hath joined together, let not man put asunder.

In the house His disciples asked Him again of the same matter. And He saith,

Whosoever shall put away his wife, and marry another, committeth adultery against her. And if a woman shall put away her husband, and be married to another, she committeth adultery.

They brought young children to Him, that He should touch them; and ***the*** *disciples rebuked those that brought them. But when Jesus saw* ***and heard them,*** *He was much displeased, and said,*

Suffer the little children to come unto me, and forbid them not; for of such is the kingdom of God. Verily I say unto you, Whosoever shall not receive the kingdom of God as a little child, he shall not enter therein.

When He was gone forth into the way, there came one running, and kneeled to Him, and asked, Good Master, what shall I do that I may inherit eternal life? Jesus said,

Why callest thou me good? None **is** good but one, that is God. Thou knowest the commandments, Do not commit adultery, Do not kill, Do not steal, Do not bear false witness, Defraud not, Honor thy father and mother.

The man *answered, Master, all these have I observed from my youth. Then Jesus beholding him loved him, and said,*

One thing thou lackest: go thy way, sell whatsoever thou hast, and give to the poor, and thou shalt have treasure in heaven: and come, take up the cross, and follow me.

The man *was sad at that saying, and went away grieved; for he had great possessions. Jesus looked round about and* ***said*** *unto His disciples,*

How hardly shall they that have riches enter into the kingdom of **my Father**! Children, how hard is it for them **who** trust in riches to enter into the kingdom of God! It is easier for a camel to go through the eye of a needle, than for a rich man to enter into the kingdom of God.

And they were astonished, saying among themselves, Who then can be saved? Jesus, looking upon them, ***said,***

With men **that trust in riches**, it is impossible; but not **impossible** with **men who trust in** God **and leave all for my sake,** for with ~~God~~ **such** all **these** things are possible.

Peter began to say, Lo, we have left all, and have followed Thee. Jesus said,

Verily I say unto you, There is no man that hath left house, or brethren, or sisters, or father, or mother, or wife, or children, or lands, for my sake, and the gospel's, but he shall receive a hundredfold now in this time, houses, and brethren, and sisters, and mothers, and children, and lands, with persecutions; and in the world to come eternal life. But **there are** many **who make themselves** first**, that** shall be last; and the last first.

This He said rebuking Peter.

And they were in the way going up to Jerusalem; and He took again the Twelve, and began to tell them what things should happen unto Him. ***And Jesus said,***

Behold, we go up to Jerusalem; and the Son of Man shall be delivered unto the chief priests, and unto the scribes; and they shall condemn Him to death; and shall deliver Him to the Gentiles. And they shall mock Him, and shall scourge Him, and shall spit upon Him, and shall kill Him: and the third day He shall rise again.

James and John, the sons of Zebedee, ***came*** *unto Him, saying, Master, we would that Thou shouldest do for us whatsoever we shall desire.*

What **will** ye that I should do **unto** you?

Grant us that we may sit, one on Thy right hand, and the other on Thy left hand, in Thy glory. But Jesus said,

Ye know not what ye ask: can ye drink of the cup that I drink of? And be baptized with the baptism that I am baptized with?

We can.

Ye shall indeed drink of the cup that I drink of; and **be baptized** with the baptism that I am baptized **with**; but to sit on my right hand, and on my left hand, is not mine to give; but **they shall receive it** for whom it is prepared.

When the ten heard, they began to be much displeased with James and John. But Jesus called them and ***said****,*

Ye know that they **who** are ~~accounted~~ **appointed** to rule over the Gentiles exercise lordship over them; and their great ones exercise authority upon them. But **it** shall not be **so** among you; but whosoever will be great among you, shall be your minister. And whosoever of you will be the chiefest, shall be servant of all. For even the Son of Man came not to be ministered unto, but to minister, and to give His life a ransom for many.

They came to Jericho: and as He went out of Jericho with His disciples and a great number of people, blind Bartimaeus, sat by the highway side begging. And when he heard that it was Jesus of Nazareth, he began to cry out, Jesus, Son of David, have mercy on me. And Jesus stood still and commanded him to be called. And he ***arose*** *and came to Jesus. And Jesus said,*

What wilt thou that I should do unto thee?

Lord, that I might receive my sight. Jesus said,

Go thy way; thy faith hath made thee whole.

Immediately he received his sight, and followed Jesus.

MARK 11

Colt—curses fig tree—moneychangers—faith

When they came nigh to Jerusalem, unto Bethphage and Bethany, at the Mount of Olives, He sendeth forth two of His disciples,

Go your way into the village over against you; and as soon as ye **have** entered into it, ye shall find a colt tied, whereon **no** man **ever** sat; loose him and bring him **to me**. And if any man say unto you, Why do ye this? Say ye that the Lord hath need of him; and straightway he will send him hither.

And they brought the colt to Jesus, and cast their garments on ***it****; and* ***Jesus*** *sat upon* ***it****. And Jesus entered into Jerusalem and into the temple. And when He had looked round about upon all things, and* ***blessed the disciples,*** *the eventide was come;* ***and*** *He went out unto Bethany with the Twelve.*

On the morrow, when they ***came*** *from Bethany He was hungry; and seeing a fig tree afar off having leaves, He* ***came to it to see*** *if He might find anything thereon.* ***There was*** *nothing but leaves; for* ***as yet the*** *figs* ***were*** *not* ***ripe****. Jesus said unto it,*

No man eat fruit of thee hereafter, forever.

They ***came*** *to Jerusalem. And Jesus went into the temple, and began to cast out them that sold and bought in the temple, and overthrew the tables of the moneychangers, and the seats of them* ***who*** *sold doves; and would not suffer that any man should carry* ***a*** *vessel through the temple. And He taught,*

Is it not written, My house shall be called of all nations the house of prayer? But ye have made it a den of thieves.

When even was come, He went out of the city. In the morning, as they passed by, they saw the fig tree dried up from the roots. Peter calling to remembrance saith, Master, behold, the fig tree which Thou cursedst is withered away. And Jesus ***said****,*

Have faith in God. For verily I say unto you, That whosoever shall say unto this mountain, Be thou removed, and be thou cast into the sea; and shall not doubt in his heart, but shall believe that those things which he saith shall come to pass; he shall have whatsoever he saith **fulfilled**. Therefore I say unto you, **Whatsoever** things ye desire, when ye pray, believe that ye receive, and ye shall have **whatsoever ye ask**. And when ye stand praying, forgive if ye have **aught** against any; that your Father also **who** is in heaven, may forgive you your trespasses. But if **you** do not forgive, neither will your Father **who** is in heaven forgive your trespasses.

They ***came*** *again to Jerusalem; and as He was walking in the temple, there* ***came*** *the chief priests, and the scribes, and the elders, and* ***said*** *unto Him, By what authority doest Thou these things? Jesus answered,*

I will also ask of you one question, answer me, and **then** I will tell you by what authority I do these things. **Was** the baptism of John from heaven, or of man? Answer me.

We cannot tell.

Neither do I tell you by what authority I do these things.

MARK 12

Parable of wicked husbandmen—paying tribute—seven husbands—the great commandment—widow's mites

And ***Jesus*** *began to speak unto them by parables****, saying,***

A man planted a vineyard, and set **a** hedge about it, and digged the ~~winefat~~ **wine vat**, and built a tower, and let it out to husbandmen, and went into a far country. And at the season he sent to the husbandmen a servant, that he might receive from the husbandmen of the fruit of the vineyard. And they caught **the servant**, and beat him, and sent him away empty. And again he sent unto them another servant; and at him they cast stones, and wounded him in the head, and sent him away shamefully handled. And again he sent another; and him they killed, and many others; beating some, and killing some. Having yet therefore one son, his wellbeloved, he sent him also last unto them, saying, They will reverence my son. But those husbandmen said among themselves, This is the heir; come, let us kill him, and the inheritance shall be ours. And they took him and cast him out of the vineyard, **and killed him**. What shall therefore the lord of the vineyard do?

Lo, he will come and destroy the husbandmen, and will give the vineyard unto others. **Again,** have ye not read this scripture; the stone which the builders rejected, is become the head of the corner; this was the Lord's doing, and it is marvelous in our eyes.

And now they were angry when they heard these words; *and they send unto Him certain of the Pharisees and of the Herodians, to catch Him in His words. They say unto Him, Is it lawful to give tribute to Caesar, or not? But He knowing their hypocrisy, said,*

Why tempt ye me? Bring me a penny, that I may see it. Whose image and superscription **is this**?

They said, Caesar's.

Render to Caesar the things **which** are Caesar's; and to God the things that are God's.

Then ***came*** *unto Him the Sadducees; and they asked, Master, Moses wrote unto us* ***in his law****, If a man's brother die, and leave* ***a*** *wife, and leave no children, that his brother should take his wife, and raise up seed unto his brother. Now there were seven brethren: and the first took a wife, and dying left no seed. And the second took her, and died, neither left he any seed: and the third likewise. And the seven had her, and left no seed: last of all the woman died also. In the resurrection therefore, whose wife shall she be of them? Jesus answering said unto them,*

Ye **do** err **therefore**, because ye know not**, and understand not** the scriptures, neither the power of God. For when they shall rise from the dead, they neither marry, nor are given in marriage; but are as the angels **of God who** are in heaven. And as touching the dead, that they rise: have ye not read in the book of Moses, how in the bush God spake unto him, saying, I am the God of Abraham, and the God of Isaac, and the God of Jacob? He is not **therefore** the God of the dead, but the God of the living; **for He raiseth them up out of their graves.** Ye therefore do greatly err.

One of the scribes asked Him, Which is the first commandment of all? And Jesus answered,

The first of all the commandments is, **Hearken, and** hear, O Israel; the Lord our God is one Lord; and thou shalt love the Lord thy God with all thy heart, and with all thy soul, and with all thy mind, and with all thy strength: this is the first commandment. And the second is like this, Thou shalt love thy neighbor as thyself. There is none other commandment greater than these.

Well, Master, Thou hast said the truth; for there is one God, and there is none other but ***Him****. And to love Him with all the heart, and with all the understanding, and with all the soul, and with all the strength, and to love his neighbor as himself, is more than all whole burnt offerings and sacrifices. When Jesus saw that he answered discreetly, He said,*

Thou art not far from the kingdom of God.

Jesus said in the temple,

How say the scribes that Christ is the Son of David? For David himself said by the Holy Ghost, The LORD said to my Lord, Sit Thou on my right hand, till I make Thine enemies Thy footstool. David therefore himself calleth Him Lord; and whence is He his Son?

*And the common people heard Him gladly****; but the high priest and the elders were offended at Him.*** *He said unto them,*

Beware of the scribes which love to go in long clothing, and ~~love~~ **have** salutations in the marketplaces, and the chief seats in the synagogues, and the uppermost rooms at feasts; **who** devour widows' houses, and for a pretense make long prayers; these shall receive greater damnation.

After this, *Jesus beheld how the people cast money into the treasury; and many that were rich cast in much. There came a poor widow, and she* ***cast*** *in two mites, which make a farthing. And* ***Jesus*** *called His disciples, and* ***said,***

Verily I say unto you, that this poor widow hath cast more in, than all they **who** have cast into the treasury; for all **the rich** did cast in of their abundance; but she, **notwithstanding** her want, did cast in all that she had; **yea**, even all her living.

MARK 13

Second Coming—parable of fig tree

As ***Jesus*** *went out of the temple, His disciples* ***came to*** *Him* ***to hear Him, saying,*** *Master,* ***show us concerning the*** *buildings* ***of the temple. He*** *said unto* ***them,***

Behold ye these **stones of the temple, and all this** great **work, and** buildings **of the temple**? **Verily I say unto you, they shall be thrown down and left unto the Jews desolate. See ye not all these things, and do ye not understand them? Verily I say unto you,** There shall not be left **here upon this temple,** one stone upon another, that shall not be thrown down.

And Jesus left them and went upon the Mount of Olives; *and* ***the disciples came unto*** *Him privately,* ***saying,*** *Tell us, when shall these things be* ***which Thou hast said, concerning the destruction of the temple, and the Jews? And what is the sign of Thy coming, and of the end of the world (or the destruction of the wicked)?*** *Jesus answered,*

Take heed **that no** man deceive you; for many shall come in my name, saying, I am Christ, and shall deceive many. **Then shall they deliver you up to be afflicted, and shall kill you, and ye** shall be hated of all ~~men~~ **nations** for my name's sake. **And then shall many be offended, and shall betray one another; and many false prophets shall arise, and shall deceive many; and because iniquity shall abound, the love of many shall wax cold;** but he that shall endure unto the end, the same shall be saved.

When ye **therefore** shall see the abomination of desolation, spoken of by Daniel the prophet **concerning the destruction of Jerusalem, then ye shall stand in the holy place. (Whoso** readeth **let him** understand.**)** Then let them **who** be in Judea flee **into** the mountains; and let him **who** is on the housetop **flee, and not return** to take anything out of his house; **neither** let him **who** is in the field, **return** back to take his ~~garment~~ **clothes**. **And** woe **unto** them that are with child, and **unto** them that give suck in those days. **Therefore** pray ye **the Lord**, that your flight be not in the winter**, neither on the Sabbath day**. For

then, in those days, shall be ~~affliction~~ **great tribulations on the Jews, and upon the inhabitants of Jerusalem;** such as was not **before sent upon Israel, of God, since** the beginning of ~~the creation which God created~~ **their kingdom (for it is written their enemies shall scatter them), until** this time**; no, nor ever** shall be **sent again upon Israel. All** these **things** are the beginnings of sorrows. And except those days **should be shortened, there should** no flesh be saved; but for the elect's sake, **according to the covenant, those days shall be** shortened.

Behold these things I have spoken unto you concerning the Jews. And then **immediately after the tribulation of those days which shall come upon Jerusalem,** if any man shall say **unto** you, Lo, here is Christ; or there; believe him not. For **in those days there shall also arise** false Christs, and false prophets, and shall show **great** signs and wonders**; insomuch, that** if possible, **they shall deceive** the **very** elect**, who are the elect according to the covenant**. Behold, I ~~have foretold~~ **speak these things unto** you**, for the elect's sake**.

And **you also** shall hear of wars, and rumors of wars**; see that ye** be not troubled; for **all I have told you** must **come to pass**, but the end **is** not yet. **Behold, I have told you before, wherefore if they shall say unto you, Behold, He is in the desert; go not forth; Behold, He is in the secret chambers; believe it not. For as the light of the morning cometh out of the East, and shineth even unto the West, and covereth the whole earth, so shall also the coming of the Son of Man be.**

And now I show unto you a parable. Behold, wheresoever the carcass is, there will the eagles be gathered together; so likewise, shall mine elect be gathered from the four quarters of the earth. And they shall hear of wars and rumors of wars. Behold, I speak unto you for mine elect's sake. For nation shall rise against nation, and kingdom against kingdom; there shall be famines, and ~~troubles~~ **pestilences, and earthquakes in divers places. And again, because iniquity shall abound, the love of men shall wax cold; but he who shall not be overcome, the same shall be saved.**

And **again this** gospel **of the kingdom shall** be ~~published~~ **preached in** all **the world, for a witness unto all nations, and then shall the end come, or the destruction of the wicked. And again shall the abomination of desolation, spoken of by Daniel the prophet, be**

fulfilled. And immediately after **the** tribulation **of those days**, the sun shall be darkened, and the moon shall not give her light, and the stars shall fall **from heaven**, and the powers **of** heaven shall be shaken. Verily I say unto you, This generation **in which these things shall be shown forth,** shall not pass **away** till all **I have told you shall** be **fulfilled**.

Although the days will come that heaven and earth shall pass away**, yet** my words shall not pass away**, but all shall be fulfilled. And as I said before, After the tribulation of those days, and the powers of the heavens shall be shaken, then shall appear the sign of the Son of Man in heaven; and then shall all the tribes of the earth mourn;** and **they** shall see the Son of Man coming in the clouds **of heaven,** with power and **great** glory. **And whoso treasureth up my words shall not be deceived. For the Son of Man shall come; and He** shall send His angels **before Him with the great sound of a trumpet**, and **they** shall gather together His elect from the four winds, from **one end** of heaven **to the other**.

Now learn a parable of the fig tree. When ~~her~~ **his branches are** yet tender, and putteth forth leaves, ye know that summer is **nigh at hand**. So **likewise, mine elect,** when **they** shall see **all** these things**, they shall** know that ~~it~~ **He** is **near,** even at the doors. But of that day and hour **no one** knoweth; no, not the angels **of God** in heaven, ~~neither the Son~~ but **my** Father **only**. **But as it was in the days of Noah, so it shall be also at the coming of the Son of Man; for it shall be with them as it was in the days which were before the flood. Until the day that Noah entered into the ark, they were eating and drinking, marrying and giving in marriage, and knew not until the flood came and took them all away; so shall also the coming of the Son of Man be.**

Then shall be fulfilled that which is written. That in the last days, two shall be in the field, one shall be taken and the other left. Two shall be grinding at the mill; the one taken, and the other left. And what I say unto **one**, I say unto all **men**. Watch **therefore, for ye know not at what hour your Lord doth come. But know this, if the goodman of the house had known in what watch the thief would come, he would have watched, and would not have suffered his house to have been broken up; but would have been ready. Therefore, be ye also ready, for in such an hour as ye think not, the Son**

of Man cometh. Who then is a faithful and wise servant, whom his lord hath made ruler over his household, to give them meat in due season? Blessed is that servant whom his lord, when he cometh, shall find so doing. And verily I say unto you, he shall make him ruler over all his goods.

But if that evil servant shall say in his heart, My lord delayeth his coming; and shall begin to smite his fellow servants, and to eat and drink with the drunken; the lord of that servant shall come in a day when he looketh not for him, and in an hour that he is not aware of, and shall cut him asunder, and shall appoint him his portion with the hypocrites. There shall be weeping and gnashing of teeth; and thus cometh the end.

MARK 14

Anointing—Passover—sacrament—Gethsemane—trial

***Jesus** being in Bethany, in the house of Simon the leper, as He sat at meat, there came a woman having an alabaster box of ointment of spikenard, very precious, and she brake the box, and poured **the ointment** on His head. And there were some **among the disciples who** had indignation within themselves, and said, Why was this waste of the ointment made? For it might have been sold for more than three hundred pence, and have been given to the poor. And Jesus said **unto them**,*

Let her alone; why trouble ye her? **For** she hath wrought a good work on me. Ye have the poor with you always, and whensoever ye will, ye may do them good; but me ye have not always. She **has** done what she could**, and this which she has done unto me, shall be had in remembrance in generations to come, wheresoever my gospel shall be preached; for verily** she **has** come **beforehand** to anoint my body to the burying. Verily I say unto you, Wheresoever this gospel shall be preached throughout the whole world, **what** she hath done shall be spoken of **also** for a memorial of her.

***Now** the first day of Unleavened Bread, when they killed the passover, His disciples said unto Him, Where wilt Thou that we go and prepare, that Thou mayest eat the passover? And He sendeth forth two of His disciples,*

Go ye into the city, and there shall meet you a man bearing a pitcher of water: follow him. And wheresoever he shall go in, say ye to the goodman of the house, The Master saith, Where is the guestchamber, where I shall eat the passover with my disciples? And he will show you a large upper room furnished and prepared: there make ready for us.

His disciples went forth and found as He had said unto them: and they made ready the passover. In the evening He cometh with the Twelve; and as they sat and did eat, Jesus said,

Verily I say unto you, One of you **who** eateth with me shall betray me.

And they all began to be ***very*** *sorrowful, and* ***began*** *to say unto Him one by one, Is it I? He answered,*

It is one of the Twelve **who** dippeth with me in the dish. The Son of Man indeed goeth, as it is written of Him: but woe to that man by whom the Son of Man is betrayed! Good were it for that man if he had never been born.

As they did eat, Jesus took bread and blessed ***it****, and brake, and gave to them, and said,*

Take **it, and** eat. **Behold, this is for you to do in remembrance of my body; for as oft as ye do this ye will remember this hour that I was with you.**

He took the cup, and when He had given thanks, He gave it to them: and they all drank of it. And He said,

This is **in remembrance of** my blood which is shed for many**, and the new testament which I give unto you; for of me, ye shall bear record unto all the world. And as oft as ye do this ordinance, ye will remember me in this hour that I was with you and drank with you of this cup, even the last time in my ministry.** Verily I say unto you, **Of this ye shall bear record; for** I will **no more** drink of the fruit of the vine **with you**, until that day that I drink it new in the kingdom of God.

Now they were grieved, and wept over Him. *And when they had sung a hymn, they went out into the Mount of Olives. And Jesus saith unto them,*

All ye shall be offended because of me this night: for it is written, I will smite the Shepherd, and the sheep shall be scattered. But after that I am risen, I will go before you **unto** Galilee.

And He said unto Judas Iscariot,

What thou doest, do quickly; but beware of innocent blood.

Nevertheless, *Judas went unto the chief priests and sought how he might conveniently betray* ***Jesus****. But Peter said unto* ***Jesus****, Although all* ***men*** *shall be offended* ***with Thee****, yet* ***I*** *will* ***never be offended****. And Jesus saith,*

Verily I say unto thee, That this day, even in this night, before the cock crow twice, thou shalt deny me thrice.

They came to a place which was named Gethsemane, ***which was a garden;*** *and* ***the disciples*** *began to be sore amazed, and to be very heavy,* ***and to complain in their hearts, wondering if this be the Messiah.*** *And* ***Jesus knowing their hearts, said*** *to His disciples,*

Sit **you** here, while I shall pray.

He taketh with Him, Peter, James and John, ***and rebuked them,***

My soul is exceeding sorrowful**, even** unto death; tarry ye here and watch.

He went forward a little and fell on the ground, and prayed that, if it were possible, the hour might pass from Him. And He said,

Abba, Father, all things are possible unto Thee; take away this cup from me; nevertheless, not **my** will, but **Thine be done**.

He cometh, and findeth them sleeping, and saith unto Peter,

Simon, sleepest thou? Couldest not thou watch one hour? Watch ye and pray, lest ye enter into temptation.

And they said unto Him, *The spirit truly is ready, but the flesh is weak. And again He went away, and prayed, and spake the same words. When He returned, He found them asleep again. And He cometh* ***to them*** *the third time, and* ***said,***

Sleep on now and take rest; it is enough, the hour is come; behold, the Son of Man is betrayed into the hands of sinners.

And after they had finished their sleep, He said,

Rise up, let us go; lo, he **who** betrayeth me is at hand.

And immediately, while He yet spake, cometh Judas, one of the Twelve, and with him a great multitude with swords and staves, from the chief priests, scribes and elders. As soon as he was come, he goeth straightway to Him, and saith, Master, Master; and kissed Him. And one of them ***who*** *stood by, drew* ***his*** *sword, and smote a servant of the high priest, and cut off his ear.* ***But Jesus commanded Him to return his sword, saying,***

He who taketh the sword shall perish with the sword.

And He put forth His finger and healed the servant of the high priest. *Jesus said unto them,*

Are ye come out as against a thief, with swords and staves to take me? I was daily with you in the temple teaching, and ye took me not: but the scriptures must be fulfilled.

And ***the disciples, when they heard this saying,*** *all forsook Him and fled. And they led Jesus away to the high priest: and with him were assembled all the chief priests and the elders and the scribes. And the chief priests and all the council* *sought for witness against Jesus, to put Him to death, **but** found none. And the high priest stood up in the midst, and asked Jesus, Art Thou the Christ, the Son of the Blessed? And Jesus said,*

I am: and ye shall see the Son of Man sitting on the right hand of power, and coming in the clouds of heaven.

*Then the high priest rent his clothes and **said**, What need we any further witnesses? Ye have heard the blasphemy; what think ye? And they all condemned Him to be guilty of death.*

MARK 15

Trial—Crucifixion

*Straightway in the morning the chief priests held a consultation with the elders and scribes; the whole council **condemned Him**, and bound **Him**, and delivered Him to Pilate. And Pilate asked Him, Art Thou the King of the Jews? And **Jesus** answering, said unto him,*

I am, even as thou sayest.

The chief priests accused Him of many things: but He answered nothing. And Pilate asked Him again, Answerest Thou nothing? Behold how many things they witness against Thee. But Jesus yet answered nothing; so that Pilate marvelled.

*Now **it was common** at **the** feast, **for Pilate to release** unto them one prisoner. And there was **a man** named Barabbas, who had committed murder. The multitude, crying aloud, began to desire him to **deliver Jesus** unto them. But Pilate answered **unto** them, Will ye that I release unto you the King of the Jews? For he knew that the chief priests had delivered Him for envy. But the chief priests moved the people that he should rather release Barabbas unto them.*

*Pilate **spake again**, What will ye then that I shall do **with** Him whom ye call the King of the Jews? They cried, **Deliver Him unto us to be crucified. Away with Him.** Crucify Him. Then Pilate said, Why, what evil hath He done? **But** they cried out the more exceedingly, Crucify Him. **Now** Pilate, willing to content the people, released Barabbas, and delivered Jesus, when he had scourged Him, to be crucified.*

*The soldiers led Him away, clothed Him with purple, [put] a crown of thorns about His head, and began to salute Him, **saying,** Hail, King of the Jews. And they smote Him on the head with a reed, and did spit upon Him, and bowing their knees worshipped Him. And when they had mocked Him, they took off the purple, and put His own clothes on Him, and led Him out to crucify Him.*

*[At] Golgotha, the place of a ~~skull~~ **burial**, they gave Him to drink ~~wine~~ **vinegar** mingled with ~~myrrh~~ **gall; and when He had tasted the vinegar,** He **would** not **drink**. And when they had crucified Him, they parted His garments, casting lots upon them, what every man should take. It was the third hour **when** they crucified Him.*

Pilate wrote *His accusation* ***and put it upon the cross,*** *THE KING OF THE JEWS.* ***There were certain of the chief priests who stood by, and* said unto Pilate, Write, that He said, I am the King of the Jews. But Pilate said unto them, What I have written, I have written.***

And with Him they ***crucified*** *two thieves****,*** *the one on His right hand, and the other on His left. And they* ***who*** *passed by railed on Him, wagging their heads, and saying, Ah, Thou* ***who*** *destroyest the temple and buildest it in three days, save Thyself, and come down from the cross. Likewise also the chief priests mocking said among themselves with the scribes, He saved others; Himself He cannot save. Let Christ the King of Israel descend now from the cross, that we may see and believe.* ***One of them who was*** *crucified with Him****,*** *reviled Him* ***also, saying, If Thou art the Christ, save Thyself and us.***

When the sixth hour was come, there was darkness over the whole land until the ninth hour. And at the ninth hour Jesus cried with a loud voice,

Eloi, Eloi, lama sabachthani *(My God, my God, why hast Thou forsaken me)?*

Some of them ***who*** *stood by, when they heard* ***Him****, said, Behold, He calleth Elias. One ran and filled a* ***sponge*** *full of vinegar, and put it on a reed and gave Him to drink****; others spake,*** *saying, Let* ***Him*** *alone; let us see whether Elias will come to take Him down.*

And Jesus cried with a loud voice and gave up the ghost.

MARK 16

Sends Apostles

When Jesus was risen, early ***on*** *the first day of the week, He appeared first to Mary Magdalene; and she told them* ***who*** *had been with Him, as they mourned and wept. And they, when they had heard that He was alive, and had been seen of her, believed not. After that, He appeared in another form unto two of them, as they walked, and went into the country. And they went and told it unto the residue: neither believed they them. Afterward, He appeared unto the eleven as they sat at meat, and upbraided them with their unbelief and hardness of heart, because they believed not them which had seen Him after He was risen. And He said unto them,*

Go ye into all the world, and preach the gospel to every creature. He that believeth and is baptized shall be saved; but he that believeth not shall be damned. And these signs shall follow them that believe; in my name shall they cast out devils; they shall speak with new tongues; they shall take up serpents; and if they drink any deadly thing, it shall not hurt them; they shall lay hands on the sick, and they shall recover.

After the Lord had spoken unto them, He was received up into heaven, and sat on the right hand of God.

Words of Christ According to Saint Luke

LUKE 2

My Father's business

The child grew, and waxed strong in spirit, ***being*** *filled with wisdom; and the grace of God was upon Him. Now His parents went to Jerusalem every year at the Feast of the Passover. When He was twelve years old, they went up to Jerusalem, after the custom,* ***to*** *the feast. And when they had fulfilled the days, as they returned, the child Jesus tarried behind, in Jerusalem; and Joseph and His mother knew not* ***that He tarried****. After three days they found Him in the temple, sitting in the midst of the doctors,* ***and they were*** *hearing* ***Him****, and asking* ***Him*** *questions. All* ***who*** *heard Him were astonished at His understanding, and answers.*

When ***His parents*** *saw Him, they were amazed; and His mother said, Son, why hast Thou thus dealt with us? Behold, Thy father and I have sought Thee sorrowing. And He said,*

Why is it **that** ye sought me? **Know** ye not that I must be about my Father's business?

And they understood not. And He went down with them, and came unto Nazareth, and was subject unto them.

LUKE 3–4

Temptation of Jesus—scripture fulfilled—casts out devil

Jesus began to be about thirty years of age, ***having lived with His father,*** *being****,*** *as was supposed* ***of the world,*** *the son of Joseph. And Jesus being full of the Holy Ghost returned from Jordan, and was led by the Spirit into the wilderness.* ***After*** *forty days, the devil* ***came unto Him, to tempt Him****. And in those days, He did eat nothing; and when they were ended, He* ***afterwards*** *hungered. The devil said, If Thou be the Son of God, command this stone that it be made bread. Jesus answered,*

It is written, That man shall not live by bread alone, but by every word of God.

The ***Spirit taketh*** *Him up into* ***a*** *high mountain* ***and He beheld*** *all the kingdoms of the world, in a moment of time. And the devil* ***came*** *unto Him and* ***said,*** *All this power I will give* ***unto*** *Thee, and the glory of them; for* ***they are*** *delivered unto me, and to whomsoever I will, I give* ***them****. If Thou therefore wilt worship me, all shall be Thine. Jesus said,*

Get thee behind me, Satan; for it is written, Thou shalt worship the Lord thy God, and Him only shalt thou serve.

__The Spirit__ brought Him to Jerusalem, and set Him on a pinnacle of the temple. __And the devil came unto Him,__ and said, If Thou be the Son of God, cast Thyself down from hence; for it is written, He shall give His angels charge over Thee, to keep Thee; and in __His__ hands they shall bear Thee up, lest at any time Thou dash Thy foot against a stone. And Jesus said,

It is ~~said~~ **written**, Thou shalt not tempt the Lord thy God.

When the devil had ended all the temptation, he departed from Him for a season. [Jesus] came to Nazareth, where He had been brought up; and as His custom was He went into the synagogue on the Sabbath day, and stood up to read. And there was delivered unto Him the book of the prophet Esaias. And when He had opened the book, He found the place where it was written,

The Spirit of the Lord is upon me, because He hath anointed me to preach the gospel to the poor; He hath sent me to heal the broken-hearted, to preach deliverance to the captives, and **the** recovering of sight to the blind; to set at liberty them that are bruised; to preach the acceptable year of the Lord.

He closed the book, and He gave it again to the minister, and __He__ sat down. And the eyes of all __those who__ were in the synagogue, were fastened on Him, and He began to say,

This day is this scripture fulfilled in your ears.

And all bare Him witness, and wondered at the gracious words which proceeded out of His mouth. And they said, Is not this Joseph's son? And He said,

Ye will surely say unto me this proverb, Physician, heal thyself. Whatsoever we have heard **was** done in Capernaum, do also here in Thy country. Verily I say unto you, No prophet is accepted in his own country. But I tell you **the** truth, many widows were in Israel in the days of Elias, when the heaven was shut up three years and six months, **and** great famine was throughout all the land; but unto none of them was Elias sent, save unto Sarepta, of Sidon, unto a woman **who** was a widow. And many lepers were in Israel, in the time of Eliseus the prophet; and none of them **were** cleansed, **save** Naaman the Syrian.

All they in the synagogue, when they heard these things, were filled with wrath, and rose up, and thrust Him out of the city, and led Him unto the brow of the hill, whereon __the__ city was built, that they might cast Him down headlong. But He passing through the midst of them went His way, and came down to Capernaum, a city of Galilee, and taught them on the Sabbath days.

In the synagogue there was a man which had a spirit of an unclean devil, and ***he*** *cried out with a loud voice, Let us alone; what have we to do with Thee, Jesus of Nazareth? Art Thou come to destroy us? I know Thee, who Thou art, The Holy One of God. Jesus rebuked him,*

Hold thy peace, and come out of him.

When the devil had thrown him in the midst, he came out of him, and hurt him not.

When the sun was setting, all they ***who*** *had any sick, with divers diseases, brought them unto Him, and He laid His hands on every one of them, and healed them. And devils also came out of many, crying out, Thou art Christ the Son of God. And He rebuking them suffered them not to speak: for they knew that He was Christ. And when it was day, He departed and went into a* ***solitary*** *place; and the people* ***desired*** *Him that He should not depart from them.* ***But*** *He said,*

I must preach the kingdom of God to other cities also, for therefore am I sent.

LUKE 5

Calls Simon Peter—forgives sins—new wine into old bottles

As the people pressed upon Him, to hear the word of God, He stood by the lake of Gennesaret, and saw two ships standing ***on*** *the lake. He entered into one of the ships, which was Simon's, and prayed him that he would thrust out a little from the land. And He sat down, and taught the people out of the ship.*

Now, when He had ***done*** *speaking, He said* ***to*** *Simon,*

Launch out into the deep, and let down your **net** for a draught.

Simon said, Master, we have toiled all the night, and have taken nothing: nevertheless, at Thy word I will let down the net. When they had this done, they enclosed a great multitude of fishes: and their net brake. When Simon Peter saw ***the multitude of fishes****, he fell down at Jesus' knees, saying, Depart from me; for I am a sinful man, O Lord. He was astonished, and all* ***who*** *were with him, and so* ***were*** *also James, and John, the sons of Zebedee,* ***who*** *were partners with Simon. Jesus said unto Simon,*

Fear not from henceforth, **for** thou shalt catch men.

When they had brought their ships to land, they forsook all, and followed Him. When He was in a certain city, a man full of leprosy: who seeing Jesus fell on his face, and besought Him, saying, Lord, if Thou wilt, Thou canst make me clean. And He put forth His hand and touched him, saying,

I will: be thou clean.

Immediately the leprosy departed from him. And He ***said,***

Go and show thyself to the **priests**, and offer for thy cleansing, according as Moses commanded, for a testimony unto them.

On a certain day, as He was teaching, there were Pharisees and doctors of the law sitting by, ***who*** *were come out of every town of Galilee, and Judea, and Jerusalem. And the power of the Lord was present to heal them. And men brought in a bed, a man* ***who*** *was taken with a palsy; and they sought to bring him in, and to lay him before* ***Jesus****. And when they* ***found that they*** *could not bring him in* ***for*** *the multitude, they went upon the housetop, and let him down through the tiling, with his couch, into the midst, before Jesus.* ***Now*** *He saw their faith,* ***and*** *said unto* ***the*** *man,*

Thy sins are forgiven thee.

The scribes and Pharisees began to reason, Who is this ***that*** *speaketh blasphemies? Who can forgive sins but God alone? But Jesus perceived their thoughts,* ***and*** *said,*

What reason ye in your hearts? ~~Whether is easier~~ **Does it require more power** to **forgive** sins **than to make the sick** rise up and walk? But, that ye may know that the Son of Man hath power upon earth to forgive sins, **I said it**.

He said unto the sick of the palsy,

I say unto thee, Arise, and take up thy couch, and go **unto thy** house.

Immediately he rose up before them, and took up that whereon he lay, and departed to his own house, glorifying God.

After these things He went forth, and saw a publican, named Levi, sitting at the ***place where they received*** *custom; and He said unto him,*

Follow me.

And he left all, rose up, and followed Him. And Levi made Him a great feast in his own house: and there was a great company of publicans and of others that sat down with them. But ***the*** *scribes and Pharisees murmured against His disciples, Why do ye eat and drink with publicans and sinners? Jesus said,*

They that are whole need not a physician; but they that are sick. I came not to call the righteous, but sinners to repentance.

They said, Why do the disciples of John fast often, and make prayers, and likewise the disciples of the Pharisees; but Thine eat and drink? He said,

Can ye make the children of the bridechamber fast, while the bridegroom is with them? But the days will come, when the bridegroom shall be taken away from them, and then shall they fast in those days.

He spake also a parable unto them, ***saying,***

No man putteth a piece of new **cloth** upon an old **garment**; if **so**, then the new maketh a rent, and agreeth not with the old. And no man putteth new wine into old bottles; else the new wine will burst the bottles, and be spilled, and the bottles shall perish. But new wine must be put into new bottles; and both are preserved. No man also, having drunk old wine, desireth new; for he saith, The old is better.

LUKE 6

Lord of Sabbath—heals on Sabbath—Sermon on the Plain

On the second Sabbath after ***this****, He went through the cornfields; and His disciples plucked ears of corn, and did eat. The Pharisees said, Why do ye that which is not lawful to do on the Sabbath days? Jesus said,*

Have ye not read so much as this, what David did, when **he** himself was an hungered, and they **who** were with him; how he went into the house of God, and did take and eat the shewbread, and gave also to them **who** were with him, which it is not lawful to eat, but for the priests alone?

And He said unto them,

The Son of Man is Lord also of the Sabbath.

On another Sabbath, He entered into the synagogue and taught: and there was a man whose right hand was withered. The scribes and Pharisees watched Him, whether He would heal on the Sabbath day; that they might find an accusation against Him. But He knew their thoughts, and said to the man,

Rise up, and stand forth in the midst.

He arose and stood forth. Said Jesus unto them,

I will ask you one thing; Is it lawful on the Sabbath days to do good, or to do evil? To save life, or to destroy?

Looking round about them all, He said unto the man,

Stretch forth thy hand.

He did so: and his hand was restored whole as the other.

In those days He went out into a mountain to pray, and continued all night in prayer to God. When it was day, He called His disciples; and of them He chose twelve, whom also He named Apostles. He came down with them and stood in the plain. And the whole multitude sought to touch Him: for there went virtue out of Him, and healed them all.

He lifted up his eyes on His disciples and said,

Blessed **are the** poor; for **theirs** is the kingdom of God. Blessed are **they who** hunger now; for **they** shall be filled. Blessed are **they who** weep now; for **they** shall laugh. Blessed are ye when men shall hate you, and when they shall separate you from **among them**, and shall reproach you, and cast out your name as evil, for the Son of Man's sake. Rejoice ye in that day, and leap for joy; for behold your reward **shall be** great in heaven; for in the like manner did their fathers unto the prophets.

But woe unto you that are rich! For ye have received your consolation. Woe unto you **who** are full! For ye shall hunger. Woe unto you **who** laugh now! For ye shall mourn and weep. Woe unto you, when all men shall speak well of you! For so did their fathers to the false prophets.

But I say unto you **who** hear **my words**, Love your enemies, do good to them **who** hate you. Bless them **who** curse you, and pray for them **who** despitefully use you **and persecute you**. And unto him **who** smiteth thee on the cheek, offer also the other; **or, in other words, it is better to offer the other, than to revile again**. And him **who** taketh away thy **cloak**, forbid not to take thy coat also. **For it is better that thou suffer thine enemy to take these things, than to contend with him. Verily I say unto you, Your Heavenly Father who seeth in secret, shall bring that wicked one into judgment.**

Therefore give to every man **who** asketh of thee; and of him **who** taketh away thy goods, ask them not again. And as ye would that men should do to you, do ye also to them likewise. For if ye love them **only who** love you, what ~~thank~~ **reward** have **you**? For sinners also love those that love them. And if ye do good to them which do good to you, what thank have ye? For sinners also do even the same. And if ye lend to them of whom ye hope to receive, what ~~thank~~ **reward** have **you**? For sinners also lend to sinners, to receive as much again. But love ye your enemies, and do good, and lend, hoping for nothing again; and your reward shall be great, and ye shall be the children of the Highest: for He is kind unto the unthankful and to the evil. Be ye therefore merciful, as your Father also is merciful.

Judge not, and ye shall not be judged: condemn not, and ye shall not be condemned: forgive, and ye shall be forgiven: give, and it shall be given unto you; good measure, pressed down, and shaken together, and running over, shall men give into your bosom. For with the same measure that ye mete withal it shall be measured to you again.

And He spake a parable unto them,

Can the blind lead the blind? Shall they not both fall into the ditch? **A** disciple is not above his master; but everyone that is perfect shall be as his master. And why beholdest thou the mote **which** is in thy brother's eye, but perceivest not the beam **which** is in thine own eye? **Again,** how canst thou say to thy brother, Let me pull out the mote that is in thine eye, when thou thyself beholdest not the beam **which** is in thine own eye? Thou hypocrite, cast out first the beam out of thine own eye, and then shalt thou see clearly to pull out the mote **which** is in thy brother's eye.

For a good tree bringeth not forth corrupt fruit; neither doth a corrupt tree bring forth good fruit. For every tree is known by his own fruit. For of thorns men do not gather figs, nor of a bramble bush gather they grapes. A good man out of the good treasure of his heart bringeth forth that which is good; and an evil man out of the evil treasure of his heart bringeth forth that which is evil: for of the abundance of the heart his mouth speaketh.

And why call ye me, Lord, Lord, and do not the things which I say? Whosoever cometh to me, and heareth my sayings, and doeth them, I will show you to whom he is like: he is like a man **who** built **a** house, and digged deep, and laid the foundation on a rock, and when the flood arose, the stream beat vehemently upon that house, and could not shake it; for it was founded upon a rock. But he that heareth, and doeth not, is like a man that without a foundation built a house upon the earth; against which the stream did beat vehemently, and immediately it fell; and the ruin of that house was great.

LUKE 7

Heals—raises dead—feet anointed—forgives sins

*When He had ended all **these** sayings in the audience of the people, he entered into Capernaum. A certain centurion's servant, who was dear unto him, was sick, and ready to die. When he heard of Jesus, he sent unto Him the elders of the Jews, beseeching Him that He would come and heal his servant. Then Jesus went with them. And when He was not far from the house, the centurion sent friends to Him, saying, Lord, trouble not Thyself: for I am not worthy that Thou shouldest enter under my roof: neither thought I myself worthy to come unto Thee: but say in a word, and my servant shall be healed. When Jesus heard these things, he marveled, and turned about, and said unto the people **who** followed Him,*

I say unto you, I have not found so great faith, no, not in Israel.

*They **who** were sent, returning to the house, found the servant whole **who** had been sick.*

The day after, He went into a city called Nain; and many of His disciples went with Him, and much people. When He came nigh to the gate of the city, there was a dead man carried out, the only son of his mother, and she was a widow; and ***many*** *people of the city* ***were*** *with her.* ***Now*** *the Lord saw her,* ***and*** *had compassion on her, and* ***He*** *said unto her,*

Weep not.

And He came and touched the bier; and they that bare ***it*** *stood still, and He said,*

Young man, I say unto thee, Arise.

And he ***who*** *was dead, sat up, and began to speak; and He delivered him to his mother.*

John calling two of his disciples, sent them to Jesus, saying, Art Thou He ***who*** *should come, or look we for another? In* ***the*** *same hour He cured many of infirmities, and plagues, and of evil spirits, and unto many blind He gave sight. Then Jesus answering, said,*

Go your way, and tell John what things ye have seen and heard; how that the blind see, the lame walk, the lepers are cleansed, the deaf hear, the dead are raised, **and** to the poor the gospel is preached. And blessed **are they who** shall not be offended in me.

When the messengers of John were departed, He began to speak unto the people concerning John,

What went ye out into the wilderness to see? A reed shaken with the wind? **Or** a man clothed in soft raiment? Behold, they **who** are gorgeously appareled, and live delicately, are in king's courts. But what went ye out for to see? A prophet? Yea, I say unto you, and much more than a prophet. This is **the one** of whom it is written, Behold I send my messenger before Thy face, **who** shall prepare Thy way before Thee. For I say unto you, Among those **who** are born of women, there is not a greater prophet than John the Baptist; but he **who** is least in the kingdom of God is greater than he.

All the people ***who*** *heard Him, and the publicans, justified God, being baptized with the baptism of John. But the Pharisees and lawyers rejected the counsel of God against themselves,* ***not*** *being baptized of him. The Lord said,*

Whereunto then shall I liken the men of this generation? And to what are they like? They are like unto children sitting in the marketplace, and calling one to another, and saying, We have piped **for** you, and ye have not danced; we have mourned **for** you, and ye have not wept. For John the Baptist came neither eating bread nor drinking wine; and ye say, He hath a devil. The Son of Man is come eating and drinking; and ye say, Behold a gluttonous man, and a winebibber, a friend of publicans and sinners! But wisdom is justified of all her children.

One of the Pharisees desired Him that He would eat with him. He went into the Pharisee's house, and sat down to meat. A woman in the city, ***who*** *was a sinner, when she knew that Jesus sat at meat in the Pharisee's house, brought an alabaster box of ointment, and stood at His feet weeping, and began to wash His feet with tears, and did wipe them with the hairs of her head, and kissed His feet, and anointed them with the ointment. Now when the Pharisee* ***who*** *had bidden Him saw* ***this****, he spake within himself, This man, if he were a prophet, would have known who,* ***or*** *what manner of woman this is* ***who*** *toucheth Him; for she is a sinner. Jesus answering said unto him,*

Simon, I have somewhat to say unto thee. There was a certain creditor, **who** had two debtors; the one owed five hundred pence, and the other fifty. And when **he found** they had nothing to pay, he frankly forgave them both. Tell me therefore, which of them will love him most?

I suppose ***the man*** *to whom he forgave most.*

Thou hast rightly judged.

Seest thou this woman? I entered into **thy** house; thou gavest me no water for my feet: but she hath washed my feet with tears, and wiped them with the hairs of her head. Thou gavest me no kiss: but this woman since the time I came in hath not ceased to kiss my feet. My head with oil thou didst not anoint: but this woman hath anointed my feet with ointment. Wherefore I say unto thee, Her sins, which are many, are forgiven; for she loved much: but to whom little is forgiven, the same loveth little.

And He said unto her,

Thy sins are forgiven. Thy faith hath saved thee; go in peace.

LUKE 8

Parables of sower; candle under a bushel—stills tempest—devils into swine—woman touches His garment—raises maiden

Afterward, He went throughout every city and village, preaching and showing the glad tidings of the kingdom of God; and the Twelve ***who were ordained of Him,*** *were with Him. When much people were gathered together, and were come to Him out of every city, He spake by a parable,*

A sower went out to sow his seed: and as he sowed, some fell by the wayside; and it was trodden down, and the fowls of the air devoured it. And some fell upon a rock; and as soon as it was sprung up, it withered away, because it lacked moisture. And some fell among thorns; and the thorns sprang up with it, and choked it. And **others** fell on good ground, and sprang up, and bare fruit a hundredfold.

He cried,

He **who** hath ears to hear, let him hear.

His disciples asked Him, What might this parable be? He said,

Unto you it is given to know the mysteries of the kingdom of God: but to others in parables; that seeing they might not see, and hearing they might not understand. Now the parable is this: The seed is the word of God. **That which fell** by the wayside are they **who** hear; **and** the devil **cometh** and taketh away the word out of their hearts, lest they should believe and be saved. **That which fell** on the rock are they, **who**, when they hear, receive the word with joy; and **they** have no root, **but** for a while believe, and in **a** time of temptation fall away.

And that which fell among **the** thorns are they, **who**, when they have heard, go forth and are choked with cares, and riches, and pleasures of life, and bring no fruit to perfection. But that **which fell** on the good ground are they, **who receive the word** in an honest and good heart, having heard the word, keep **what they hear**, and bring forth fruit with patience. **For** no man, when he hath lighted a candle, covereth it with a vessel, or putteth it under a bed; but setteth it on a candlestick, that they **who** enter in may see the light. For nothing is secret, **which** shall not be made manifest; neither hid, **which** shall not be **made** known, and **go** abroad. Take heed therefore how ye hear; for whosoever ~~hath~~ **receiveth**, to him shall be given; and whosoever ~~hath~~ **receiveth** not, from him shall be taken even that which he seemeth to have.

*Then came to Him His mother and His brethren, and could not **speak to** Him for the **multitude**. **Some who stood by,** said **unto Him**, Thy mother and Thy brethren stand without, desiring to see Thee. He answered,*

My mother and my brethren are **those who** hear the word of God, and do it.

On a certain day, He went into a ship with His disciples: and He said,

Let us go over unto the other side of the lake.

As they sailed, He fell asleep; and there came down a storm of wind on the lake; and they were filled with ***fear*** *and were in* ***danger****. And they awoke Him, saying, Master, Master, we perish. Then He arose, and rebuked the wind and the raging of the* ***waters****, and they ceased; and there was a calm. He said unto them,*

Where is your faith?

They arrived at the country of the Gadarenes, and when He went forth to land, there met Him out of the city a man ***who*** *had devils. When he saw Jesus, he cried out, and fell down before Him, and with a loud voice said, What have I to do with Thee, Jesus, Thou Son of God Most High? I beseech Thee, torment me not (for He had commanded the unclean spirit to come out of the man). Jesus asked,*

What is thy name?

Legion. And they besought Him that He would suffer them to enter into the ***swine****.* ***And He said unto them,***

Come out of the man.

Then went the devils out of the man, and entered into the swine: and the herd ran violently down a steep place into the lake, and were choked.

Then the whole multitude of the country of the Gadarenes besought ***Jesus*** *to depart from them; for they were taken with great fear.* ***Jesus*** *went up into the ship. The man out of whom the devils were departed besought Him that he might be with Him: but Jesus sent him away, saying,*

Return to thine own house, and show how great things God hath done unto thee.

And he went his way.

When Jesus was returned, the people were all waiting for Him. And there came a man named Jairus, and he was a ruler of the synagogue: and he fell down at Jesus' feet, and besought Him that He would come into his house: for he had ***an*** *only daughter, about twelve years of age, and she lay a-dying. But as He went, the people thronged Him. And a woman, having an issue of blood twelve years came behind* ***Jesus*** *and touched the border of His garment; and immediately her issue of blood* ***staunched****. Jesus said,*

Who touched me?

When all denied, Peter and they that were with him, said, Master, the multitude throng Thee, and press ***upon*** *Thee, and sayest Thou, Who touched me?*

Someone hath touched me; for I perceive that virtue is gone out of me.

When the woman ***found*** *that she was not hid, she came trembling, and falling down before Him, she declared unto Him for what cause she had touched Him, and how she was healed immediately. He said,*

Daughter, be of good comfort: thy faith hath made thee whole; go in peace.

*While He yet spake, there cometh one from the ruler of the synagogue's house, saying to him, Thy daughter is dead; trouble not the Master. But Jesus **said unto the ruler of the synagogue**,*

Fear not; believe only, and she shall be made whole.

When He came into the house, He suffered no man to go in, save Peter, James, and John, and the father and mother of the maiden. He said,

Weep not; she is not dead, but sleepeth.

And they laughed Him to scorn, knowing that she was dead. He put them all out, and took her by the hand, and He called,

Maid, arise.

Her spirit came again, and she arose straightway: and He commanded to give her meat.

LUKE 9

Sends Twelve—feeds five thousand—Jesus is the Christ

*Then He called His twelve disciples together, and **He** gave them power and authority over all devils, and to cure diseases. And He sent them to preach the kingdom of God, and to heal the sick. He said unto them,*

Take nothing for your journey, neither staves, nor scrip, neither bread, neither money; neither have two coats apiece. And **into** whatsoever house ye enter, there abide **until ye** depart **thence**. And whosoever will not receive you, when ye go out of that city, shake off the very dust from your feet for a testimony against them.

They departed, and went through the towns, preaching the gospel, and healing everywhere.

*The Apostles, when they returned, told **Jesus** all that they had done. And He took them, and went aside privately into a **solitary** place. The people followed Him; and he received them, and spake unto them of the kingdom of God, and healed them **who** had need of healing. When the day began to wear away, then came the Twelve, and said unto Him, Send the multitude away, that they may go into the towns and country round about, and lodge, and get victuals; for we are here in a **solitary** place. But He said,*

Give ye them to eat.

*They said, We have but five loaves and two fishes; **and** except we should go and buy meat, **we can provide no more food** for all this **multitude**, for they were **in number** about five thousand men.*

***Jesus** said **unto** His disciples,*

Make them sit down by fifties in a company.

They did so, and made them all sit down. Then He took the five loaves and the two fishes, and looking up to heaven, He blessed them, and brake, and gave to the disciples to set before the multitude. They did eat, and were all filled. And there was taken up of ***the*** *fragments* ***which*** *remained, twelve baskets.*

As He ***went*** *alone* ***with*** *His disciples* ***to pray****, He asked them,*

Who say the people that I am?

Some say*, John the Baptist; but* ***others*** *say, Elias; and others that one of the old prophets is risen again.*

But **who** say ye that I am?

Peter answering said, The Christ, ***the Son*** *of God.*

The Son of Man must suffer many things, and be rejected of the elders and chief priests and scribes, and be slain, and be raised the third day. If any man will come after me, let him deny himself, and take up his cross daily, and follow me. For whosoever will save his life, ~~shall~~ **must be willing to** lose it **for my sake; and** whosoever will **be willing to** lose his life for my sake, the same shall save it. For what **doth it profit a man** if he gain the whole world, **and yet he receive Him not whom God hath ordained,** and **he** lose **his own soul, and he** himself be **a** castaway? For whosoever shall be ashamed of me, and of my words, of him shall the Son of Man be ashamed, when He shall come in His own **kingdom, clothed in the glory of His Father, with** the holy angels. **Verily,** I tell you of a truth, there **are** some standing here **who** shall not taste of death, until they see the kingdom of God **coming in power**.

Eight days after these sayings, He took Peter, John, and James, and went up into a mountain to pray. As He prayed, the fashion of His countenance was ***changed****, and His raiment* ***became*** *white and* ***glittering****. There* ***came and*** *talked with Him two men,* ***even*** *Moses and Elias. A cloud overshadowed them* ***all;*** *and there came a voice out of the cloud, saying, This is my Beloved Son: hear Him. When the voice was past, Jesus was found alone.*

On the next day, when they were come down from the hill, much people met Him. A man of the company cried out, Master, I beseech Thee, look upon my son: for he is mine only child. And, lo, a spirit taketh him, and I besought Thy disciples to cast him out: and they could not. Jesus said,

O faithless and perverse generation, how long shall I be with you, and suffer you? Bring thy son hither.

Jesus rebuked the unclean spirit and healed the child.

While they wondered at all things which Jesus did, He said unto His disciples,

Let these sayings sink down into your ~~ears~~ **hearts**; for the Son of Man shall be delivered into the hands of men.

But they understood not, and they feared to ask Him of that saying.

Then there arose a reasoning among them, ***who*** *of them should be greatest. And Jesus perceiving the* ***thoughts*** *of their* ***hearts****, took a child, and set him* ***in the midst;*** *and said unto them,*

Whosoever shall receive this child in my name, receiveth me; and whosoever shall receive me, receiveth Him **who** sent me; for he **who** is least among you all, the same shall be great.

John said, Master, we saw one casting out devils in Thy name; and we ***forbade*** *him, because he followeth not with us. Jesus said,*

Forbid not **any**; for he **who** is not against us is for us.

When the time was come that He should be received up, He steadfastly set His face to go to Jerusalem, and sent messengers before His face: and they went, and entered into a village of the Samaritans to make ready for Him. ***The Samaritans would*** *not receive Him, because His face was* ***turned*** *as though He would go to Jerusalem. When His disciples, James and John, saw* ***that they would not receive Him****, they said, Lord, wilt Thou that we command fire to come down from heaven and consume them, even as Elias did? But He turned and rebuked them,*

Ye know not what manner of spirit ye are of. For the Son of Man is not come to destroy men's lives, but to save them.

And they went to another village.

In the way, a certain man said unto Him, Lord, I will follow Thee whithersoever Thou goest. And Jesus said,

Foxes have holes, and birds of the air have nests; but the Son of Man hath not where to lay His head.

And He said unto another,

Follow me.

But he said, Lord, suffer me first to go and bury my father. Jesus said,

Let the dead bury their dead: but go thou and preach the kingdom of God.

Another also said, Lord, I will follow Thee; but let me first go ***and*** *bid them farewell* ***who*** *are at my house. And Jesus said unto him,*

No man, having put his hand to the plow, and looking back, is fit for the kingdom of God.

LUKE 10

Instructs Seventy—parable of good Samaritan

After these things the Lord appointed other Seventy also, and sent them two and two before His face, into every city and place ***where*** *He Himself would come.* ***He*** *said unto them,*

The harvest truly is great, but the laborers few; pray ye therefore the Lord of the Harvest, that He would send forth laborers into His harvest. Go your ways: behold, I send you forth as lambs among wolves. Carry neither purse, nor scrip, nor shoes; **nor** salute **any** man by the way. And into whatsoever house ye enter, first say, Peace to this house. And if the son of peace be there, your peace shall rest upon it: if not, it shall turn to you again. And **into whatsoever** house **they receive you**, remain, eating and drinking such things as they give; for the laborer is worthy of his hire. Go not from house to house.

And into whatsoever city ye enter, and they receive you, eat such things as are set before you: and heal the sick that are therein, and say, The kingdom of God is come nigh unto you. But into whatsoever city ye enter, and they receive you not, go your ways out into the streets of the same, and say, Even the very dust of your city which cleaveth on us, we do wipe off against you; notwithstanding, be sure of this, that the kingdom of God is nigh unto you. But I say unto you, that it shall be more tolerable in **the** Day **of Judgment** for Sodom, than for that city.

Then He began to upbraid the people in every city wherein His mighty works were done, who received Him not, saying,

Woe unto thee, Chorazin! Woe unto thee, Bethsaida! For if the mighty works had been done in Tyre and Sidon, which have been done in you, they **would have** repented, sitting in sackcloth and ashes. But it shall be more tolerable for Tyre and Sidon at the **Day of** Judgment, than for you. And thou, Capernaum, which art exalted to heaven, shalt be **cast** down to hell.

And He said unto His disciples,

He that heareth you, heareth me; and he that despiseth you, despiseth me; and he that despiseth me, despiseth Him **who** sent me.

*The Seventy returned again with joy, saying, Lord, even the devils are subject **to** us through Thy name. And He said,*

As lightning **falleth** from heaven**, I beheld Satan also falling**. Behold, I **will** give unto you power ~~to tread on~~ **over** serpents and scorpions, and over all the power of the enemy; and nothing shall by any means hurt you. Notwithstanding in this rejoice not, that the spirits are subject unto you; but rather rejoice, because your names are written in heaven.

In that hour Jesus rejoiced in spirit, and said,

I thank Thee, O Father, Lord of Heaven and Earth, that Thou hast hid these things from ~~the~~ **them who think they are** wise and prudent, and hast revealed them unto babes; even so, Father; for so it seemed good in Thy sight. All things are delivered to me of my Father; and no man knoweth ~~who~~ **that** the Son is ~~but~~ the Father, and ~~who~~ the Father is ~~but~~ the Son, ~~and he~~ **but him** to whom the Son will reveal ~~him~~ **it**.

*And He turned unto **the** disciples, and said privately,*

Blessed are the eyes which see the things that ye see. For I tell you, that many prophets and kings have desired to see those things which ye see, and have not seen them; and to hear those things which ye hear, and have not heard them.

A lawyer tempted Him, saying, Master, what shall I do to inherit eternal life? He said unto him,

What is written in the law? How readest thou?

He answering said, Thou shalt love the Lord thy God with all thy heart, and with all thy soul, and with all thy strength, and with all thy mind; and thy neighbor as thyself. And He said,

Thou hast answered right: this do, and thou shalt live.

But he, willing to justify himself, said, Who is my neighbor? Jesus answering said,

A certain man went down from Jerusalem to Jericho, and fell among thieves, which stripped him of his raiment, and wounded him, and departed, leaving him half dead. And by chance, there came down a certain priest that way; and when he saw him, he passed by on the other side **of the way**. And likewise a Levite, when he was at the place, came and looked **upon** him, and passed by on the other side **of the way; for they desired in their hearts that it might not be known that they had seen him**.

But a certain Samaritan, as he journeyed, came where he was: and when he saw him, he had compassion on him, and went to him, and bound up his wounds, pouring in oil and wine, and set him on his own beast, and brought him to an inn, and took care of him. And on the morrow, when he departed, he took **money**, and gave to the host, and said unto him, Take care of him, and whatsoever thou spendest more, when I come again, I will repay thee. **Who** now of these three, thinkest thou, was neighbor unto him that fell among the thieves?

*And he said, He **who** showed mercy on him. Then said Jesus,*

Go, and do likewise.

They *entered into a certain village; and a certain woman named Martha received Him into her house. She had a sister, called Mary,* ***who*** *also sat at Jesus' feet, and heard His* ***words****. But Martha was cumbered about much serving, and came to Him, and said, Lord, dost Thou not care that my sister hath left me to serve alone? Bid her therefore that she help me. Jesus said,*

Martha, Martha, thou art careful and troubled about many things: But one thing is needful: and Mary hath chosen that good part, which shall not be taken away from her.

LUKE 11

Lord's Prayer—parable of friend at midnight—ask and receive—house divided—signs—unwashed hands

As ***Jesus*** *was praying in a certain place, when He ceased, one of His disciples said unto Him, Lord, teach us to pray, as John also taught his disciples. And He said,*

When ye pray, say, Our Father **who** art in heaven, hallowed be Thy name. Thy kingdom come. Thy will be done as in heaven, so in earth. Give us day by day our daily bread. And forgive us our sins; for we also forgive everyone **who** is indebted to us. And ~~lead~~ **let** us not **be led** into temptation; but deliver us from evil; **for Thine is the kingdom and power. Amen.**

Your Heavenly Father will not fail to give unto you whatsoever ye ask of Him.

And He spake a parable, saying,

Which of you shall have a friend, and shall go unto him at midnight, and say unto him, Friend, lend me three loaves; for a friend of mine **has** come to me **in his journey**, and I have nothing to set before him; and he from within shall answer and say, Trouble me not: the door is now shut, and my children are with me in bed; I cannot rise and give thee. I say unto you, Though he will not rise and give him, because he is his friend, yet because of his importunity he will rise and give him as many as he needeth.

And I say unto you, Ask, and it shall be given you; seek, and ye shall find; knock, and it shall be opened unto you. For everyone **who** asketh, receiveth; and he that seeketh, findeth; and to him **who** knocketh, it shall be opened. If a son shall ask bread of any of you **who** is a father, will he give him a stone? Or, if a fish, will he for a fish give him a serpent? Or if he shall ask an egg, will he offer him a scorpion? If ye then, being evil, know how to give good gifts unto your children, how much more shall your Heavenly Father **give good gifts, through** the Holy Spirit, to them **who** ask Him.

He was casting a devil ***out of a man****, and* ***he*** *was dumb. When the devil was gone out, the dumb spake; and the people wondered. But some of them said, He casteth out devils through Beelzebub the chief of the devils. Others tempting, sought of Him a sign from heaven. But He, knowing their thoughts, said unto them,*

Every kingdom divided against itself is brought to desolation; and a house divided **cannot stand, but** falleth. If Satan also be divided against himself, how **can** his kingdom stand? **I say this,** because **you** say I cast out devils through Beelzebub. And if I, by Beelzebub, cast out devils, by whom do your sons cast out **devils**? Therefore shall they be your judges. But if I, with the finger of God cast out devils, no doubt the kingdom of God **has** come upon you.

When a strong man armed keepeth his palace, his goods are in peace: but when a stronger than he shall come upon him, and overcome him, he taketh from him all his armor wherein he trusted and divideth his ~~spoils~~ **goods**. He that is not with me, is against me: and he that gathereth not with me scattereth.

When the unclean spirit is gone out of a man, **it** walketh through dry places, seeking rest; and finding none, **it** saith, I will return unto my house whence I came out. And when **it** cometh, **it** findeth **the house** swept and garnished. Then goeth **the evil spirit**, and taketh seven other spirits more wicked than himself, and they enter in, and dwell there; and the last ~~state~~ **end** of that man is worse than the first.

As He spake these things, a certain woman of the company, lifted up her voice, Blessed is the womb ***which*** *bare Thee, and the paps which Thou hast sucked.* ***And*** *He said,*

Yea**, and** blessed are **all** they **who** hear the word of God, and keep it.

When the people were gathered thick together, He began to say,

This is an evil generation; they seek a sign, and there shall no sign be given **them**, but the sign of Jonas the prophet. For as Jonas was a sign unto the Ninevites, so also **shall** the Son of Man be to this generation. The queen of the south shall rise up in the **Day of** Judgment with the men of this generation, and condemn them; for she came from the utmost parts of the earth, to hear the wisdom of Solomon; and, behold, a greater than Solomon is here. The men of **Nineveh** shall rise up in the

Day of Judgment with this generation; and shall condemn it; for they repented at the preaching of Jonas; and, behold, a greater than Jonas is here.

No man when he hath lighted a candle, putteth it in a secret place, neither under a bushel, but on a candlestick, that they **who** come in may see the light. The light of the body is the eye: therefore when thine eye is single, thy whole body also is full of light; but when thine eye is evil, thy body also is full of darkness. Take heed therefore that the light which is in thee be not darkness. If thy whole body therefore **is** full of light, having no part dark, the whole shall be full of light, as when the bright shining of a candle **lighteneth a room and** doth give **the** light **in all the room**.

As He spake, a certain Pharisee besought Him to dine with him: and He went in, and sat down to meat. When the Pharisee saw ***Him****, he marveled that He had not first washed before dinner. And the Lord said unto him,*

Now do **you** Pharisees make clean the outside of the cup and the platter; but your inward **parts are** full of ravening and wickedness. **O** fools, did not he **who** made that which is without, make that which is within also? But **if ye would** rather give alms of such things as ye have; and ~~behold~~ **observe to do** all things **which I have commanded you, then would your inward parts be** clean **also**. But **I say unto you**, Woe **be** unto you, Pharisees! For ye tithe mint, and rue, and all manner of herbs, and pass over judgment, and the love of God; these ought ye to have done, and not to leave the other undone. Woe unto you, Pharisees! For **you** love the uppermost seats in the **synagogue**, and greetings in the markets. Woe unto you, scribes and Pharisees, hypocrites! For ye are as graves which appear not, and the men **who** walk over are not aware of them.

Then answered one of the lawyers, Master, thus saying Thou reproachest us also.

Woe unto you, lawyers**, also**! For ye lade men with burdens grievous to be borne, and ye yourselves touch not the burdens with one of your fingers. Woe unto you! For **you** build the sepulchres of the prophets, and your fathers killed them. Truly ye bear witness that ye allow the deeds of your fathers: for they indeed killed them, and ye build their sepulchres.

Therefore also said the wisdom of God, I will send them prophets and apostles, and some of them they shall slay and persecute: that the blood of all the prophets, which was shed from the foundation of the world, may be required of this generation; from the blood of Abel unto the blood of Zacharias, **who** perished between the altar and the temple. Verily I say unto you, It shall be required of this generation. Woe unto you, lawyers! For ye have taken away the key of knowledge**, the fulness of the scriptures;** ye entered not in yourselves **into the kingdom**; and **those who** were entering in, ye hindered.

LUKE 12

Leaven—blasphemies—covetousness—treasures—
parable of foolish rich man—discern this time

When there were gathered together an innumerable multitude of people, insomuch that they trod one upon another, He began to say unto His disciples first of all,

Beware ye of the leaven of the Pharisees, which is hypocrisy. For there is nothing covered **which** shall not be revealed; neither hid **which** shall not be known. Therefore whatsoever ye have spoken in darkness shall be heard in the light; and that which ye have spoken in the ear in closets shall be proclaimed upon the housetops.

And I say unto you my friends, Be not afraid of them **who** kill the body, and after that have no more that they can do; but I will forewarn you whom ye shall fear; fear Him, **who** after He hath killed, hath power to cast into hell; yea, I say unto you, Fear Him. Are not five sparrows sold for two farthings, and not one of them is forgotten before God? But even the very hairs of your head are all numbered. Fear not therefore: ye are of more value than many sparrows. Also I say unto you, Whosoever shall confess me before men, him shall the Son of Man also confess before the angels of God: but he **who** denieth me before men, shall be denied before the angels of God.

Now His disciples knew that He said this, because they had spoken evil against Him before the people; for they were afraid to confess Him before men. And they reasoned among themselves, saying, He knoweth our hearts, and He speaketh to our condemnation, and we shall not be forgiven. But He answered them, and said unto them,

Whosoever shall speak a word against the Son of Man, **and repenteth,** it shall be forgiven him; but unto him **who** blasphemeth against the Holy Ghost, it shall not be forgiven. And **again I say unto you,**

They **shall** bring you unto the synagogues, and **before** magistrates, and powers. **When they do this,** take ye no thought how, or what thing ye shall answer, or what ye shall say; for the Holy Ghost shall teach you in the same hour what ye ought to say.

One of the company said unto Him, Master, speak to my brother, that he divide the inheritance with me. And He said unto him,

Man, who made me a judge or a divider over you?

He said unto them,

Take heed, and beware of covetousness: for a man's life consisteth not in the abundance of the things which he possesseth.

And He spake a parable unto them, saying,

The ground of a certain rich man brought forth plentifully: and he thought within himself, saying, What shall I do, because I have no room where to bestow my fruits? And he said, This will I do: I will pull down my barns, and build greater; and there will I bestow all my fruits and my goods. And I will say to my soul, Soul, thou hast much goods laid up for many years; take thine ease, eat, drink, and be merry. But God said unto him, Thou fool, this night thy soul shall be required of thee: then whose shall those things be, which thou hast provided? So **shall it be with him who** layeth up treasure for himself, and is not rich toward God.

And He said unto His disciples,

Therefore I say unto you, Take no thought for your life, what ye shall eat; neither for the body, what ye shall put on. **For** the life is more than meat, and the body than raiment. Consider the ravens; for they neither sow nor reap; which neither have storehouse nor barn; **nevertheless,** God feedeth them. Are ye **not** better than the fowls? And **who** of you **by** taking thought, can add to his stature one cubit? If ye then be not able to do that which is least, why take ye thought for the rest?

Consider the lilies how they grow: they toil not, they spin not; and yet I say unto you, that Solomon in all his glory was not arrayed like one of these. If then God so clothe the grass, which is today in the field, and tomorrow is cast into the oven; how much more will He **provide for** you, **if** ye **are not** of little faith? **Therefore,** seek not what ye shall eat, or what ye shall drink, neither be ye of doubtful mind; For all these things do the nations of the world seek after; and your Father **who is in heaven**, knoweth that ye have need of these things. **And ye are sent unto them to be their ministers, and the laborer is worthy**

of his hire; for the law saith, That a man shall not muzzle the ox that treadeth out the corn. ~~But rather~~ **Therefore,** seek ye **to bring forth** the kingdom of God, and all these things shall be added unto you. Fear not, little flock; for it is your Father's good pleasure to give you the kingdom.

This He spake unto His disciples, saying,

Sell that ye have and give alms; provide **not for** yourselves bags which wax old, **but rather provide** a treasure in the heavens, that faileth not; where no thief approacheth, neither moth corrupteth. For where your treasure is, there will your heart be also. Let your loins be girded about and **have** your lights burning; **that** ye yourselves **may be** like unto men **who** wait for their lord, when he will return from the wedding; that, when he cometh and knocketh, they may open unto him immediately. **Verily I say unto you,** Blessed are those servants, whom the Lord when He cometh shall find watching; **for** He shall gird Himself, and make them to sit down to meat, and will come forth and serve them. **For, behold, He cometh in the first watch of the night, and He shall also come in the second watch, and again He shall come in the third watch.**

And verily I say unto you, He hath already come, as it is written of Him; and ~~if~~ **again when** He shall come in the second watch, or come in the third watch, blessed are those servants **when He cometh, that He shall find so doing; for the Lord of those servants shall gird Himself, and make them to sit down to meat, and will come forth and serve them.**

And now, verily I say these things unto you, that ye may know this, that the coming of the Lord is as a thief in the night. And it is like unto a man who is a householder, who, if he watcheth not his goods, the thief cometh in an hour of which he is not aware, and taketh his goods, and divideth them among his fellows. Verily I say unto you, be ye therefore ready also; for the Son of Man cometh at an hour when ye think not.

Peter said unto Him, Lord, speakest Thou this parable unto us, or ***unto*** *all?*

I speak unto those whom **the** Lord shall make **rulers** over His household, to give **His children** their portion of meat in due season.

They said, Who then is that faithful and wise servant? And the Lord said unto them,

It is that servant who watcheth, to impart his portion of meat in due season. Blessed **be** that servant whom his Lord **shall find**, when He cometh, so doing. Of a truth I say unto you, that He will make him ruler over all that He hath.

But **the evil servant is he who is not found watching.** And if that servant **is not found watching, he will** say in his heart, My Lord delayeth his coming; and shall begin to beat the menservants and **the** maidens, and to eat and drink, and to be drunken. The Lord of that servant will come in a day he looketh not for, and at an hour when he is not aware, and will cut him **down**, and will appoint him his portion with the unbelievers.

And that servant **who** knew his Lord's will, and prepared not **for his Lord's coming**, neither did according to His will, shall be beaten with many stripes. But he that knew not **his Lord's will**, and did commit things worthy of stripes, shall be beaten with few. For unto whomsoever much is given, of him shall much **be** required; and to whom ~~men have~~ **the Lord has** committed much, of him will **men** ask the more. **For they are not well pleased with the Lord's doings; therefore** I am come to send fire on the earth; and what **is it to you**, if **I will that** it be already kindled? But I have a baptism to be baptized with; and how am I **straightened** until it be accomplished!

Suppose ye that I am come to give peace on earth? I tell you, Nay; but rather division: for from henceforth there shall be five in one house divided, three against two, and two against three. The father shall be divided against the son, and the son against the father; the mother against the daughter, and the daughter against the mother; the mother-in-law against her daughter-in-law, and the daughter-in-law against her mother-in-law.

*He said also **unto** the people,*

When **you** see a cloud rise out of the West, **ye say** straightway, There cometh a shower; and so it is. And when the south wind **blows**, ye say, There will be heat; and it cometh to pass. **O** hypocrites! Ye can discern the face of the sky, and of the earth; but how is it that ye do not discern this time? Yea, and why even of yourselves judge ye not what is right? **Why** goest **thou to** thine adversary **for a** magistrate, **when** thou art in the way **with thine enemy? Why not** give diligence that thou mayest be delivered from him, lest he hale thee to the judge, and the judge deliver thee to the officer, and the officer cast thee into prison? I tell thee, thou shalt not depart thence, till thou hast paid the very last mite.

LUKE 13

Parables of barren fig tree; mustard seed; leaven—
heals on Sabbath—enter strait gate

*There were present at that **time**, some **who spake unto** Him of the **Galileans**, whose blood Pilate had mingled with their sacrifices. And Jesus said,*

Suppose ye that these **Galileans** were sinners above all the **Galileans**, because they suffered such things? I tell you, Nay: but except ye repent, ye shall all likewise perish. Or those eighteen, **on** whom the tower in Siloam fell, and slew them; think ye that they were sinners above all men that dwelt in Jerusalem? I tell you, Nay: but, except ye repent, ye shall all likewise perish.

He spake also this parable,

A certain **husbandman** had a fig tree planted in his vineyard. He came and sought fruit thereon and found none. Then said he unto the dresser of his vineyard, Behold, these three years I come seeking fruit on this fig tree, and find none: cut it down; why cumbereth it the ground? And he answering said unto him, Lord, let it alone this year also, till I shall dig about it, and dung it: and if it bear fruit, **the tree is saved,** and if not, after that thou shalt cut it down.

***After this,** as He was teaching in one of the synagogues on the Sabbath: there was a woman **who** had a spirit of infirmity eighteen years, and was bowed together, and could in no wise **straighten** up. When Jesus saw her, He said unto her,*

Woman, thou art loosed from thine **infirmities**.

*He laid hands on her; and immediately she was made straight, and glorified God. The ruler of the synagogue **was filled** with indignation, because Jesus had healed on the Sabbath day, and said unto the people, There are six days in which men ought to work; in them therefore come and be healed, and not on the Sabbath day. The Lord then **said unto** him,*

O hypocrite! Doth not each one of you on the Sabbath loose **an** ox or **an** ass from the stall, and lead him away to watering? And ought not this woman, being a daughter of Abraham, whom Satan hath bound, lo, these eighteen years, be loosed from this bond on the Sabbath day?

*When He had said these things, all His adversaries were ashamed; and all **His disciples** rejoiced for all the glorious things **which** were done by Him. Then said He,*

Unto what is the kingdom of God like? And whereunto shall I resemble it? It is like a grain of mustard seed, which a man took, and cast into his garden; and it grew, and waxed a great tree; and the fowls of the air lodged in the branches of it. Whereunto shall I liken the kingdom of God? It is like leaven, which a woman took and hid in three measures of meal, till the whole was leavened.

He went through the cities and villages, teaching, and journeying toward Jerusalem. ***There*** *said one unto Him, Lord, are there few* ***only*** *that be saved? He* ***answered,***

Strive to enter in at the strait gate; for I say unto you, **Many shall** seek to enter in, and shall not be able**; for the Lord shall not always strive with man. Therefore,** when once the **Lord** of the ~~house~~ **kingdom** is risen up, and hath shut the door **of the kingdom**, **then** ye **shall** stand without, and knock at the door, saying, Lord, Lord, open unto us. **But the Lord** shall answer and say unto you, **I will not receive you, for** ~~I~~ **ye** know ~~you~~ not **from** whence ye are. Then shall ye begin to say, We have eaten and drunk in Thy presence, and Thou hast taught in our streets. But He shall say, I tell you, ~~I~~ **ye** know not **from** whence ye are; depart from me, all workers of iniquity.

There shall be weeping and gnashing of teeth **among you**, when ye shall see Abraham, and Isaac, and Jacob, and all the prophets, in the kingdom of God, and you **are** thrust out. And **verily I say unto you**, They shall come from the East, and the West; and from the North, and the South, and shall sit down in the kingdom of God; and, behold, there are last which shall be first, and there are first which shall be last**, and shall be saved therein**.

As He was thus teaching, *there came* ***to Him*** *certain of the Pharisees, saying unto Him, Get Thee out, and depart hence; for Herod will kill Thee. He said,*

Go ye and tell ~~that fox~~ **Herod**, Behold, I cast out devils, and do cures today and tomorrow, and the third day I shall be perfected. Nevertheless, I must walk today and tomorrow, and the **third** day; for it cannot be that a prophet perish out of Jerusalem.

This He spake, signifying of His death. And in this very hour He began to weep over Jerusalem, saying,

O Jerusalem, Jerusalem, **thou who** killest the prophets, and stonest them **who** are sent unto thee; how often would I have gathered thy children together, as a hen her brood under her wings, and ye would not. Behold, your house is left unto you desolate. And verily I say unto you, Ye shall not ~~see~~ **know** me, **until ye have received from the hand of the Lord a just recompense for all your sins;** until the time come when ye shall say, Blessed is He that cometh in the name of the Lord.

LUKE 14

Heals on Sabbath—humility—parables of wedding guests; great supper—count cost—disciples forsake all

As He went into the house of one of the chief Pharisees to eat bread on the Sabbath day, they watched Him. There was a man before Him, ***who*** *had the dropsy. Jesus spake unto the lawyers and Pharisees,*

Is it lawful to heal on the Sabbath day?

They held their peace. And He took ***the man****, and healed him, and let him go; and* ***spake unto*** *them* ***again****, saying,*

Which of you shall have an ass or an ox fallen into a pit and will not straightway pull him out on the Sabbath day?

They could not answer Him to these things. And He put forth a parable ***unto them concerning*** *those* ***who*** *were bidden* ***to a wedding; for He knew*** *how they chose out the chief rooms****, and exalted themselves one above another; wherefore He spake unto them,***

When thou art bidden of any man to a wedding, sit not down in the highest room; lest a more honorable man than thou be bidden of him; And he **who** bade thee, **with** him **who is more honorable**, come, and say to thee, Give this man place; and thou begin with shame to take the lowest room. But when thou art bidden, go and sit down in the lowest room; that when he **who** bade thee, cometh, he may say unto thee, Friend, go up higher; then shalt thou have ~~worship~~ **honor of God,** in the presence of them **who** sit at meat with thee. For whosoever exalteth himself shall be abased; and he **who** humbleth himself shall be exalted.

Then said He also ***concerning*** *him* ***who*** *bade* ***to the wedding****,*

When thou makest a dinner, or a supper, call not thy friends, nor thy brethren, neither thy kinsmen, nor rich neighbors; lest they also bid thee again, and a recompense be made thee. But when thou makest a feast, call the poor, the maimed, the lame, the blind: and thou shalt be blessed; for they cannot recompense thee: for thou shalt be recompensed at the Resurrection of the Just.

When one of them ***who*** *sat at meat with Him, heard these things, he said unto Him, Blessed is he* ***who*** *shall eat bread in the kingdom of God. Then said He unto him,*

A certain man made a great supper, and bade many: and sent his **servants** at suppertime, to say to them **who** were bidden, Come, for all things are now ready. And they all with one consent began to make excuse. The first said unto him, I have bought a piece of ground, and I must needs go and see it: I pray thee have me excused. And another said, I have bought five yoke of oxen, and I go to prove them: I pray thee have me excused. And another said, I have married a wife, therefore I cannot come. So that servant came and showed his lord these things.

Then the master of the house, being angry, said to his **servants**, Go out quickly into the streets and lanes of the city, and bring hither the poor, and the maimed, the halt and the blind. And the servant said, Lord, it is done as thou hast commanded, and yet there is room. The lord said unto **his** servant, Go out into the highways, and hedges, and compel **men** to come in, that my house may be filled; for I say unto you, That none of those men **who** were bidden, shall taste of my supper.

When He had finished these sayings, He departed thence, *and there went great multitudes with Him, and He turned and said,*

If any man come to me, and hate not his father, and mother, and wife, and children, and brethren, and sisters, **or husband,** yea and his own life also**; or in other words, is afraid to lay down their life for my sake,** he cannot be my disciple. And whosoever doth not bear his cross, and come after me, cannot be my disciple.

Wherefore, settle this in your hearts, that ye will do the things which I shall teach, and command you. For which of you intending to build a tower, sitteth not down first, and counteth the cost, whether he have ~~sufficient~~ **money** to finish **his work**? Lest, ~~haply~~ **unhappily**, after he **has** laid the foundation and is not able to finish **his work**, all **who** behold, begin to mock him, saying, This man began to build, and was not able to finish.

And this He said, signifying there should not any man follow Him, unless he was able to continue; saying,

Or what king, going to make war against another king, sitteth not down first, and consulteth whether he be able with ten thousand, to meet him **who** cometh against him with twenty thousand. Or else, while the other is yet a great way off, he sendeth an ambassage, and desireth conditions of peace. So likewise, whosoever of you forsaketh not all that he hath he cannot be my disciple.

Then certain of them came to Him, saying, Good Master, we have Moses and the prophets, and whosoever shall live by them, shall he not have life? And Jesus answered,

Ye know not Moses, neither the prophets; for if ye had known them, ye would have believed on me; for to this intent they were written. For I am sent that ye might have life. Therefore I will liken it unto salt **which** is good; but if the salt **has** lost **its** savor, wherewith shall it be seasoned? It is neither fit for the land, nor yet for the dunghill; men cast it out. He **who** hath ears to hear, let him hear.

These things He said, signifying that which was written, verily must all be fulfilled.

LUKE 15

Parables of lost sheep; lost piece of silver; prodigal son

Then drew near unto Him, ***many of*** *the publicans, and sinners, to hear Him. The Pharisees and scribes murmured, This man receiveth sinners, and eateth with them. And He spake this parable unto them,*

What man of you having **a** hundred sheep, if he lose one of them, doth not leave the ninety and nine**, and go into** the wilderness after that which is lost, until he find it? And when he hath found it, he layeth it on his shoulders, rejoicing. And when he cometh home, he calleth together his friends and neighbors, **and saith** unto them, Rejoice with me; for I have found my sheep which was lost. I say unto you, that likewise joy shall be in heaven over one sinner that repenteth, more than over ninety and nine just persons, **who** need no repentance.

Either what woman having ten pieces of silver, if she lose one piece, doth not light a candle, and sweep the house, and seek diligently till she find it? And when she hath found it, she calleth her friends and her neighbors together, saying, Rejoice with me; for I have found the piece which I had lost. Likewise I say unto you, there is joy in the presence of the angels of God over one sinner **who** repenteth.

A certain man had two sons: and the younger of them said to his father, Father, give me the portion of goods **which** falleth to me. And he divided unto them his living. And not many days after, the younger son gathered all together, and took his journey into a far country, and there wasted his substance with riotous living. And when he had spent all, there arose a mighty famine in that land; and he began to be in want. And he went and joined himself to a citizen of that country; and he sent him into his fields to feed swine. And he would fain have filled his belly with the husks **which** the swine did eat; and no man gave unto him.

And when he came to himself, he said, How many hired servants of my father's have bread enough and to spare, and I perish with hunger! I will arise and go to my father, and will say unto him, Father, I have sinned against heaven, and before thee, and am no more worthy to be called thy son: make me as one of thy hired servants. And he arose, and came to his father. But when he was yet a great way off, his father saw him, and had compassion, and ran, and fell on his neck, and kissed him. And the son said unto him, Father, I have sinned against heaven, and in thy sight, and am no more worthy to be called thy son. But the father said **unto the** servants, Bring forth the best robe, and put it on him; and put a ring on his ~~hand~~ **finger**, and shoes on his feet; and bring hither the fatted calf, and kill it; and let us eat, and be merry: for this my son was dead, and is alive again; he was lost, and is found. And they began to be merry.

Now his elder son was in the field: and as he came and drew nigh to the house, he heard music and dancing. And he called one of the servants, and asked what these things meant. And he said unto him, Thy brother is come; and thy father hath killed the fatted calf, because he hath received him safe and sound. And he was angry, and would not go in: therefore came his father out, and entreated him. And he answering, said to his father, Lo, these many years do I serve thee, neither transgressed I at any time thy commandment; and thou never gavest me a kid, that I might make merry with my friends; but as soon as this thy son was come, **who** hath devoured thy living with harlots, thou hast killed for him the fatted calf. And he said unto him, Son, thou art ever with me, and all that I have is thine. It was meet that we should make merry, and be glad; for this thy brother was dead, and is alive again; was lost, and is found.

LUKE 16

Parables of unjust steward; Lazarus and rich man—divorce

He said also unto His disciples,

There was a certain rich man **who** had a steward; and the same was accused unto him, that he had wasted his goods. And he called him, and said unto him, How is it that I hear this of thee? Give an account of thy stewardship; for thou mayest be no longer steward. Then the steward said within himself, What shall I do? For my lord taketh away from me the stewardship: I cannot dig; to beg I am ashamed. I am resolved what to do, that, when I am put out of the stewardship, they may receive me into their houses.

So he called every one of his lord's debtors, and said unto the first, How much owest thou unto my lord? And he said, A hundred measures of oil. And he said unto him, Take thy bill, and sit down quickly, and write fifty. Then said he to another, And how much owest thou? And he said, A hundred measures of wheat. And he said unto him, Take thy bill, and write fourscore. And the lord commended the unjust steward, because he had done wisely; for the children of this world are **wiser** in their generation, than the children of light.

And I say unto you, Make to yourselves friends of the mammon of unrighteousness; that, when ye fail, they may receive you into everlasting habitations. He **who** is faithful in that which is least, is faithful also in much; and he **who** is unjust in the least, is also **unjust** in much. If therefore ye have not been faithful in the unrighteous mammon, who will commit to your trust the true riches? And if ye have not been faithful in that which is another man's, who shall give **unto** you that which is your own? No servant can serve two masters: for either he will hate the one, and love the other; or else he will hold to the one, and despise the other. Ye cannot serve God and mammon.

The Pharisees also, who were covetous, heard all these things: and they derided Him. And He said,

Ye are they **who** justify yourselves before men; but God knoweth your hearts; for that which is highly esteemed among men, is **an** abomination in the sight of God.

And they said unto Him, we have the law, and the prophets; but as for this man we will not receive Him to be our ruler; for He maketh Himself to be a judge over us. Then said Jesus,

The law and the prophets **testify of me; yea, and all the prophets who have written, even unto** John, **have foretold of these days**. Since that time, the kingdom of God is preached, and every man **who seeketh truth** presseth into it. And it is easier for heaven and earth to pass, than **for** one tittle of the law to fail. **And why teach ye the law, and deny that which is written; and condemn Him whom the Father hath sent to fulfill the law, that ye might all be redeemed? O fools! For you have said in your hearts, There is no God. And you pervert the right way; and the kingdom of heaven suffereth violence of you; and you persecute the meek; and in your violence you seek to destroy the kingdom; and ye take the children of the kingdom by force. Woe unto you, ye adulterers!**

They reviled Him again, being angry for the saying, that they were adulterers. But He continued,

Whosoever putteth away his wife, and marrieth another, committeth adultery; and whosoever marrieth her **who** is put away from her husband, committeth adultery.

Verily I say unto you, I will liken you unto the rich man. For there was a certain rich man, **who** was clothed in purple, and fine linen, and fared sumptuously every day. And there was a certain beggar named Lazarus, **who** was laid at his gate, full of sores, and desiring to be fed with the crumbs which fell from the rich man's table: moreover the dogs came and licked his sores. And it came to pass, that the beggar died, and was carried **of** the angels into Abraham's bosom. The rich man also died, and was buried. And in hell he **lifted** up his eyes, being in torments, and **saw** Abraham afar off, and Lazarus in his bosom. And he cried and said, Father Abraham, have mercy on me, and send Lazarus, that he may dip the tip of his finger in water, and cool my tongue; for I am tormented in this flame. But Abraham said, Son, remember that thou in thy lifetime receivedst thy good things, and likewise Lazarus evil things: but now he is comforted, and thou art tormented.

And beside all this, between us and you, there is a great gulf fixed; so that they **who** would pass from hence to you, cannot; neither can they pass to us that would come from thence. Then he said, I pray thee therefore, father, that thou wouldest send him to my father's house: for I have five brethren; that he may testify unto them, lest they also come into this place of torment. Abraham saith unto him, They have Moses and the prophets; let them hear them. And he said, Nay, father Abraham: but if one went unto them from the dead, they will repent. And he said unto him, If they hear not Moses and the prophets, neither will they be persuaded, though one **should rise** from the dead.

LUKE 17

Offenses—forgiveness—faith—parable of unprofitable servants—ten lepers—Second Coming

Then said He unto the disciples,

It is impossible but that offenses will come; but woe **to** him through whom they come. It were better for him that a millstone were hanged about his neck, and he cast into the sea, than that he should offend one of these little ones. Take heed to yourselves. If **your** brother trespass against **you**, rebuke him; and if he repent, forgive him. And if he trespass against **you** seven times in a day, and seven times in a day turn to **you again**, saying, I repent; **you shall** forgive him.

The Apostles said unto ***Him, Lord****, increase our faith. The Lord said,*

If **you** had faith as a grain of mustard seed, **you** might say unto this **sycamore** tree, Be thou plucked up by the **roots**, and be thou planted in the sea; and it should obey you. But **who** of you, having a servant plowing, or feeding cattle, will say unto him when he is come from the field, Go and sit down to meat? Will **he** not rather say unto him, Make ready wherewith I may sup, and gird **yourself** and serve me till I have eaten and drunken; and afterward, **by and by, you** shalt eat and drink? Doth he thank that servant because he **doeth** the things **which** were commanded him? I ~~trow not~~ **say unto you, Nay**. So likewise ye, when ye shall have done all those things which are commanded you, say, We are unprofitable servants. We have done that which was **no more than** our duty to do.

As He went to Jerusalem, he passed through the midst of ***Galilee*** *and* ***Samaria****. And as He entered into a village, there met Him ten men* ***who*** *were lepers,* ***who*** *stood afar off; and they lifted up their voices, Jesus, Master, have mercy on us. And He said,*

Go show yourselves unto the priests.

As they went, they were cleansed. One of them, when he saw he was healed, turned back, and with a loud voice glorified God, and fell down on his face at ***Jesus'*** *feet, giving Him thanks; and he was a Samaritan.*

Were there not ten cleansed? But where are the nine? There are not found that returned to give glory to God, save this stranger.

He said unto him,

Arise, go thy way: thy faith hath made thee whole.

When He was demanded of the Pharisees, when the kingdom of God should come, He answered,

The kingdom of God cometh not with observation: neither shall they say, Lo, here! or, Lo, there! For, behold, the kingdom of God ~~is within~~ **has already come unto** you.

He said unto the disciples,

The days will come, when ~~ye~~ **they will** desire to see one of the days of the Son of Man, and ~~ye~~ **they** shall not see it. And **if** they shall say to you, See here! or, See there! Go not after them, nor follow them. For as the ~~lightning~~ **light of the morning**, that **shineth** out of the one part under heaven, **and lighteneth to** the other part under heaven; so shall also the Son of Man be in His day. But first **He** must suffer many things, and be rejected of this generation. And as it was in the days of Noah, so shall it be also in the days of the Son of Man. They did eat, they drank, they married wives, they were given in marriage, until the day that Noah entered into the ark, and the flood came, and destroyed them all. Likewise also as it was in the days of Lot; they did eat, they drank, they bought, they sold, they planted, they builded; but the same day that Lot went out of Sodom it rained fire and brimstone from heaven, and destroyed them all. Even thus shall it be in the day when the Son of Man is revealed.

In that day, **the disciple who** shall be **on** the housetop, and his stuff in the house, let him not come down to take it away; and he **who** is in the field, let him likewise not return back. Remember Lot's wife. Whosoever shall seek to save his life shall lose it; and whosoever shall lose his life shall preserve it. I tell you, in that night there shall be two in one bed; the one shall be taken, and the other shall be left. Two shall be grinding together; the one shall be taken, and the other left. Two shall be in the field; the one shall be taken, and the other left.

*They answered, Where, Lord, **shall they be taken**? And He said,*

Wheresoever the body is **gathered; or, in other words, whithersoever the saints are gathered;** thither will the eagles be gathered together**; or, thither will the remainder be gathered together**.

This He spake, signifying the gathering of His saints; and of angels descending and gathering the remainder unto them; the one from the bed, the other from the grinding, and the other from the field, whithersoever He listeth. For verily there shall be new heavens, and a new earth, wherein dwelleth righteousness. And there shall be no unclean thing; for the earth becoming old, even as a garment, having waxed in corruption, wherefore it vanisheth away, and the footstool remaineth sanctified, cleansed from all sin.

LUKE 18

Parables of unjust judge; Pharisee and publican—little children—rich ruler—riches—heals blind

He spake a parable unto them, ***saying,*** *that men ought always to pray and not faint.*

There was in a city a judge, **who** feared not God, **nor** regarded man. And there was a widow in that city; and she came unto him, saying, Avenge me of mine adversary. And he would not for a while: but afterward he said within himself, Though I fear not God, nor regard man; yet because this widow troubleth me, I will avenge her, lest by her continual coming she weary me. Hear what the unjust judge saith. And shall not God avenge His own elect, **who** cry day and night unto Him, though He bear long with **men**? I tell you that He will **come, and when He does come, He will** avenge **His saints** speedily. Nevertheless, when the Son of Man cometh, shall He find faith on the earth?

He spake this parable unto certain ***men who*** *trusted in themselves that they were righteous, and despised others.*

Two men went up into the temple to pray; the one a Pharisee, and the other a publican. The Pharisee stood and prayed thus with himself, God, I thank Thee, that I am not as other men are, extortioners, unjust, adulterers, or even as this publican. I fast twice in the week, I give tithes of all that I possess. **But** the publican, standing afar off, would not lift up so much as his eyes unto heaven, but smote upon his breast, saying, God be merciful to me a sinner. I tell you, this man went down to his house justified, rather than the other; for everyone **who** exalteth himself, shall be abased; and he **who** humbleth himself, shall be exalted.

They brought unto Him also, infants, that He ***might*** *touch them; but when His disciples saw it, they rebuked them. But Jesus called them,*

Suffer little children to come unto me, and forbid them not; for of such is the kingdom of God. Verily I say unto you, Whosoever **will** not receive the kingdom of God as a little child, shall in no wise enter therein.

A certain ruler asked Him, Good Master, what shall I do to inherit eternal life? Jesus said,

Why callest thou me good? None is good, save one, that is, God. Thou knowest the commandments, Do not commit adultery, Do not kill, Do not steal, Do not bear false witness, Honor thy father and thy mother.

All these have I kept from my youth up.

Yet **thou** lackest one thing; sell all that thou hast, and distribute unto the poor, and thou shalt have treasure in heaven, and come, follow me.

When he heard this, he was very sorrowful: for he was very rich. And when Jesus saw that he was very sorrowful, He said,

How hardly shall they **who** have riches enter into the kingdom of God! For it is easier for a camel to go through a needle's eye, than for a rich man to enter into the kingdom of God.

*They that heard said **unto Him**, Who then can be saved? And He said,*

It is impossible **for them who trust in riches, to enter into the kingdom of God; but he who forsaketh the things which are of this world, it is** possible with God**, that he should enter in**.

Peter said, Lo, we have left all, and followed Thee.

Verily I say unto you, There is no man **who** has left house, or parents, or brethren, or wife, or children, for the kingdom of God's sake, who shall not receive manifold more in this present time, and in the world to come life everlasting.

Then He took the Twelve, and said unto them,

Behold, we go up to Jerusalem, and all things **which** are written by the prophets concerning the Son of Man, shall be accomplished. For He shall be delivered unto the Gentiles, and shall be mocked, and spitefully entreated, and spitted on: and they shall scourge and put Him to death; and the third day He shall rise again.

*They understood none of these things; and this saying was hid from them; neither **remembered** they the things which were spoken.*

As He was come nigh unto Jericho, a blind man sat by the wayside begging. He cried, Jesus, Son of David, have mercy on me. And Jesus stood and commanded him to be brought unto Him: and when he was come near, He asked,

What wilt thou that I shall do unto thee?

Lord, that I may receive my sight.

Receive thy sight: thy faith hath saved thee.

Immediately he received his sight; and ***he*** *followed Him, glorifying God.*

LUKE 19

Parable of pounds—colt—weeps over Jerusalem

Jesus entered and passed through Jericho. And there was a man named Zacchaeus, ***who*** *was chief among the publicans; and he was rich. He sought to see Jesus; and he ran before, and climbed up into a sycamore tree to see Him. When Jesus came to the place, He looked up, and saw him, and said,*

Zacchaeus, make haste, and come down; for today I must abide at thy house.

He made haste, and came down, and received Him joyfully.

When ***the disciples*** *saw it, they all murmured, That He was gone to be guest with a man* ***who*** *is a sinner. And Zacchaeus stood, and said unto the Lord, Behold, Lord, the half of my goods I give to the poor, and if I have taken anything from any man by* ***unjust means,*** *I restore fourfold.*

This day is salvation come to this house, **forasmuch** as he also is a son of Abraham. For the Son of Man is come to seek and to save that which was lost.

He added and spake a parable because He was nigh to Jerusalem, and because ***the Jews taught*** *that the kingdom of God should immediately appear.*

A certain nobleman went into a far country to receive for himself a kingdom, and to return. And he called his ten servants, and delivered them ten pounds, and said unto them, Occupy till I come. But his citizens hated him, and sent a **messenger** after him, saying, We will not have this man to reign over us. And it came to pass, that when he was returned, having received the kingdom, then he commanded these servants to be called unto him, to whom he had given the money, that he might know how much every man had gained by trading. Then came the first, saying, Lord, thy pound hath gained ten pounds. And he said unto him, Well **done**, thou good servant; because thou hast been faithful in a very little, have thou authority over ten cities.

And the second came, saying, Lord, thy pound hath gained five pounds. And he said likewise to him, Be thou also over five cities. And another came, saying, Lord, behold thy pound which I have kept laid up in a napkin; for I feared thee, because thou art an austere man; thou takest up that thou layedst not down, and reapest that **which** thou didst not sow. And he **said** unto him, Out of thine own mouth will I judge thee, **O** wicked servant. Thou knewest that I was an austere man, taking up that I laid not down, and reaping that I did not sow. Wherefore then, gavest not thou my money into the bank, that at my coming I might have ~~required~~ **received** mine own with usury?

And he said unto them **who** stood by, Take from him the pound, and give it to him **who** hath ten pounds. For I say unto you, That unto everyone **who** ~~hath~~ **occupieth**, shall be given; and from him **who** ~~hath~~ **occupieth** not, even that he hath **received** shall be taken away from him. But those mine enemies, **who** would not that I should reign over them, bring hither, and slay them before me.

When He had thus spoken, he went before, ascending up to Jerusalem. When He was come nigh to Bethphage and Bethany, at the mount called the Mount of Olives, He sent two of His disciples,

Go ye into the village over against you, in the which at your entering ye shall find a colt tied, whereon yet never man sat; loose him, and bring him **to me**. And if any man ask you, Why do ye loose **the colt**? Thus shall ye say unto him, Because the Lord hath need of him.

*They **who** were sent, went their way, and found even as He had said unto them. And they brought him to Jesus: and they cast their garments upon the colt, and they set Jesus thereon.*

*When He was come nigh, even now at the descent of the Mount of Olives, the whole multitude of the disciples began to rejoice and praise God with a loud voice for all the mighty works that they had seen, Blessed **is** the King that cometh in the name of the Lord, peace in heaven, and glory in the highest! Some of the Pharisees said, Master, rebuke Thy disciples. He answered,*

If these should hold their peace, the stones would immediately cry out.

When He was come near, He beheld the city, and wept over it,

If thou hadst known, even thou, at least in this thy day, the things which belong unto thy peace! But now they are hid from thine eyes. For the days shall come upon thee, that thine enemies shall cast a trench about thee, and compass thee round, and keep thee in on every side, and shall lay thee even with the ground, and thy children within thee; and they shall not leave in thee one stone upon another; because thou knewest not the time of thy visitation.

*He went into the temple, and began to cast out them that sold therein, and them **who** bought, saying,*

It is written, My house is **a** house of prayer; but ye have made it a den of thieves.

LUKE 20

Parable of wicked husbandmen—paying tribute—seven husbands

*On one of those days, as He taught the people in the temple, and preached the gospel, the chief priests and the scribes came upon Him with the elders, saying, Tell us, by what authority doest Thou these things? Or, who is he **who** gave Thee this authority? And He answered,*

I will also ask you one thing; answer me: The baptism of John, was it from heaven, or of men?

They answered that they could not tell whence it was. Jesus said,

Neither tell I you, by what authority I do these things.

Then began He to speak to the people, this parable:

A certain man planted a vineyard, and let it ~~forth~~ **out** to husbandmen, and went into a far country for a long time. And at the season **of the harvest**, he sent **his** servant to the husbandmen, that they should give him of the fruit of the vineyard; but the husbandmen beat him, and sent him away empty. And again he sent another servant: and they beat him also, and entreated him shamefully, and sent him away empty. And again he sent a third: and they wounded him also, and cast him out.

Then said the lord of the vineyard, What shall I do? I will send my beloved son: it may be they will reverence him when they see him. But when the husbandmen saw him, they reasoned among themselves, saying, This is the heir: come, let us kill him, that the inheritance may be ours. So they cast him out of the vineyard, and killed him. What therefore shall the lord of the vineyard do unto them? He shall come and destroy these husbandmen, and shall give the vineyard to others.

They said, God forbid! And He beheld them, and said,

What is this then **which** is written, The stone which the builders rejected, the same is become the head of the corner? Whosoever shall fall upon that stone, shall be broken; but on whomsoever it shall fall, it **shall** grind him to powder.

The chief priests, and the scribes, sought to lay hands on Him; for they perceived that He had spoken this parable against them. They watched Him, and sent forth spies. They asked Him, Is it lawful for us to give tribute unto Caesar, or no? But He perceived their craftiness, and said,

Why tempt ye me? Show me a penny. Whose image and superscription hath it?

Caesar's.

Render therefore unto Caesar the things which be Caesar's, and unto God the things which be God's.

Then came to Him certain of the Sadducees, saying, Master, Moses wrote unto us, ***saying,*** *If any man's brother die, having a wife, and he die without children, that his brother should take his wife, and raise up seed unto his brother. There were therefore seven brethren: and the first took a wife, and died without children. And the second took her to wife, and died childless. And the third took her, and in like manner the seven also: and they left no children, and died.* ***And*** *last of all, the woman died also. Therefore in the resurrection whose wife of them is she? Jesus said,*

The children of this world marry, and are given in marriage: but they **who** shall be accounted worthy to obtain that world, ~~and the~~ **through** resurrection from the dead, neither marry nor are given in marriage. Neither can they die any more: for they are equal unto the angels; and are the children of God, being the children of the resurrection. Now that the dead are raised, even Moses showed at the bush, when he calleth the Lord the God of Abraham, and the God of Isaac, and the God of Jacob. For He is not a God of the dead, but of the living: for all live unto Him.

After that they durst not ask Him any question at all. And He said unto them,

How say they that Christ is David's Son? And David himself saith in the book of Psalms, The LORD said unto my Lord, Sit Thou on my right hand, till I make Thine enemies Thy footstool. David therefore calleth Him Lord, how is He then his Son?

Then in the audience of all the people He said unto His disciples,

Beware of the scribes, **who** desire to walk in long robes, and love greetings in the markets, and the highest seats in the synagogues, and the chief rooms at feasts; **who** devour widows' houses, and for a show, make long prayers; the same shall receive greater damnation.

LUKE 21

Widow's mites—destruction of Jerusalem—
Second Coming—parable of fig tree

He looked up, and saw the rich men casting ***in*** *their gifts into the treasury; and saw also, a poor widow casting in thither two mites. He said,*

Of a truth I say unto you, that this poor widow hath cast in more than they all: for all these have of their abundance cast in unto the offerings of God: but she of her penury hath cast in all the living that she had.

As some spake of the temple, how it was adorned with goodly stones and gifts, He said,

These things which ye behold, the days will come, in the which there shall not be left one stone upon another, **which** shall not be thrown down.

The disciples *asked, Master, when shall these things be? And what sign* ***wilt Thou show****, when these things shall come to pass? He said,*

The time draweth near, and therefore take heed that ye be not deceived; for many shall come in my name, saying, I am Christ; go ye not therefore after them. **And** when ye shall hear of wars and commotions, be not terrified; for these things must first come to pass; but **this** is not **the end**. Nation shall rise against nation, and kingdom against kingdom: and great earthquakes shall be in divers places, and famines, and pestilences; and fearful sights and great signs shall there be from heaven.

But before all these **things shall come**, they shall lay their hands on you, and persecute you; delivering you up to the synagogues, and into prisons; being brought before kings and rulers for my name's sake. Settle **this** therefore in your hearts, not to meditate before what ye shall answer; for I will give you a mouth and wisdom, which all your adversaries shall not be able to gainsay nor resist. And it shall turn to you for a testimony. And ye shall be betrayed both by parents, and brethren, and kinsfolk, and friends; and some of you shall they cause to be put to death. And ye shall be hated of all ~~men~~ **the world** for my name's sake. But there shall not a hair of your head perish.

In your patience possess ye your souls. And when ye shall see Jerusalem compassed with armies, then know that the desolation thereof is nigh. Then let them which are in Judea flee to the mountains; and let them **who** are in the midst of it, depart out; and let not them **who** are in the countries, **return to** enter **into the city**. For these be the days of vengeance, that all things which are written may be fulfilled.

But woe unto them **who** are with child, and to them **who** give suck, in those days! For there shall be great distress in the land, and wrath upon this people. And they shall fall by the edge of the sword, and shall be led away captive into all nations: and Jerusalem shall be trodden down of the Gentiles, until the times of the Gentiles be fulfilled.

These things He spake, concerning the destruction of Jerusalem. Then His disciples asked, Master, tell us concerning Thy coming? He answered,

In the generation in which the times of the Gentiles shall be fulfilled, there shall be signs in the sun, and in the moon, and in the stars; and upon the earth distress of nations with perplexity, **like** the sea and the waves roaring. **The earth also shall be troubled, and the waters of the great deep;** men's hearts failing them for fear, and for looking after those things which are coming on the earth: for the powers of heaven shall be shaken. And when these things begin to come to pass, then look up and lift up your heads, for **the day of** your redemption draweth nigh. And then shall they see the Son of Man coming in a cloud, with power and great glory.

Behold the fig tree, and all the trees. When they now shoot forth, ye see and know of your own selves that summer is now nigh at hand. So likewise ye, when ye see these things come to pass, know ye that the kingdom of God is nigh at hand. Verily I say unto you, This generation, **the generation when the times of the Gentiles be fulfilled,** shall not pass away till all be fulfilled. Heaven and earth shall pass away: but my words shall not pass away.

Let my disciples therefore take heed to ~~yourselves~~ **themselves**, lest at any time ~~your~~ **their** hearts be overcharged with surfeiting, and drunkenness, and cares of this life, and that day come upon ~~you~~ **them** unawares. For as a snare shall it come on all them **who** dwell on the face of the whole earth. **And what I say unto one, I say unto all,** Watch ye therefore, and pray always, **and keep my commandments,** that ye may be **counted** worthy to escape all these things **which** shall come to pass, and to stand before the Son of Man **when He shall come clothed in the glory of His Father**.

LUKE 22

Passover—sacrament—Gethsemane—trial

Then came the day of Unleavened Bread, when the passover must be killed. He sent Peter and John,

Go and prepare us the passover, that we may eat.

They said, Where wilt Thou that we prepare? He said,

Behold, when ye **have** entered into the city, there shall a man meet you, bearing a pitcher of water; follow him into the house where he entereth in. And ye shall say unto the goodman of the house, The Master saith unto **you**, Where is the guestchamber, where I shall eat the passover with my disciples? And he shall show you a large upper room furnished: there make ready.

They went, and found as He had said unto them: and they made ready the passover. When the hour was come, He sat down, and the Twelve Apostles with Him. He said unto them,

With desire I have desired to eat this passover with you before I suffer: for I say unto you, I will not anymore eat thereof, until it be fulfilled **which is written in the prophets concerning me. Then I will partake with you,** in the kingdom of God.

He took the cup, and gave thanks, and said,

Take this and divide among yourselves; for I say unto you, **That** I will not drink of the fruit of the vine, until the kingdom of God shall come.

And He took bread, and gave thanks, and brake, and gave unto them, saying,

This is my body which is given for you; this do in remembrance of me.

Likewise also the cup after supper, saying,

This cup is the new testament in my blood, which is shed for you. But, behold, the hand of him **who** betrayeth me is with me on the table. And truly the Son of Man goeth, as it was determined: but woe unto that man by whom He is betrayed!

They began to inquire among themselves, which of them it was that should do this thing. There was also a strife among them, which of them should be accounted the greatest. And He said unto them,

The kings of the Gentiles exercise lordship over them, and they **who** exercise authority upon them, are called benefactors. But **it ought** not **to** be so **with you**; but he **who** is greatest among you, let him be as the younger; and he **who** is chief, as he **who** doth serve. For whether is **he** greater, **who** sitteth at meat, or he **who** serveth? **I am** not **as** he **who** sitteth at meat, but I am among you as he **who** serveth. Ye are they **who** have continued with me in my temptations. And I appoint unto you a kingdom, as my Father hath appointed unto me; that **you** may eat and drink at my table in my kingdom; and sit on **twelve** thrones, judging the twelve tribes of Israel.

Simon, Simon, behold Satan hath desired you, that he may sift **the children of the kingdom** as wheat. But I have prayed for **you**, that **your** faith fail not; and when **you are** converted strengthen **your** brethren.

*He said, Lord, I am ready to go with **you**, both into prison, and **unto** death. **The Lord** said,*

I tell **you**, Peter, **that** the cock shall not crow this day, before that **you will** thrice deny that **you know** me.

And He said unto them,

When I sent you without purse, and scrip, and shoes, lacked ye anything?

Nothing.

I say unto you again, He **who** hath a purse, let him take it, and likewise his scrip; and he **who** hath no sword, let him sell his garment and buy one. For I say unto you, This that is written must be accomplished in me, and he was reckoned among the transgressors; for the things concerning me have an end.

They said, Lord, here are two swords.

It is enough.

*And He came out, and went, as He was **accustomed**, to the Mount of Olives; and His disciples followed Him. When He was at the place, He said unto them,*

Pray that ye enter not into temptation.

And He was withdrawn from them about a stone's cast, and kneeled down, and prayed, saying,

Father, if Thou be willing, remove this cup from me: nevertheless, not my will, but Thine, be done.

*And there appeared an angel unto Him from heaven, strengthening Him. And being in an agony, He prayed more earnestly; and **He** sweat as it were great drops of blood falling down to the ground. When He rose up from prayer, and was come to His disciples, He found them sleeping; for **they were filled with** sorrow. **He** said,*

Why sleep ye? Rise and pray, lest ye enter into temptation.

*While He yet spake, behold, a multitude, and he **who** was called Judas, one of the Twelve, went before them, and drew near unto Jesus to kiss Him. But Jesus said,*

Judas, betrayest thou the Son of Man with a kiss?

*They **who** were about Him said, Lord, shall we smite with **a** sword? One of them smote the servant of the high priest, and cut off his right ear. Jesus answered,*

Suffer ye thus far.

*And He touched his ear, and healed him. Then Jesus said unto the chief priests, and captains of the temple, and the elders, **who** were come to Him,*

Are ye come out as against a thief, with swords and staves? When I was daily with you in the temple, ye stretched forth no hands against me: but this is your hour, and the power of darkness.

Then [they] took Him, and led Him, and brought Him into the high priest's house.

As soon as it was day, the elders of the people and the chief priests and the scribes came together, and led Him into their council, saying, Art Thou the Christ? And He said,

If I tell you, ye will not believe. And if I also ask you, ye will not answer me, nor let me go. Hereafter shall the Son of Man sit on the right hand of the power of God.

Art Thou then the Son of God?

Ye say that I am.

*What need **ye** any further witness? We have heard of His own mouth.*

LUKE 23

Trial—Crucifixion

*The whole multitude of them arose, and led Him unto Pilate. And they began to accuse Him, saying, We found this **man** perverting the nation, and forbidding to give tribute to Caesar, saying, that He Himself is Christ**,** a king. Pilate asked Him, Art Thou the King of the Jews? And He answered,*

Yea, thou sayest it.

Then said Pilate to the chief priests and to the people, I find no fault in this man. And they were the more fierce, saying, He stirreth up the people, teaching throughout all Jewry, beginning from Galilee to this place. When Pilate heard of Galilee, he asked whether the man were a Galilaean. And as soon as he knew that He belonged unto Herod's jurisdiction, he sent Him to Herod, who himself also was at Jerusalem at that time.

*And when Herod saw Jesus, he was exceeding glad; for he was desirous to see Him**,** of a long **time**, because he had heard many things of Him; and hoped to have seen some miracle done by Him. Then he questioned with Him in many words; but He answered him nothing. The chief priests and scribes stood and vehemently accused Him. And Herod with his men of war set Him at **naught**, and mocked Him, and arrayed Him in a gorgeous robe, and sent Him again to Pilate.*

*Pilate, when he had called together the chief priests and the rulers and the people, said, **You** have brought this man unto me, as one **who** perverteth the* *people;* *and behold, I, having examined Him before you, have found no fault in this man, touching those things whereof ye accuse Him.* *No, nor yet Herod: for I sent you to him; and, lo, nothing worthy of death is done unto Him. I will therefore chastise Him, and release Him. (For of necessity he must release one unto them at the feast.)* ***But*** *they cried out all at once, saying, Away with this man, and release unto us Barabbas. (Who for a certain sedition made in the city, and for murder, was cast into prison.)*

Pilate therefore, willing to release Jesus, spake again to them. But they cried, Crucify Him, crucify Him. And he said unto them the third time, Why, what evil hath He done? I have found no cause of death in Him: I will therefore chastise Him, and let Him go. And they were instant ***in*** *loud voices, requiring that He might be crucified;* *and the voices of them, and of the chief priests,* *prevailed. And Pilate gave sentence that it should be as they required. And he released unto them him* ***who*** *for sedition and murder was cast into prison, whom they had desired;* ***and*** *delivered Jesus to their will.*

As they led Him away, there followed a great company of people, and of women, which also bewailed and lamented Him. But Jesus ***turned*** *unto them* ***and*** *said,*

Daughters of Jerusalem, weep not for me, but weep for yourselves, and for your children. For behold, the days are coming, in the which they shall say, Blessed are the barren, and the wombs **which** never bare, and the paps which never gave suck. Then shall they begin to say to the mountains, Fall on us; and to the hills, Cover us. **And** if these things **are done** in **the** green tree, what shall be done in the dry **tree**?

This He spake, signifying the scattering of Israel, and the desolation of the heathen, or in other words, the Gentiles.

And there were also two ***others****, malefactors, led with Him to be put to death. When they were come to the place called Calvary, there they crucified Him, and the malefactors, one on the right hand, and the other on the left. Then said Jesus,*

Father, forgive them; for they know not what they do ***(meaning the soldiers who crucified Him)***.

And they parted His raiment, and cast lots. And the people stood, beholding, and the rulers also with them, derided, saying, He saved others; let Him save Himself, if He be the Christ, the Chosen of God. And the soldiers also mocked Him, coming to Him, and offering Him vinegar, and saying, If Thou be the King of the Jews, save Thyself. And a superscription also was written over Him in letters of Greek, Latin, and Hebrew, THIS IS THE KING OF THE JEWS.

One of the malefactors ***who was crucified with Him*** *railed on Him, If Thou be* ***the*** *Christ, save Thyself and us. But the other answering,* *rebuked him, Dost thou* ***not*** *fear God, seeing thou art in the same condemnation? And we indeed* *justly; for we receive the due reward of our deeds: but this man hath done nothing amiss. And he said* ***to*** *Jesus, Lord, remember me when Thou comest into Thy kingdom. Jesus said,*

Verily I say unto thee, Today shalt thou be with me in **the world of spirits**.

It was about the sixth hour, and there was darkness over all the earth until the ninth hour. And the sun was darkened, and the veil of the temple was rent in the midst. When Jesus had cried with a loud voice, He said,

Father, into Thy hands I commend my spirit.

And He gave up the ghost.

LUKE 24

Resurrection—road to Emmaus

Now upon the first day of the week, very early in the morning, ***the women*** *came unto the sepulchre, bringing the spices which they had prepared, and certain others with them. They found the stone rolled away from the sepulchre****, and two angels standing by it in shining garments****. They entered* ***into the sepulchre,*** *and not* ***finding*** *the body of the Lord Jesus, they were much perplexed thereabout; and were* ***affrighted****, and bowed down their faces to the earth.* ***But the angels*** *said unto them, Why seek ye the living among the dead? He is not here, but is risen: remember how He spake unto you when He was yet in Galilee, saying, The Son of Man must be delivered into the hands of sinful men, and be crucified, and the third day rise again.*

They remembered His words, and returned from the sepulchre, and told all these things unto the eleven, and to all the rest. Their words seemed to them as idle tales, and they believed them not. Then arose Peter, and ran unto the sepulchre and ***went in, and*** *he beheld the linen clothes laid by themselves; and departed, wondering in himself at that which was come to pass.*

Two of them went that same day to a village called Emmaus. While they communed together and reasoned, Jesus Himself drew near, and went with them. But their eyes were holden, ***or covered,*** *that they* ***could*** *not know Him. And He said unto them,*

What manner of communications are these **which** ye have one **with** another, as ye walk and are sad?

One of them, whose name was Cleopas, answering, said unto Him, Art Thou a stranger in Jerusalem, and hast not known the things which are come to pass there in these days? And He said unto them,

What things?

And they said, Concerning Jesus of Nazareth, ***who*** *was a prophet mighty in deed and word before God and all the people; and how the chief priests and our* *rulers delivered Him to be condemned to death, and have crucified Him. But we trusted that it had been He* ***who*** *should have redeemed Israel.* ***Besides*** *all this, today is the third day since these things were done; Yea, and certain women also of our company made us astonished,* ***who*** *were early at the sepulchre; and when they found not His body, they came, saying, that they had also seen a vision of angels,* ***who*** *said that He was alive. And certain of them* ***who*** *were with us, went to the sepulchre, and found it even so as the women had said; but Him they saw not. Then He said,*

O fools, and slow of heart to believe all that the prophets have spoken: Ought not Christ to have suffered these things, and to enter into His glory?

And beginning at Moses and all the prophets, He expounded unto them in all the scriptures the things concerning Himself. And they drew nigh unto the village whither they went; and He made as though He would have gone ***farther****. But they constrained Him, saying, Abide with us: for it is toward evening, and the day is far spent. And He went in to tarry with them. As He sat at meat with them, He took bread, and blessed, and brake, and gave to them. And their eyes were opened, and they knew Him; and He* ***was taken up*** *out of their sight. And they said one to another, Did not our* ***hearts*** *burn within us, while He talked with us by the way, and while He opened to us the scriptures?*

And they rose up the same hour and returned to Jerusalem, and found the eleven gathered together, and ***those who*** *were with them, saying, The Lord is risen indeed, and hath appeared to Simon. And they told what things* ***they saw and heard*** *in the way, and how He was known* ***to*** *them, in breaking of bread. As they thus spake, Jesus Himself stood in the midst of them, and saith unto them,*

Peace be unto you.

But they were terrified and affrighted, and supposed that they had seen a spirit. He said,

Why are **you** troubled? And why do thoughts arise in your hearts? Behold my hands and my feet, that it is I: myself, handle me, and see; for a spirit hath not flesh and bones, as ye see me have.

When He had thus spoken, He showed them His hands and His feet. While they yet ***wondered and*** *believed not for joy, He said unto them,*

Have ye here any meat?

They gave Him a piece of a broiled fish, and ***a*** *honey comb. And He took it, and did eat before them. He said,*

These are the words which I spake unto you, while I was yet with you, that all things must be fulfilled, which were written in the law of Moses, and in the prophets, and in the psalms, concerning me.

Then opened He their understanding, that they might understand the scriptures.

Thus it is written, and thus it behooved Christ to suffer, and to rise from the dead the third day: and that repentance and remission of sins should be preached in His name among all nations, beginning at Jerusalem. And ye are witnesses of these things. And, behold, I send the promise of my Father upon you: but tarry ye in the city of Jerusalem, until ye be endued with power from on high.

He led them out as far as Bethany, and He lifted up His hands and blessed them. While He blessed them, He was ***taken*** *from them, and carried up into heaven.*

Words of Christ According to Saint John

JOHN 1

John—Andrew—Simon Peter—Philip—Nathanael

John seeth Jesus coming unto him, and ***said****, Behold the Lamb of God,* ***who*** *taketh away the sin of the world!* ***And John bare record of Him unto the people, saying,*** *This is He of whom I said; After me cometh a man* ***who*** *is preferred before me; for He was before me, and I knew Him,* ***and*** *that He should be made manifest to Israel; therefore am I come baptizing with water. And John bare record, saying,* ***When He was baptized of me,*** *I saw the Spirit descending from heaven like a dove, and it abode upon Him. And I knew Him;* ***for*** *He* ***who*** *sent me to baptize with water, the same said unto me; Upon whom thou shalt see the Spirit descending, and remaining on Him, the same is He* ***who*** *baptizeth with the Holy Ghost. And I saw, and bare record that this is the Son of God.*

These things were done in Bethabara, beyond Jordan, where John was baptizing. Again the next day after John stood, and two of his disciples; and looking upon Jesus as He walked, he ***said****; Behold the Lamb of God! And the two disciples heard him speak, and they followed Jesus. Then Jesus turned, and saw them following* ***Him****, and* ***said****,*

What seek ye?

They ***say****, Rabbi (Master), where dwellest Thou?*

Come and see.

And *they came and saw where He dwelt.*

One of the two ***who*** *heard John, and followed* ***Jesus****, was Andrew, Simon Peter's brother. He first findeth his own brother Simon, and saith unto him, We have found the Christ. He brought him to Jesus. When Jesus beheld him, He said,*

Thou art Simon, the son of Jona; thou shalt be called Cephas *(a* ***seer, or a*** *stone).*

They were fishermen. And they straightway left all, and followed Jesus. *The day following, Jesus would go forth into Galilee, and findeth Philip, and saith unto him,*

Follow me.

Philip findeth Nathanael, and saith, We have found Him, of whom Moses in the law, and the prophets, did write, Jesus of Nazareth, the son of Joseph. And Nathanael said, Can there any good thing come out of Nazareth? Philip saith, Come and see. Jesus saw Nathanael coming and ***said*** *of him,*

Behold an Israelite indeed, in whom is no guile!

*Nathanael **said**, Whence knowest thou me? Jesus **answering**, said,*

Before Philip called thee, when thou wast under the fig tree, I saw thee.

Rabbi, Thou art the Son of God; Thou art the King of Israel. Jesus said,

Because I said unto thee, I saw thee under the fig tree, believest thou? Thou shalt see greater things than these. Verily, verily, I say unto you, Hereafter ye shall see heaven open, and the angels of God ascending and descending upon the Son of Man.

JOHN 2

Water to wine—moneychangers

*On the third day **of the week**, there was a marriage in Cana of Galilee; and the mother of Jesus was there. Jesus was called, and His disciples, to the marriage. When they wanted wine, **His** mother **said** unto Him, They have no wine. Jesus **said**,*

Woman, what **wilt thou** have ~~I~~ **me** ~~to~~ do ~~with~~ **for** thee? **That will I do; for** mine hour is not yet come.

*His mother **said** unto the servants, Whatsoever He saith unto you, **see that ye** do it.*

There were set there six waterpots of stone, after the manner of the purifying of the Jews, containing two or three firkins apiece. Jesus saith,

Fill the waterpots with water.

They filled them up to the brim.

Draw out now, and bear unto the governor of the feast.

*They bare **unto him**. When the **governor** of the feast had tasted the water **which** was made wine (and **he** knew not whence it was, but the servants **who** drew the water knew), the governor of the feast called the bridegroom, and saith unto him, Every man at the beginning doth set forth good wine; and when men have well drunk, then that which is worse: but thou hast kept the good wine until now.*

*The Jews' Passover was at hand, and Jesus went up to Jerusalem, and found in the temple those **who** sold oxen, and sheep, and doves, and the changers of money sitting. When He had made a scourge of small cords, He drove them all out of the temple, and the sheep, and the oxen; and poured out the changers' money, and overthrew the tables; and said unto them **who** sold doves,*

Take these things hence; make not my Father's house **a** house of merchandise.

*Then **spake** the Jews, What sign showest Thou unto us, seeing Thou doest these things? Jesus answered,*

Destroy this temple, and in three days I will raise it up.

JOHN 3

Born of water and Spirit—Only Begotten Son

There was a man of the Pharisees, named Nicodemus, a ruler of the Jews: the same came to Jesus by night, and said, Rabbi, we know that Thou art a teacher come from God; for no man can do these miracles ***which*** *Thou doest, except God be with Him. Jesus answered,*

Verily, verily, I say unto thee, Except a man be born again, he cannot see the kingdom of God.

How can a man be born when he is old? Can he enter the second time into his mother's womb, and be born?

Verily, verily, I say unto thee, Except a man be born of water, and the Spirit, he cannot enter into the kingdom of God. That which is born of the flesh is flesh; and that which is born of the Spirit is spirit. Marvel not that I said unto thee, Ye must be born again. The wind bloweth where it listeth, and thou hearest the sound thereof, but canst not tell whence it cometh, and whither it goeth; so is everyone **who** is born of the Spirit.

Nicodemus answered, How can these things be? Jesus said,

Art thou a master of Israel, and knowest not these things? Verily, verily, I say unto thee, We speak that we do know, and testify that we have seen; and ye receive not our witness. If I have told you earthly things, and ye believe not, how shall ye believe if I tell you heavenly things? **I tell you,** No man hath ascended up to heaven, but He **who** came down from heaven, the Son of Man **who** is in heaven. And as Moses lifted up the serpent in the wilderness, even so must the Son of Man be lifted up: that whosoever believeth ~~in~~ **on** Him should not perish, but have eternal life. For God so loved the world, that He gave His Only Begotten Son, that whosoever believeth ~~in~~ **on** Him should not perish; but have everlasting life. For God sent not His Son into the world to condemn the world; but that the world through Him might be saved.

He **who** believeth on Him is not condemned; but he **who** believeth not is condemned already, because he hath not believed ~~in~~ **on** the name of the Only Begotten Son of God**, which before was preached by the mouth of the holy prophets; for they testified of me.** And this is the condemnation, that light is come into the world, and men **love** darkness rather than light, because their deeds **are** evil. For everyone **who** doeth evil hateth the light, neither cometh to the light, lest his deeds should be reproved. But he **who** ~~doeth~~ **loveth** truth, cometh to the light, that his deeds may be made manifest. **And he who obeyeth the truth, the works which he doeth** they are **of** God.

JOHN 4

Woman of Samaria—heals nobleman's son

He *cometh to* ***the*** *city of Samaria which is called Sychar, near to the parcel of ground* ***which*** *Jacob gave to his son Joseph****; the place where Jacob's well was.*** *Now Jesus being* ***weary*** *with* ***the*** *journey,* ***it being about the sixth hour,*** *sat* ***down*** *on the well;* ***and*** *there* ***came*** *a woman of Samaria to draw water. Jesus* ***said,***

Give me to drink.

Wherefore, He being alone, the woman of Samaria said, *How is it that Thou being a Jew, askest drink of me,* ***who*** *am a woman of Samaria? The Jews have no dealings with the Samaritans. Jesus answered,*

If thou knewest the gift of God, and who it is that saith to thee, Give me to drink; thou wouldest have asked of Him, and He would have given thee living water.

The woman saith, Sir, Thou hast nothing to draw with, and the well is deep: from whence then hast Thou that living water? Art Thou greater than our father Jacob, ***who*** *gave us the well, and drank thereof himself, and his children, and his cattle? Jesus answered,*

Whosoever **shall drink** of this ~~water~~ **well**, shall thirst again; But whosoever drinketh of the water **which** I shall give him shall never thirst; but the water that I shall give him shall be in him a well of water springing up into everlasting life.

Sir, give me ***of*** *this water that I thirst not, neither come hither to draw. Jesus saith,*

Go, call thy husband, and come hither.

I have no husband. Jesus said unto her,

Thou hast well said, I have no husband: for thou hast had five husbands; and he whom thou now hast is not thy husband: in that saidst thou truly.

Sir, I perceive that Thou art a prophet. Our fathers worshiped in this mountain; and ye say, that in Jerusalem is the place where men ought to worship.

Woman, believe me, the hour cometh, when ye shall neither in this mountain, nor yet at Jerusalem, worship the Father. Ye worship ye know not what; we know what we worship; **and** salvation is of the Jews. **And** the hour cometh, and now is, when the true worshipers shall worship the Father in spirit and in truth; for the Father seeketh such to worship Him. **For unto such hath** God ~~is a~~ **promised His** Spirit. And they **who** worship Him, must worship in spirit and in truth.

*The woman **said**, I know that Messias cometh, **who** is called Christ; when He is come, He will tell us all things. Jesus **said**,*

I **who** speak unto thee am **the Messias**.

*Upon this came His disciples, and marveled that He talked with the woman. The woman then left her waterpot, and went her way into the city, and saith to the men, Come see a man **who** told me all things that I **have ever done**. Is not this the Christ? Then they went out of the city, and came unto Him.*

*In the **meantime** His disciples prayed Him, saying, Master, eat. But He said,*

I have meat to eat that ye know not of.

*Therefore said the disciples one to another, Hath any man brought Him **meat** to eat? Jesus **said**,*

My meat is to do the will of Him **who** sent me, and to finish His work. Say not ye, There are yet four months, and then cometh harvest? Behold, I say unto you, Lift up your eyes, and look on the fields; for they are white already to harvest. And he **who** reapeth, receiveth wages, and gathereth fruit unto life eternal; that both he **who** soweth, and he **who** reapeth, may rejoice together. And herein is that saying true, One soweth, and another reapeth. I **have** sent you to reap that whereon ye bestowed no labor; ~~other men~~ **the prophets have** labored, and ye **have** entered into their labors.

Jesus came again into Cana of Galilee, where He made the water wine. And there was a certain nobleman, whose son was sick at Capernaum. When he heard that Jesus was come out of Judea into Galilee, he went unto Him, and besought Him that He would come down, and heal his son: for he was at the point of death. Then said Jesus,

Except ye see signs and wonders, ye will not believe.

*The nobleman **said**, Sir, come down **before** my child die.*

Go thy way, thy son liveth.

*The man believed the word **which** Jesus had spoken unto him, and he went his way. As he was going down **to his house**, his servants met him, saying, Thy son liveth. Then inquired he of them the hour when he began to **mend**. And they said unto him, Yesterday at the seventh hour the fever left him. So the father knew that **this son** was **healed in** the same hour in the which Jesus said unto him, Thy son liveth; and himself believed, and his whole house.*

JOHN 5

Bethesda—all be judged of Son of Man

After this, there was a feast of the Jews; and Jesus went up to Jerusalem. Now there is at Jerusalem by the sheep market a pool, which is called in the Hebrew tongue Bethesda. And a certain man was there, ***who*** *had an infirmity thirty and eight years. Jesus saw him lie, and knew that he had been now a long time* ***afflicted; and*** *He* ***said****,*

Wilt thou be made whole?

The impotent man answered, Sir, I have no man, when the water is troubled, to put me into the pool: but while I am coming, another steppeth down before me. Jesus saith,

Rise, take up thy bed, and walk.

Immediately the man was made whole, and took up his bed, and walked. And ***it was*** *on the Sabbath.*

Afterward, Jesus findeth him in the temple, and said,

Behold, thou art made whole: sin no more, lest a worse thing come unto thee.

The man departed, and told the Jews that it was Jesus ***who*** *had made him whole; therefore did the Jews persecute Jesus, and sought to slay Him, because He had done these things on the Sabbath day. But Jesus answered them,*

My Father worketh hitherto, and I work.

Therefore the Jews sought the more to kill Him, because He not only had broken the Sabbath, but said also that God was His Father, making Himself equal with God. Then Jesus said,

Verily, verily, I say unto you, The Son can do nothing of Himself, but what he seeth the Father do: for what things soever he doeth, these also doeth the Son likewise. For the Father loveth the Son, and showeth Him all things that Himself doeth: and He will show Him greater works than these, that ye may marvel. For as the Father raiseth up the dead, and quickeneth them; even so the Son quickeneth whom He will. For the Father judgeth no man, but hath committed all judgment unto the Son: that all should honor the Son, even as they honor the Father. He **who** honoreth not the Son, honoreth not the Father **who** hath sent Him.

Verily, verily, I say unto you, He **who** heareth my word, and believeth on Him **who** sent me, hath everlasting life, and shall not come into condemnation; but is passed from death **into** life. Verily, verily, I say unto you, The hour is coming, and now is, when the dead shall hear the voice of the Son of God; and they **who** hear shall live. For as the Father hath life in Himself; so hath He given to the Son to have life in Himself; and hath given Him authority to execute judgment also, because He is the Son of Man.

Marvel not at this; for the hour is coming, in the which all **who** are in **their** graves shall hear His voice, and shall come forth; they **who** have done good, **in** the Resurrection of the Just; and they **who** have done evil, **in** the Resurrection of the Unjust. **And shall all be judged of the Son of Man. For** as I hear, I judge, and my judgment is just; **for I can of mine own self do nothing;** because I seek not mine own will, but the will of the Father **who** hath sent me. **Therefore** if I bear witness of myself, **yet** my witness is true. **For I am not alone,** there is another **who** beareth witness of me, and I know that the **testimony** which He **giveth** of me is true. Ye sent unto John, and he bare witness **also** unto the truth. **And he received** not **his** testimony **of** man, but **of God, and ye yourselves say that he is a prophet, therefore ye ought to receive his testimony.** These things I say that ye might be saved.

He was a burning and a shining light: and ye were willing for a season to rejoice in his light. But I have **a** greater witness than **the testimony** of John; for the works which the Father hath given me to finish, the same works that I do, bear witness of me, that the Father hath sent me. And the Father Himself **who** hath sent me, hath borne witness of me. **And verily I testify unto you, that** ye have ~~neither~~ **never** heard His voice at any time, nor seen His shape; **for** ye have not His word abiding in you; **and Him** whom He hath sent, ye believe not.

Search the scriptures; for in them ye think ye have eternal life: and they are they which testify of me. And ye will not come to me that ye might have life**, lest ye should honor me**. I receive not honor from men. But I know you, that ye have not the love of God in you. I am come in my Father's name, and ye receive me not: if another shall come in his own name, him ye will receive. How can ye believe, **who** ~~receive~~ **seek** honor one of another, and seek not the honor **which** cometh from God only?

Do not think that I will accuse you to the Father; there is **Moses who** accuseth you, in whom ye trust. For had ye believed Moses, ye would have believed me: for he wrote of me. But if ye believe not his writings, how shall ye believe my words?

JOHN 6

Feeds five thousand—walks on sea

After these things, Jesus went over the sea of Galilee, which is the sea of Tiberias. And a great multitude followed Him, because they saw His miracles which He did on them that were diseased. Jesus went up into a mountain, and there He sat with His disciples. The Passover, a feast of the Jews, was nigh. When Jesus then lifted up His eyes, and saw a great company come unto Him, He saith unto Philip,

Whence shall we buy bread, that these may eat?

Philip answered, Two hundred pennyworth of bread is not sufficient for them, that every one of them may take a little. Andrew saith, There is a lad here, which hath five barley loaves, and two small fishes: but what are they among so many? Jesus said,

Make the men sit down.

The men sat down, in number about five thousand. Jesus took the loaves; and when He had given thanks, He distributed to the disciples, and the disciples to them that were set down; and likewise of the fishes as much as they would. When they ***had eaten and*** *were* ***satisfied****, He said unto His disciples,*

Gather up the fragments that remain, that nothing be lost.

They gathered them together, and filled twelve baskets with the fragments of the five barley loaves, which remained.

When Jesus perceived that they would come and take him by force, to make Him a king, He departed again into a mountain Himself alone. When even was come, His disciples went down unto the sea, and entered into a ship, and went over the sea toward Capernaum. It was now dark, and Jesus ***had*** *not come to them. The sea arose by reason of a great wind that blew. When they had rowed about five and twenty or thirty furlongs, they* ***saw*** *Jesus walking on the sea, and drawing nigh unto the ship; and they were afraid. But He saith,*

It is I; be not afraid.

Then they willingly received Him into the ship: and immediately the ship was at the land whither they went. The day following, when the people found Him on the other side of the sea, they said unto Him, Rabbi, ***how*** *camest Thou hither? Jesus answered,*

Verily, verily, I say unto you, Ye seek me, not because **ye desire to keep my sayings, neither because** ye saw the miracles, but because ye did eat of the loaves and were filled. Labor not for the meat which perisheth, but for that meat which endureth unto everlasting life, which the Son of Man ~~shall~~ **hath power to** give unto you; for Him hath God the Father sealed.

Then said they, What shall we do, that we might work the works of God? Jesus answered,

This is the work of God, that ye believe on Him whom He hath sent.

They said, What sign showest Thou then, that we may see, and believe Thee? What dost Thou work? Our fathers did eat manna in the desert; as it is written, He gave them bread from heaven to eat. Then Jesus said,

Verily, verily, I say unto you, Moses gave you not that bread from heaven; but my Father giveth you the True Bread from heaven. For the Bread of God is He which cometh down from heaven, and giveth life unto the world.

Then said they, Lord, evermore give us this bread. Jesus said,

I am the Bread of Life: he that cometh to me shall never hunger; and he that believeth on me shall never thirst. But I said unto you, That ye also have seen me, and believe not. All that the Father giveth me shall come to me; and him that cometh to me I will in no wise cast out. For I came down from heaven, not to do mine own will, but the will of Him that sent me. And this is the Father's will which hath sent me, that of all which He hath given me I should lose nothing, but should raise it up again at the last day. And this is the will of Him that sent me, that everyone which seeth the Son, and believeth on Him, may have everlasting life; and I will raise him up **in the Resurrection of the Just** at the last day.

The Jews murmured, Is not this Jesus, the son of Joseph, whose father and mother we know? How is it then that He saith, I came down from heaven? Jesus said,

Murmur not among yourselves. No man can come to me, except **he doeth the will of my** Father **who** hath sent me. **And this is the will of Him who hath sent me, that ye receive the Son; for the Father beareth record of Him; and he who receiveth the testimony, and doeth the will of Him who sent me,** I will raise up **in the Resurrection of the Just. For** it is written in the prophets, And **these** shall all **be** taught of God. Every man therefore that hath heard, and hath learned of the Father, cometh unto me. Not that any man hath seen the Father, save he which is of God, he hath seen the Father. Verily, verily, I say unto you, he that believeth on me hath everlasting life.

I am that Bread of Life. This is the bread which cometh down from heaven, that a man may eat thereof, and not die. Your fathers did eat manna in the wilderness, and are dead. **But** I am the Living Bread which came down from heaven; if any man eat of this bread, he shall live forever; and the bread that I will give is my flesh, which I will give for the life of the world.

The Jews strove among themselves, saying, How can this man give us His flesh to eat? Then Jesus said,

Verily, verily, I say unto you, Except ye eat the flesh of the Son of Man, and drink His blood, ye have no life in you. Whoso eateth my flesh, and drinketh my blood, hath eternal life; and I will raise him up **in the Resurrection of the Just** at the last day; for my flesh is meat indeed, and my blood is drink indeed. He that eateth my flesh, and drinketh my blood, dwelleth in me, and I in him. As the living Father hath sent me, and I live by the Father: so he that eateth me, even he shall live by me. This is that bread which came down from heaven: not as your fathers did eat manna, and are dead: he that eateth of this bread shall live forever.

Many of His disciples said, This is a hard saying; who can hear it?

Doth this offend you? What and if ye shall see the Son of Man ascend up where He was before? It is the spirit that quickeneth; the flesh profiteth nothing: the words that I speak unto you, they are spirit, and they are life. But there are some of you that believe not.

For Jesus knew who they were that believed not, and who should betray Him.

Therefore said I unto you, that no man can come unto me, except **he doeth the will** of my Father **who hath sent me**.

From that time many of His disciples went back, and walked no more with Him. Then said Jesus unto the Twelve,

Will ye also go away?

Simon Peter answered, Lord, to whom shall we go? Thou hast the words of eternal life. And we believe and are sure that Thou art that Christ, the Son of the living God. Jesus answered,

Have not I chosen you twelve, and one of you is a devil?

JOHN 7

Feast of Tabernacles

After these things, Jesus walked in Galilee: for He would not walk in Jewry, because the Jews sought to kill Him. Now the Jews' Feast of Tabernacles was at hand. His brethren therefore said unto Him, Depart hence, and go into Judea, that Thy disciples ***there*** *also may see the works that Thou doest. Then Jesus said,*

My time is not yet come: but your time is always ready. The world cannot hate you; but me it hateth, because I testify of it, that the works thereof are evil. Go ye up unto this feast: I go not up yet unto this feast; for my time is not yet full come.

After *His brethren were gone up, then went He also up unto the feast, not openly, but as it were in secret. Now about the midst of the feast Jesus went up into the temple, and taught. And the Jews marveled, How knoweth this man letters, having never learned? Jesus answered,*

My doctrine is not mine, but His that sent me. If any man will do His will, he shall know of the doctrine, whether it be of God, or whether I speak of myself. He that speaketh of himself seeketh his own glory: but he that seeketh his glory that sent him, the same is true, and no unrighteousness is in him. Did not Moses give you the law, and yet none of you keepeth the law? Why go ye about to kill me?

The people answered, Thou hast a devil: who goeth about to kill Thee? Jesus said,

I have done one work, and ye all marvel. Moses therefore gave unto you circumcision (not because it is of Moses, but of the fathers); and ye on the Sabbath day circumcise a man. If a man on the Sabbath day receive circumcision, that the law of Moses should not be broken; are ye angry at me, because I have made a man every whit whole on the Sabbath day? Judge not according to ~~the appearance~~ **your traditions**, but judge righteous judgment.

Then said some, Is not this He, whom they seek to kill? But, lo, He speaketh boldly, and they say nothing unto Him. Do the rulers know indeed that this is the very Christ? Howbeit we know this man whence He is: but when Christ cometh, no man knoweth whence He is. Then cried Jesus in the temple as He taught,

Ye both know me, and ye know whence I am: and I am not come of myself, but He that sent me is true, whom ye know not. But I know Him: for I am from Him, and He hath sent me.

The Pharisees and the chief priests sent officers to take Him. Then said Jesus unto them,

Yet a little while I **am** with you, and then I go unto Him that sent me. Ye shall seek me, and shall not find me: and where I am, thither ye cannot come.

In the last day, that great day of the feast, Jesus stood and cried,

If any man thirst, let him come unto me, and drink. He that believeth on me, as the scripture hath said, out of His belly shall flow rivers of living water.

JOHN 8

Cast first stone—truth shall make you free

Jesus went unto the Mount of Olives. And early in the morning He came again into the temple, and all the people came unto Him; and He taught them. The scribes and Pharisees brought unto Him a woman taken in adultery; and when they had set her in the midst ***of the people****, they say, Master, this woman was taken in adultery, in the very act. Now Moses in the law commanded us, that such should be stoned: but what sayest Thou?*

He that is without sin among you, let him first cast a stone at her.

And they, being convicted by their own conscience, went out one by one. When Jesus saw none ***of her accusers, and*** *the woman* ***standing****, He said unto her,*

Woman, where are those thine accusers? Hath no man condemned thee?

No man, Lord.

Neither do I condemn thee; go, and sin no more.

Then spake Jesus again unto them,

I am the Light of the World: he that followeth me shall not walk in darkness, but shall have the light of life.

The Pharisees said, Thou bearest record of Thyself; Thy record is not true.

Though I bear record of myself, yet my record is true: for I know whence I came, and whither I go; but ye cannot tell whence I come, and whither I go. Ye judge after the flesh; I judge no man. And yet if I judge, my judgment is true: for I am not alone, but I and the Father that sent me. It is also written in your law, that the testimony of two men is true. I am one that bear witness of myself, and the Father that sent me beareth witness of me.

They [said], Where is Thy Father?

Ye neither know me, nor my Father: if ye had known me, ye should have known my Father also. I go my way, and ye shall seek me, and shall die in your sins: whither I go, ye cannot come.

Then said the Jews, Will He kill Himself? Because He saith, Whither I go, ye cannot come. And He said,

Ye are from beneath; I am from above: ye are of this world; I am not of this world. I said therefore unto you, that ye shall die in your sins: for if ye believe not that I am He, ye shall die in your sins.

Then said they, Who art Thou?

Even the same that I said unto you from the beginning. I have many things to say and to judge of you: but He that sent me is true; and I speak to the world those things which I have heard of Him.

They understood not that He spake to them of the Father. Then said Jesus,

When ye have lifted up the Son of Man, then shall ye know that I am He, and that I do nothing of myself; but as my Father hath taught me, I speak these things. And He that sent me is with me: the Father hath not left me alone; for I do always those things that please Him.

As He spake these words, many believed on Him. Then said Jesus to those Jews,

If ye continue in my word, then are ye my disciples indeed; and ye shall know the truth, and the truth shall make you free.

They answered, We be Abraham's seed, and were never in bondage to any man: how sayest Thou, Ye shall be made free?

Verily, verily, I say unto you, Whosoever committeth sin is the servant of sin. And the servant abideth not in the house forever: but the Son abideth ever. If the Son therefore shall make you free, ye shall be free indeed. I know that ye are Abraham's seed; but ye seek to kill me, because my word hath no place in you. I speak that which I have seen with my Father: and ye do that which ye have seen with your father.

They said, Abraham is our father. Jesus saith,

If ye were Abraham's children, ye would do the works of Abraham. But now ye seek to kill me, a man that hath told you the truth, which I have heard of God: this did not Abraham. Ye do the deeds of your father.

We be not born of fornication; we have one Father, even God.

If God were your Father, ye would love me: for I proceeded forth and came from God; neither came I of myself, but He sent me. Why do ye not understand my speech? Even because ye cannot ~~hear~~ **bear** my word.

Ye are of your father the devil, and the lusts of your father ye will do. He was a murderer from the beginning, and abode not in the truth, because there is no truth in him. When he speaketh a lie, he speaketh of his own: for he is a liar, and the father of it. And because I tell you the truth, ye believe me not. Which of you convinceth me of sin? And if I say the truth, why do ye not believe me? He that is of God ~~heareth~~ **receiveth** God's words; ye therefore ~~hear~~ **receive** them not, because ye are not of God.

Then answered the Jews, Say we not well that Thou art a Samaritan, and hast a devil?

I have not a devil; but I honor my Father, and ye do dishonor me. And I seek not mine own glory: there is one that seeketh and judgeth. Verily, verily, I say unto you, If a man keep my saying, he shall never see death.

Now we know that Thou hast a devil. Abraham is dead, and the prophets; and Thou sayest, If a man keep my saying, he shall never taste of death. Art Thou greater than our father Abraham, which is dead? And the prophets are dead: whom makest Thou Thyself? Jesus answered,

If I honor myself, my honor is nothing: it is my Father that honoreth me; of whom ye say, that He is your God: yet ye have not known Him; but I know Him: and if I should say, I know Him not, I shall be a liar like unto you: but I know Him, and keep His saying. Your father Abraham rejoiced to see my day: and he saw it, and was glad.

Thou art not yet fifty years old, and hast Thou seen Abraham?

Verily, verily, I say unto you, Before Abraham was, I Am.

JOHN 9

Heals blind

As Jesus passed by, He saw a man which was blind from his birth. His disciples asked, Master, who did sin, this man, or his parents, that he was born blind? Jesus answered,

Neither hath this man sinned, nor his parents: but that the works of God should be made manifest in him. I must work the works of Him that sent me, while ~~it is day~~ **I am with you**; the ~~night~~ **time** cometh when **I shall have finished my** work**, then I go unto the Father**. As long as I am in the world, I am the Light of the World.

He spat on the ground, and made clay of the spittle, and He anointed the eyes of the blind man with the clay, and said,

Go, wash in the pool of Siloam.

He went his way, and washed, and came seeing.

*Then said [the Jews], What did He to thee? How opened He thine eyes? The man said, since the world began was it not heard that any man opened the eyes of one that was born blind**, except He be of God**. If this man were not of God, He could do nothing. They answered, Thou wast altogether born in sins, and dost thou teach us? And they cast him out. Jesus heard that they had cast him out; and when He had found him, said unto him,*

Dost thou believe on the Son of God?

Who is He, Lord, that I might believe on Him?

Thou hast both seen Him, and it is He that talketh with thee.

Lord, I believe. Jesus said,

For judgment I am come into this world, that they which see not might see; and that they which see might be made blind.

Some of the Pharisees said, Are we blind also?

If ye were blind, ye should have no sin: but now ye say, We see; therefore your sin remaineth.

JOHN 10

Parable of the Good Shepherd—other sheep

Verily, verily, I say unto you, He that entereth not by the door into the sheepfold, but climbeth up some other way, the same is a thief and a robber. But he that entereth in by the door is the shepherd of the sheep. To him the porter openeth; and the sheep hear his voice: and he calleth his own sheep by name, and leadeth them out. And when he putteth forth his own sheep, he goeth before them, and the sheep follow him: for they know his voice. And a stranger will they not follow, but will flee from him: for they know not the voice of strangers.

This parable spake Jesus unto them: but they understood not what things they were which He spake unto them. Then said Jesus,

Verily, verily, I say unto you, I am the Door of the **Sheepfold**. All that ever came before me **who testified not of me** are thieves and robbers; but the sheep did not hear them. I am the door: by me if any man enter in, he shall be saved, and shall go in and out, and find pasture. The thief cometh not, but for to steal, and to kill, and to destroy: I am come that they might have life, and that they might have it more abundantly.

I am the Good Shepherd; the Good Shepherd giveth His life for **His** sheep. **And the shepherd** is not **as a hireling**, whose own the sheep are not, **who** seeth the wolf coming, and leaveth the sheep, and fleeth; and the wolf catcheth **the sheep** and scattereth **them**. **For** I am the Good Shepherd, and know my sheep, and am known of mine. **But he who is a** hireling fleeth, because he is **a** hireling, and careth not for the sheep. As the Father knoweth me, even so know I the Father: and I lay down my life for the sheep. And other sheep I have, which are not of this fold: them also I must bring, and they shall hear my voice; and there shall be one fold, and one shepherd. Therefore doth my Father love me, because I lay down my life, that I might take it again. No man taketh it from me, but I lay it down of myself. I have power to lay it down, and I have power to take it again. This commandment have I received of my Father.

It was at Jerusalem the Feast of the Dedication, and it was winter. Jesus walked in the temple in Solomon's porch. Then came the Jews round about Him, and said, How long dost Thou make us to doubt? If Thou be the Christ, tell us plainly. Jesus answered,

I told you, and ye believed not: the works that I do in my Father's name, they bear witness of me. But ye believe not, because ye are not of my sheep, as I said unto you. My sheep hear my voice, and I know them, and they follow me: and I give unto them eternal life; and they shall never perish, neither shall any man pluck them out of my hand. My Father, which gave them me, is greater than all; and no man is able to pluck them out of my Father's hand. I and my Father are one.

Then the Jews took up stones again to stone Him. Jesus answered,

Many good works have I showed you from my Father; for which of those works do ye stone me?

For a good work we stone Thee not; but for blasphemy; and because that Thou, being a man, makest Thyself God. Jesus answered,

Is it not written in your law, I said, Ye are gods? If he called them gods, unto whom the word of God came, and the scripture cannot be broken; say ye of Him, whom the Father hath sanctified, and sent into the world, Thou blasphemest; because I said, I am the Son of God? If I do not the works of my Father, believe me not. But if I do, though ye believe not me, believe the works: that ye may know, and believe, that the Father is in me, and I in Him.

JOHN 11

Raises Lazarus

*Now a certain man was sick, **whose name was** Lazarus, of **the town of** Bethany; **and** Mary**, his sister who** anointed the Lord with ointment and wiped His feet with her hair, **lived with her sister Martha, in** whose **house her** brother Lazarus was sick. Therefore his sisters sent unto Him, saying, Lord, behold, he whom Thou lovest is sick. **And** when Jesus heard, He said,*

This sickness is not unto death, but for the glory of God, that the Son of God might be glorified thereby.

Jesus tarried two days, after** He heard that **Lazarus** was sick, in the same* *place where He was. After that,* ***He said unto *His disciples,*

Let us go into Judea again.

But *His disciples* ***said****, Master, the Jews of late sought to stone Thee; and goest Thou thither again? Jesus answered,*

Are there not twelve hours in the day? If any man walk in the day, he stumbleth not, because he seeth the light of this world. But if a man walk in the night, he stumbleth, because there is no light in him.

Our friend Lazarus sleepeth; but I go, that I may awake him out of sleep.

Then said His disciples, Lord, if he sleep, he shall do well. Howbeit Jesus spake of his death: but they thought that He had spoken of taking of rest in sleep. Then said Jesus plainly,

Lazarus is dead. And I am glad for your sakes that I was not there, to the intent ye may believe; nevertheless, let us go unto him.

Martha, as soon as she heard that Jesus was coming, went and met Him: but Mary sat still in the house. Then said Martha, Lord, if Thou hadst been here, my brother had not died. But I know that even now, whatsoever Thou wilt ask of God, God will give it Thee. Jesus saith,

Thy brother shall rise again.

I know that he shall rise again in the Resurrection at the last day. Jesus said,

I am the Resurrection, and the Life: he that believeth in me, though he were dead, yet shall he live: and whosoever liveth and believeth in me shall never die. Believest thou this?

Yea, Lord: I believe that Thou art the Christ, the Son of God, which should come into the world.

When Mary was come where Jesus was, and saw Him, she fell down at His feet, saying, Lord, if Thou hadst been here, my brother had not died. When Jesus saw her weeping, and the Jews also weeping which came with her, He groaned in the spirit, and was troubled, and said,

Where have ye laid him?

They said, Lord, come and see. Jesus wept. Then said the Jews, Behold how He loved him! Jesus again groaning in Himself cometh to the grave. It was a cave, and a stone lay upon it. Jesus said,

Take ye away the stone.

Martha saith, Lord, by this time he stinketh: for he hath been dead four days.

Said I not unto thee, that, if thou wouldest believe, thou shouldest see the glory of God?

Then they took away the stone from the place where the dead was laid. Jesus lifted up His eyes, and said,

Father, I thank Thee that Thou hast heard me. And I knew that Thou hearest me always: but because of the people which stand by I said it, that they may believe that Thou hast sent me.

When He thus had spoken, He cried with a loud voice,

Lazarus, come forth.

And he that was dead came forth, bound hand and foot with graveclothes. Jesus saith unto them,

Loose him, and let him go.

JOHN 12

Feet anointed—foretells Resurrection

Then Jesus six days before the Passover came to Bethany, where Lazarus was which had been dead, whom He raised from the dead. There they made Him a supper; and Martha served: but Lazarus was one of them that sat at the table with Him. Then took Mary a pound of ointment of spikenard, very costly, and anointed the feet of Jesus, and wiped His feet with her hair: and the house was filled with the odor of the ointment. Then saith one of His disciples, Judas Iscariot, Why was not this ointment sold for three hundred pence, and given to the poor? Then said Jesus,

Let her alone; for she **hath preserved** this **ointment until now, that she might anoint me in token of my burial**. For the poor always ye have with you; but me ye have not always.

There were certain Greeks among them that came up to worship at the feast: the same came therefore to Philip, which was of Bethsaida of Galilee, and desired Him, saying, Sir, we would see Jesus. Philip cometh and telleth Andrew: and again Andrew and Philip tell Jesus. And Jesus answered,

The hour is come, that the Son of Man should be glorified. Verily, verily, I say unto you, Except a corn of wheat fall into the ground and die, it abideth alone: but if it die, it bringeth forth much fruit. He that loveth his life shall lose it; and he that hateth his life in this world shall keep it unto life eternal. If any man serve me, let him follow me; and where I am, there shall also my servant be: if any man serve me, him will my Father honor. Now is my soul troubled; and what shall I say? Father, save me from this hour: but for this cause came I unto this hour. Father, glorify Thy name.

Then came there a voice from heaven, saying, I have both glorified it, and will glorify it again. The people that stood by heard it. Jesus said,

This voice came not because of me, but for your sakes. Now is the judgment of this world: now shall the prince of this world be cast out.

And I, if I be lifted up from the earth, will draw all men unto me.

The people answered, We have heard out of the law that Christ abideth forever: and how sayest Thou, The Son of Man must be lifted up? Who is this Son of Man? Then Jesus said,

Yet a little while is the light with you. Walk while ye have the light, lest darkness come upon you: for he that walketh in darkness knoweth not whither he goeth. While ye have light, believe in the light, that ye may be the children of light.

These things spake Jesus, and departed, and did hide Himself from them.

Among the chief rulers also many believed on Him; but because of the Pharisees they did not confess Him, lest they should be put out of the synagogue: for they loved the praise of men more than the praise of God. Jesus cried,

He that believeth on me, believeth not on me, but on Him that sent me. And he that seeth me seeth Him that sent me. I am come a light into the world, that whosoever believeth on me should not abide in darkness. And if any man hear my words, and believe not, I judge him not: for I came not to judge the world, but to save the world. He that rejecteth me, and receiveth not my words, hath one that judgeth him: the word that I have spoken, the same shall judge him in the last day. For I have not spoken of myself; but the Father which sent me, He gave me a commandment, what I should say, and what I should speak. And I know that His commandment is life everlasting: whatsoever I speak therefore, even as the Father said unto me, so I speak.

JOHN 13

Passover—washing of feet

Before the Feast of the Passover, when Jesus knew that His hour was come that He should depart out of this world unto the Father, having loved His own which were in the world, He loved them unto the end. And supper being ended, the devil having now put into the heart of Judas Iscariot, to betray Him; Jesus knowing that the Father had given all things into His hands, and that He was come from God, and went to God; He riseth from supper, and laid aside His garments; and took a towel, and girded Himself.

After that, He poureth water into a basin, and began to wash the disciples' feet, and to wipe them with the towel wherewith He was girded. Then cometh He to Simon Peter, and Peter saith, Lord, dost Thou wash my feet?

What I do thou knowest not now; but thou shalt know hereafter.

Peter saith, Thou ***needest not to*** *wash my feet.*

If I wash thee not, thou hast no part with me.

Lord, not my feet only, but also my hands and my head.

He that **has** washed **his hands and his head**, needeth not save to wash his feet, but is clean every whit; and ye are clean, but not all.

Now this was the custom of the Jews under their law; wherefore, Jesus did this that the law might be fulfilled. *For He knew who should betray Him; therefore said He,*

Ye are not all clean.

After He had washed their feet, and had taken His garments, and was set down again, He said,

Know ye what I have done to you? Ye call me Master and Lord: and ye say well; for so I am. If I then, your Lord and Master, have washed your feet; ye also ought to wash one another's feet. For I have given you an example, that ye should do as I have done to you. Verily, verily, I say unto you, The servant is not greater than his lord; neither he that is sent greater than he that sent him. If ye know these things, happy are ye if ye do them.

I speak not of you all: I know whom I have chosen: but that the scripture may be fulfilled, He that eateth bread with me hath lifted up his heel against me. Now I tell you before it come, that, when it is come to pass, ye may believe that I am **the Christ**. Verily, verily, I say unto you, He that receiveth whomsoever I send receiveth me; and he that receiveth me receiveth Him that sent me. Verily, verily, I say unto you, that one of you shall betray me.

One of His disciples, whom Jesus loved, saith unto Him, Lord, who is it?

He it is, to whom I shall give a sop, when I have dipped it.

When He had dipped the sop, He gave it to Judas Iscariot. Then said Jesus unto him,

That thou doest, do quickly.

He then having received the sop went immediately out: and it was night. When he was gone out, Jesus said,

Now is the Son of Man glorified, and God is glorified in Him. If God be glorified in Him, God shall also glorify Him in Himself, and shall straightway glorify Him. Little children, yet a little while I am with you. Ye shall seek me: and as I said unto the Jews, Whither I go, ye cannot come; so now I say to you. A new commandment I give unto you, That ye love one another; as I have loved you, that ye also love one another. By this shall all men know that ye are my disciples, if ye have love one to another.

Simon Peter said unto Him, Lord, whither goest Thou?

Whither I go, thou canst not follow me now; but thou shalt follow me afterwards.

Peter said, Lord, why cannot I follow Thee now? I will lay down my life for Thy sake. Jesus answered,

Wilt thou lay down thy life for my sake? Verily, verily, I say unto thee, The cock shall not crow, till thou hast denied me thrice.

JOHN 14

I am the Way—Comforter

Let not your heart be troubled: ye believe in God, believe also in me. In my Father's ~~house~~ **kingdom** are many mansions: if it were not so, I would have told you. I go to prepare a place for you. And **when** I go, **I will** prepare a place for you, **and** come again, and receive you unto myself; that where I am, ye may be also. And whither I go ye know, and the way ye know.

Thomas saith unto Him, Lord, we know not whither Thou goest; and how can we know the way?

I am the Way, the Truth, and the Life: no man cometh unto the Father, but by me. If ye had known me, ye should have known my Father also: and from henceforth ye know Him, and have seen Him.

Philip saith, Lord, show us the Father, and it sufficeth us.

Have I been so long time with you, and yet hast thou not known me, Philip? He that hath seen me hath seen the Father; and how sayest thou then, Show us the Father? Believest thou not that I am in the Father, and the Father in me? The words that I speak unto you I speak not of myself: but the Father that dwelleth in me, He doeth the works. Believe me that I am in the Father, and the Father in me: or else believe me for the very works' sake. Verily, verily, I say unto you, he that believeth on me, the works that I do shall he do also; and greater works than these shall he do; because I go unto my Father. And whatsoever ye shall ask in my name, that will I do, that the Father may be glorified in the Son. If ye shall ask anything in my name, I will do it.

If ye love me, keep my commandments. And I will pray the Father, and He shall give you another Comforter, that He may abide with you forever; even the Spirit of Truth; whom the world cannot receive, because it seeth Him not, neither knoweth Him: but ye know Him; for

He dwelleth with you, and shall be in you. I will not leave you comfortless: I will come to you. Yet a little while, and the world seeth me no more; but ye see me: because I live, ye shall live also. At that day ye shall know that I am in my Father, and ye in me, and I in you. He that hath my commandments, and keepeth them, he it is that loveth me: and he that loveth me shall be loved of my Father, and I will love him, and will manifest myself to him.

Judas (not Iscariot) saith, Lord, how is it Thou wilt manifest Thyself unto us, and not unto the world?

If a man love me, he will keep my words: and my Father will love him, and we will come unto him, and make our abode with him. He that loveth me not keepeth not my sayings: and the word which ye hear is not mine, but the Father's which sent me. These things have I spoken unto you, being yet present with you. But the Comforter, which is the Holy Ghost, whom the Father will send in my name, He shall teach you all things, and bring all things to your remembrance, whatsoever I have said unto you.

Peace I leave with you, my peace I give unto you: not as the world giveth, give I unto you. Let not your heart be troubled, neither let it be afraid. Ye have heard how I said unto you, I go away, and come again unto you. If ye loved me, ye would rejoice, because I said, I go unto the Father: for my Father is greater than I. And now I have told you before it come to pass, that, when it is come to pass, ye might believe. Hereafter I will not talk much with you; for the prince of **darkness, who is of** this world, cometh, **but** hath **no power over** me**, but he hath power over you. And I tell you these things,** that ~~the world~~ **ye** may know that I love the Father; and as the Father gave me commandment, even so I do. Arise, let us go hence.

JOHN 15

True Vine—Spirit of Truth

I am the True Vine, and my Father is the Husbandman. Every branch in me that beareth not fruit He taketh away: and every branch that beareth fruit, He purgeth it, that it may bring forth more fruit. Now ye are clean through the word which I have spoken unto you. Abide in me, and I in you. As the branch cannot bear fruit of itself, except it abide in the vine; no more can ye, except ye abide in me. I am the Vine, ye are the branches: He that abideth in me, and I in him, the same bringeth forth much fruit: for without me ye can do nothing. If a man abide not in me, he is cast forth as a branch, and is withered; and men gather them, and cast them into the fire, and they are burned. If ye abide in me, and my words abide in you, ye shall ask what ye will, and it shall be done unto you. Herein is my Father glorified, that ye bear much fruit; so shall ye be my disciples.

As the Father hath loved me, so have I loved you: continue ye in my love. If ye keep my commandments, ye shall abide in my love; even as I have kept my Father's commandments, and abide in His love. These things have I spoken unto you, that my joy might remain in you, and that your joy might be full. This is my commandment, That ye love one another, as I have loved you. Greater love hath no man than this, that a man lay down his life for his friends. Ye are my friends, if ye do whatsoever I command you.

Henceforth I call you not servants; for the servant knoweth not what his lord doeth: but I have called you friends; for all things that I have heard of my Father I have made known unto you. Ye have not chosen me, but I have chosen you, and ordained you, that ye should go and bring forth fruit, and that your fruit should remain: that whatsoever ye shall ask of the Father in my name, He may give it you.

These things I command you, that ye love one another. If the world hate you, ye know that it hated me before it hated you. If ye were of the world, the world would love his own: but because ye are not of the world, but I have chosen you out of the world, therefore the world hateth you. Remember the word that I said unto you, The servant is not greater than his lord. If they have persecuted me, they will also persecute you; if they have kept my saying, they will keep yours also. But all these things will they do unto you for my name's sake, because they know not Him that sent me. If I had not come and spoken unto them, they had not had sin: but now they have no cloak for their sin.

He that hateth me hateth my Father also. If I had not done among them the works which none other man did, they had not had sin: but now have they both seen and hated both me and my Father. But this cometh to pass, that the word might be fulfilled that is written in their law, They hated me without a cause. But when the Comforter is come, whom I will send unto you from the Father, even the Spirit of Truth, which proceedeth from the Father, He shall testify of me: and ye also shall bear witness, because ye have been with me from the beginning.

JOHN 16

Holy Ghost—foretells Resurrection

These things have I spoken unto you, that ye should not be offended. They shall put you out of the synagogues: yea, the time cometh, that whosoever killeth you will think that he doeth God service. And these things will they do unto you, because they have not known the Father, nor me. But these things have I told you, that when the time shall come, ye may remember that I told you of them.

And these things I said not unto you at the beginning, because I was with you. But now I go my way to Him that sent me; and none of you asketh me, Whither goest Thou? But because I have said these things unto you, sorrow hath filled your heart. Nevertheless I tell you the truth; It is expedient for you that I go away: for if I go not away, the Comforter will not come unto you; but if I depart, I will send Him unto you. And when He is come, He will reprove the world of sin, and of righteousness, and of judgment: of sin, because they believe not on me; of righteousness, because I go to my Father, and ~~ye~~ **they** see me no more; of judgment, because the prince of this world is judged.

I have yet many things to say unto you, but ye cannot bear them now. Howbeit when He, the Spirit of Truth, is come, He will guide you into all truth: for He shall not speak of Himself; but whatsoever He shall hear, that shall He speak: and He will show you things to come. He shall glorify me: for He shall receive of mine, and shall show it unto you. All things that the Father hath are mine: therefore said I, that He shall take of mine, and shall show it unto you. A little while, and ye shall not see me: and again, a little while, and ye shall see me, because I go to the Father.

Then said some of His disciples, What is this that He saith unto us, A little while, and ye shall not see me: and again, a little while, and ye shall see me: and, Because I go to the Father? What is this that He saith, A little while? We cannot tell what He saith. Now Jesus knew that they were desirous to ask Him, and said,

Do ye inquire among yourselves of that I said, A little while, and ye shall not see me: and again, a little while, and ye shall see me? Verily, verily, I say unto you, That ye shall weep and lament, but the world shall rejoice: and ye shall be sorrowful, but your sorrow shall be turned into joy. A woman when she is in travail hath sorrow, because her hour is come: but as soon as she is delivered of the child, she remembereth no more the anguish, for joy that a man is born into the world. And ye now therefore have sorrow: but I will see you again, and your heart shall rejoice, and your joy no man taketh from you.

And in that day ye shall ask me nothing **but it shall be done unto you**. Verily, verily, I say unto you, Whatsoever ye shall ask the Father in my name, He will give it you. Hitherto have ye asked nothing in my name: ask, and ye shall receive, that your joy may be full. These things have I spoken unto you in proverbs: but the time cometh, when I shall no more speak unto you in proverbs, but I shall show you plainly of the Father. At that day ye shall ask in my name: and I say not unto you, that I will pray the Father for you: for the Father Himself loveth you, because ye have loved me, and have believed that I came out from God. I came forth from the Father, and am come into the world: again, I leave the world, and go to the Father.

His disciples said, Lo, now speakest Thou plainly, and speakest no proverb. Now are we sure that Thou knowest all things, and needest not that any man should ask Thee: by this we believe that Thou camest forth from God. Jesus answered,

Do ye now believe? Behold, the hour cometh, yea, is now come, that ye shall be scattered, every man to his own, and shall leave me alone: and yet I am not alone, because the Father is with me. These things I have spoken unto you, that in me ye might have peace. In the world ye shall have tribulation: but be of good cheer; I have overcome the world.

JOHN 17

Intercessory Prayer

Jesus lifted up His eyes to heaven, and said,

Father, the hour is come; glorify Thy Son, that Thy Son also may glorify Thee: as Thou hast given Him power over all flesh, that He should give eternal life to as many as Thou hast given Him. And this is life eternal, that they might know Thee the only true God, and Jesus Christ, whom Thou hast sent. I have glorified Thee on the earth: I have finished the work which Thou gavest me to do. And now, O Father, glorify Thou me with Thine own self with the glory which I had with Thee before the world was. I have manifested Thy name unto the men which Thou gavest me out of the world: Thine they were, and Thou gavest them me; and they have kept Thy word. Now they have known that all things whatsoever Thou hast given me are of Thee. For I have given unto them the words which Thou gavest me; and they have received them, and have known surely that I came out from Thee, and they have believed that Thou didst send me.

I pray for them: I pray not for the world, but for them which Thou hast given me; for they are Thine. And all mine are Thine, and Thine are mine; and I am glorified in them. And now I am no more in the world, but these are in the world, and I come to Thee. Holy Father, keep through Thine own name those whom Thou hast given me, that they may be one, as we are. While I was with them in the world, I kept them in Thy name: those that Thou gavest me I have kept, and none of them is lost, but the son of perdition; that the scripture might be fulfilled. And now come I to Thee; and these things I speak in the world, that they might have my joy fulfilled in themselves.

I have given them Thy word; and the world hath hated them, because they are not of the world, even as I am not of the world. I pray not that Thou shouldest take them out of the world, but that Thou shouldest keep them from the evil. They are not of the world, even as I am not of the world. Sanctify them through Thy truth: Thy word is truth. As Thou hast sent me into the world, even so have I also sent them into the world. And for their sakes I sanctify myself, that they also might be sanctified through the truth. Neither pray I for these alone, but for them also which shall believe on me through their word; that they all may be one; as Thou, Father, art in me, and I in Thee, that they also may be one in us: that the world may believe that Thou hast sent me. And the glory which Thou gavest me I have given them; that they may be one, even as we are one: I in them, and Thou in me, that they may be made perfect in one; and that the world may know that Thou hast sent me, and hast loved them, as Thou hast loved me.

Father, I will that they also, whom Thou hast given me, be with me where I am; that they may behold my glory, which Thou hast given me: for Thou lovedst me before the foundation of the world. O righteous Father, the world hath not known Thee: but I have known Thee, and these have known that Thou hast sent me. And I have declared unto them Thy name, and will declare it: that the love wherewith Thou hast loved me may be in them, and I in them.

JOHN 18

Gethsemane—trial

When Jesus had spoken these words, He went forth with His disciples over the brook Cedron, where was a garden, into the which He entered, and His disciples. And Judas also, which betrayed Him, knew the place: for Jesus ofttimes resorted thither with His disciples. Judas then, having received a band of men and officers from the chief priests and Pharisees, cometh thither with lanterns and torches and weapons. Jesus therefore, knowing all things that should come upon Him, went forth, and said,

Whom seek ye?

They answered, Jesus of Nazareth. Jesus saith,

I am He.

As soon then as He had said unto them, I am He, they went backward, and fell to the ground. Then asked He them again,

Whom seek ye?

Jesus of Nazareth.

I have told you that I am He: if therefore ye seek me, let these go their way.

Simon Peter having a sword drew it, and smote the high priest's servant, and cut off his right ear. Then said Jesus,

Put up thy sword into the sheath: the cup which my Father hath given me, shall I not drink it?

Then the band and the captain and officers of the Jews took Jesus, and bound Him, and led Him away to Annas first; for he was father-in-law to Caiaphas, which was the high priest that same year. The high priest then asked Jesus of His disciples, and of His doctrine. Jesus answered,

I spake openly to the world; I ever taught in the synagogue, and in the temple, whither the Jews always resort; and in secret have I said nothing. Why askest thou me? Ask them which heard me, what I have said unto them: behold, they know what I said.

One of the officers which stood by struck Jesus with the palm of his hand, saying, Answerest Thou the high priest so? Jesus answered him,

If I have spoken evil, bear witness of the evil: but if well, why smitest thou me?

Then led they Jesus from Caiaphas unto the hall of judgment. Pilate then went out unto them, and said, What accusation bring ye against this man? They answered, If He were not a malefactor, we would not have delivered Him up unto thee. Then said Pilate unto them, Take ye Him, and judge Him according to your law. The Jews therefore said unto him, It is not lawful for us to put any man to death.

Then Pilate entered the judgment hall again, and called Jesus, and said, Art Thou the King of the Jews? Jesus answered,

Sayest thou this thing of thyself, or did others tell it thee of me?

Pilate answered, Am I a Jew? Thine own nation and the chief priests have delivered Thee unto me: what hast Thou done?

My kingdom is not of this world: if my kingdom were of this world, then would my servants fight, that I should not be delivered to the Jews: but now is my kingdom not from hence.

Art Thou a king then?

Thou sayest that I am a king. To this end was I born, and for this cause came I into the world, that I should bear witness unto the truth. Every one that is of the truth heareth my voice.

Pilate saith unto Him, What is truth? And when he had said this, he went out again unto the Jews, and saith unto them, I find in Him no fault. But ye have a custom, that I should release unto you one at the passover: will ye therefore that I release unto you the King of the Jews? Then cried they all again, saying, Not this man, but Barabbas. Now Barabbas was a robber.

JOHN 19

Trial—Crucifixion

Then Pilate therefore took Jesus, and scourged Him. And the soldiers platted a crown of thorns, and put it on His head, and they put on Him a purple robe, and said, Hail, King of the Jews! And they smote Him with their hands. Pilate went forth again, and saith, Behold, I bring Him forth to you, that ye may know that I find no fault in Him. Then came Jesus forth, wearing the crown of thorns, and the purple robe, and Pilate saith unto them, Behold the man!

When the chief priests and officers saw Him, they cried out, Crucify Him, crucify Him. Pilate saith unto them, Take ye Him, and crucify Him: for I find no fault in Him. The Jews answered, We have a law, and by our law He ought to die, because He made Himself the Son of God. When Pilate heard that saying, he was the more afraid; and went again into the judgment hall, and saith unto Jesus, Whence art Thou? But Jesus gave him no answer. Then saith Pilate, Speakest Thou not unto me? Knowest Thou not that I have power to crucify Thee, and have power to release Thee?

Thou couldest have no power against me, except it were given thee from above; therefore he that delivered me unto thee hath the greater sin.

From thenceforth Pilate sought to release Him: but the Jews cried out, saying, If thou let this man go, thou art not Caesar's friend: whosoever maketh himself a king speaketh against Caesar. When Pilate heard that saying, he brought Jesus forth, and sat down in the judgment seat in a place called the Pavement, but in the Hebrew, Gabbatha. And it was the preparation of the passover, and about the sixth hour: and he saith unto the Jews, Behold your King! But they cried out, Away with Him, away with Him, crucify Him. Pilate saith unto them, Shall I crucify your King? The chief priests answered, We have no king but Caesar.

Then delivered he Him unto them to be crucified. And they took Jesus, and led Him away into the place of a ~~skull~~ ***burial*** *called Golgotha, where they crucified Him, and two other with Him, on either side one, and Jesus in the midst. And Pilate wrote a title, and put it on the cross. And the writing was, JESUS OF NAZARETH THE KING OF THE JEWS, in Hebrew, Greek, and Latin. Then said the chief priests of the Jews to Pilate, Write not, The King of the Jews; but that He said, I am King of the Jews. Pilate answered, What I have written I have written.*

Then the soldiers, when they had crucified Jesus, took His garments, and made four parts, to every soldier a part; and also His coat: now the coat was without seam, woven from the top throughout. They said therefore among themselves, Let us not rend it, but cast lots for it, whose it shall be.

Now there stood by the cross of Jesus His mother, and His mother's sister, Mary the wife of Cleophas, and Mary Magdalene. When Jesus saw His mother, and the disciple standing by, whom He loved, He saith unto His mother,

Woman, behold thy son!

To the disciple,

Behold thy mother!

And from that hour that disciple took her unto his own home. After this, Jesus knowing that all things were now accomplished, that the scripture might be fulfilled, saith,

I thirst.

Now there was a vessel full of vinegar, ***mingled with gall,*** *and they filled a* ***sponge*** *with* ***it****, and put upon hyssop, and put to His mouth. When Jesus had received the vinegar, He said,*

It is finished.

And He bowed His head, and gave up the ghost.

JOHN 20

Resurrection—Thomas believes

*The first day of the week cometh Mary Magdalene early, when it was yet dark, unto the sepulchre, and seeth the stone taken away from the sepulchre****, and two***

***angels sitting thereon**. Then she runneth, and cometh to Simon Peter, and to the other disciple, whom Jesus loved, and saith unto them, They have taken away the Lord out of the sepulchre, and we know not where they have laid Him. Peter went forth, and that other disciple, and came to the sepulchre. So they ran both together: and the other disciple did outrun Peter, and came first to the sepulchre. And he stooping down, and looking in, saw the linen clothes lying; yet went he not in. Then cometh Simon Peter following him, and went into the sepulchre, and seeth the linen clothes lie, and the napkin, that was about His head, not lying with the linen clothes, but wrapped together in a place by itself. Then went in also that other disciple, which came first to the sepulchre, and he saw, and believed. For as yet they knew not the scripture, that He must rise again from the dead.*

*Then the disciples went away again unto their own **homes**. But Mary stood without at the sepulchre weeping: and as she wept, she stooped down, and looked into the sepulchre, and seeth two angels in white sitting, the one at the head, and the other at the feet, where the body of Jesus had lain. And they say unto her, Woman why weepest thou? She saith unto them, Because they have taken away my Lord, and I know not where they have laid Him. And when she had thus said, she turned herself back, and saw Jesus standing, and knew not that it was Jesus. Jesus saith,*

Woman, why weepest thou? Whom seekest thou?

She, supposing Him to be the gardener, saith, Sir, if thou have borne Him hence, tell me where thou hast laid Him, and I will take Him away.

Mary.

Rabboni (Master)!

~~Touch~~ **Hold** me not; for I am not yet ascended to my Father; but go to my brethren, and say unto them, I ascend unto my Father, and your Father; and to my God, and your God.

Mary Magdalene came and told the disciples that she had seen the Lord, and that He had spoken these things unto her. Then the same day at evening, being the first day of the week, when the doors were shut where the disciples were assembled for fear of the Jews, came Jesus and stood in the midst, and saith unto them,

Peace be unto you.

He showed unto them His hands and His side. Then were the disciples glad, when they saw the Lord. Then said Jesus to them again,

Peace be unto you: as my Father hath sent me, even so send I you.

When He had said this, He breathed on them, and saith,

Receive ye the Holy Ghost: whose soever sins ye remit, they are remitted unto them; and whose soever sins ye retain, they are retained.

But Thomas, one of the Twelve, called Didymus, was not with them when Jesus came. The other disciples therefore said unto him, We have seen the Lord. But he said unto them, Except I shall see in His hands the print of the nails, and put my finger into the print of the nails, and thrust my hand into His side, I will not believe. And after eight days again His disciples were within, and Thomas with them: then came Jesus, the doors being shut, and stood in the midst, and said,

Peace be unto you.

Saith He to Thomas,

Reach hither thy finger, and behold my hands; and reach hither thy hand, and thrust it into my side: and be not faithless, but believing.

Thomas said, My Lord and My God.

Thomas, because thou hast seen me, thou hast believed: blessed are they that have not seen, and yet have believed.

JOHN 21

Jesus shows Himself—feed my sheep

After these things, Jesus showed Himself again to the disciples at the sea of Tiberias; and on this wise showed He Himself. There were together Simon Peter, and Thomas called Didymus, and Nathanael of Cana in Galilee, and the sons of Zebedee, and two other of His disciples. Simon Peter saith unto them, I go a fishing. They say unto Him, We also go with Thee. They went forth, and entered into a ship immediately; and that night they caught nothing.

When the morning was come, Jesus stood on the shore: but the disciples knew not that it was Jesus. Then Jesus saith unto them,

Children, have ye any meat?

They answered, No. And He said,

Cast the net on the right side of the ship, and ye shall find.

They cast therefore, and now they were not able to draw it for the multitude of fishes. Therefore that disciple whom Jesus loved saith unto Peter, It is the Lord. And the other disciples came in a little ship; dragging the net with fishes.

As soon then as they were come to land, they saw a fire of coals there, and fish laid thereon, and bread. Jesus saith unto them,

Bring of the fish which ye have now caught.

Simon Peter went up, and drew the net to land full of great fishes, a hundred and fifty and three: and for all there were so many, yet was not the net broken. Jesus saith,

Come and dine.

Jesus then cometh, and taketh bread, and giveth them, and fish likewise. This is now the third time that Jesus showed Himself to His disciples, after that He was risen from the dead. So when they had dined, Jesus saith to Simon Peter,

Simon, son of Jonas, lovest thou me more than these?

Yea, Lord; Thou knowest that I love Thee.

Feed my lambs. Simon, son of Jonas, lovest thou me?

Yea, Lord; Thou knowest that I love Thee.

Feed my sheep. Simon, son of Jonas, lovest thou me?

Lord, Thou knowest all things; Thou knowest that I love Thee.

Feed my sheep. Verily, verily, I say unto thee, When thou wast young, thou girdedst thyself, and walkedst whither thou wouldest: but when thou shalt be old, thou shalt stretch forth thy hands, and another shall gird thee, and carry thee whither thou wouldest not.

This spake He, signifying by what death he should glorify God. And when He had spoken this, He saith unto him,

Follow me.

Then Peter, turning about, seeth the disciple whom Jesus loved following; which also leaned on His breast at supper, and said, Lord, which is he that betrayeth Thee? Peter seeing him saith to Jesus, Lord, and what shall this man do? Jesus saith,

If I will that he tarry till I come, what is that to thee? Follow thou me.

Then went this saying abroad among the brethren, that that disciple should not die.

Words of Christ From The Acts of the Apostles

ACTS 1

Instructs Apostles—Ascension

Being ***with [the Apostles] when they were*** *assembled together, [Jesus] commanded them that they should not depart from Jerusalem, but,*

Wait for the promise of the Father, which ye have heard of me. For John truly baptized with water; but ye shall be baptized with the Holy Ghost not many days hence.

They asked, Lord, wilt Thou at this time restore again the kingdom to Israel?

It is not for you to know the times or the seasons, which the Father hath put in His own power. But ye shall receive power, after that the Holy Ghost is come upon you: and ye shall be witnesses unto me both in Jerusalem, and in all Judea, and in Samaria, and unto the uttermost part of the earth.

While they beheld, He was taken up; and a cloud received Him out of their sight. And while they looked steadfastly toward heaven as He went up, behold, two men stood by them in white apparel; which also said, Ye men of Galilee, why stand ye gazing up into heaven? This same Jesus, which is taken up from you into heaven, shall so come in like manner as ye have seen Him go into heaven.

Words of Christ From Third Nephi

3 NEPHI 11

Heavenly Father announces Christ—Christ descends—multitude witnesses His wounds—gives power to baptize

There were a great multitude gathered together, of the people of Nephi, round about the temple which was in the land Bountiful; and they were marveling and wondering one with another, and were showing one to another the great and marvelous change which had taken place. They were also conversing about this Jesus Christ, of whom the sign had been given concerning His death.

While they were thus conversing one with another, they heard a voice as if it came out of heaven; and they cast their eyes round about, for they understood not the voice which they heard; and it was not a harsh voice, neither was it a loud voice; nevertheless, and notwithstanding it being a small voice, it did pierce them that did hear to the center, insomuch that there was no part of their frame that it did not cause to quake; yea, it did pierce them to the very soul, and did cause their hearts to burn.

Again they heard the voice, and they understood it not. The third time they did hear the voice, and did open their ears to hear it; and their eyes were towards the sound thereof; and they did look steadfastly towards heaven, from whence the sound came. And behold, the third time they did understand the voice which they heard; and it said unto them, Behold my Beloved Son, in whom I am well pleased, in whom I have glorified my name: hear ye Him.

As they understood they cast their eyes up again towards heaven; and behold, they saw a man descending out of heaven; and He was clothed in a white robe; and He came down and stood in the midst of them; and the eyes of the whole multitude were turned upon Him, and they durst not open their mouths, even one to another, and wist not what it meant, for they thought it was an angel that had appeared unto them. He stretched forth His hand and spake unto the people, saying,

Behold, I am Jesus Christ, whom the prophets testified shall come into the world. And behold, I am the Light and the Life of the World; and I have drunk out of that bitter cup which the Father hath given me, and have glorified the Father in taking upon me the sins of the world, in the which I have suffered the will of the Father in all things from the beginning.

When Jesus had spoken these words, the whole multitude fell to the earth; for they remembered that it had been prophesied among them that Christ should show Himself unto them after His ascension into heaven. The Lord spake unto them saying,

Arise and come forth unto me, that ye may thrust your hands into my side, and also that ye may feel the prints of the nails in my hands and in my feet, that ye may know that I am the God of Israel, and the God of the Whole Earth, and have been slain for the sins of the world.

The multitude went forth, and thrust their hands into His side, and did feel the prints of the nails in His hands and in His feet; and this they did do, going forth one by one until they had all gone forth, and did see with their eyes, and did feel with their hands, and did know of a surety and did bear record, that it was He, of whom it was written by the prophets that should come.

When they had all gone forth and had witnessed for themselves, they did cry out with one accord, saying, Hosanna! Blessed be the name of the Most High God! And they did fall down at the feet of Jesus, and did worship Him. He spake unto Nephi (for Nephi was among the multitude) and He commanded him that he should come forth. Nephi arose and went forth, and bowed himself before the Lord and did kiss His feet. The Lord commanded him that he should arise. And he arose and stood before Him. The Lord said unto him,

I give unto you power that ye shall baptize this people when I am again ascended into heaven.

The Lord called others, and said unto them likewise; and He gave unto them power to baptize. He said unto them,

On this wise shall ye baptize; and there shall be no disputations among you. Verily I say unto you, that whoso repenteth of his sins through your words, and desireth to be baptized in my name, on this wise shall ye baptize them: Behold, ye shall go down and stand in the water, and in my name shall ye baptize them.

And now behold, these are the words which ye shall say, calling them by name, saying, Having authority given me of Jesus Christ, I baptize you in the name of the Father, and of the Son, and of the Holy Ghost. Amen. And then shall ye immerse them in the water, and come forth again out of the water. And after this manner shall ye baptize in my name; for behold, verily I say unto you, that the Father, and the Son, and the Holy Ghost are one; and I am in the Father, and the Father in me, and the Father and I are one.

And according as I have commanded you thus shall ye baptize. And there shall be no disputations among you, as there have hitherto been; neither shall there be disputations among you concerning the points of my doctrine, as there have hitherto been. For verily, verily, I say unto you, he that hath the spirit of contention is not of me, but is of the devil, who is the father of contention, and he stirreth up the hearts of men to contend with anger, one with another. Behold, this is not my doctrine, to stir up the hearts of men with anger, one against another; but this is my doctrine, that such things should be done away.

Behold, verily, verily, I say unto you, I will declare unto you my doctrine. And this is my doctrine, and it is the doctrine which the Father hath given unto me; and I bear record of the Father, and the Father beareth record of me, and the Holy Ghost beareth record of the Father and me; and I bear record that the Father commandeth all men, everywhere, to repent and believe in me.

And whoso believeth in me, and is baptized, the same shall be saved; and they are they who shall inherit the kingdom of God. And whoso believeth not in me, and is not baptized, shall be damned. Verily, verily, I say unto you, that this is my doctrine, and I bear record of it from the Father; and whoso believeth in me, believeth in the Father also; and unto him will the Father bear record of me; for He will visit him with fire, and with the Holy Ghost. And thus will the Father bear record of me, and the Holy Ghost will bear record unto him of the Father and me; for the Father, and I, and the Holy Ghost are one.

And again I say unto you, ye must repent, and become as a little child, and be baptized in my name, or ye can in nowise receive these things. And again I say unto you, ye must repent, and be baptized in my name, and become as a little child, or ye can in nowise inherit the kingdom of God.

Verily, verily, I say unto you, that this is my doctrine, and whoso buildeth upon this, buildeth upon my rock, and the gates of hell shall not prevail against them. And whoso shall declare more or less than this, and establish it for my doctrine, the same cometh of evil, and is not built upon my rock; but he buildeth upon a sandy foundation, and the gates of hell stand* open to receive such, when the floods come and the winds beat upon them. Therefore, go forth unto this people, and declare the words which I have spoken, unto the ends of the earth.

3 NEPHI 12

Sermon at the Temple

When Jesus had spoken these words unto Nephi, and to those who had been called (the number of them who had been called, and received power and authority to baptize, was twelve), He stretched forth His hand unto the multitude, and cried unto them, saying,*

Blessed are ye if ye shall give heed unto the words of these twelve whom I have chosen from among you to minister unto you, and to be your servants; and unto them I have given power, that they may baptize you with water; and after that ye are baptized with water, behold, I will baptize you with fire and with the Holy Ghost; therefore, blessed are ye if ye shall believe in me, and be baptized, after that ye have seen me and know that I am.

And again, more blessed are they who shall believe in your words because that ye shall testify that ye have seen me, and that ye know that I am. Yea, blessed are they who shall believe in your words, and come down into the depths of humility and be baptized, for they shall be visited with fire and with the Holy Ghost, and shall receive a remission of their sins.

Yea, blessed are the poor in spirit who come unto me, for theirs is the kingdom of heaven. And again, blessed are all they that mourn, for they shall be comforted. And blessed are the meek, for they shall inherit the earth. And blessed are all they who do hunger and thirst after righteousness, for they shall be filled with the Holy Ghost. And blessed are the merciful, for they shall obtain mercy. And blessed are all the pure in heart, for they shall see God. And blessed are all the peacemakers, for they shall be called the children of God. And blessed are all they who are persecuted for my name's sake, for theirs is the kingdom of heaven. And blessed are ye when men shall revile you and persecute, and shall say all manner of evil against you falsely, for my sake; for ye shall have great joy and be exceedingly glad, for great shall be your reward in heaven; for so persecuted they the prophets who were before you.

Verily, verily, I say unto you, I give unto you to be the salt of the earth; but if the salt shall lose its savor wherewith shall the earth be salted? The salt shall be thenceforth good for nothing, but to be cast out, and to be trodden under foot of men.

Verily, verily, I say unto you, I give unto you to be the light of this people. A city that is set on a hill cannot be hid. Behold, do men light a candle and put it under a bushel? Nay, but on a candlestick, and it giveth light to all that are in the house; therefore let your light so shine before this people, that they may see your good works and glorify your Father who is in heaven.

Think not that I am come to destroy the law or the prophets. I am not come to destroy but to fulfil; for verily I say unto you, one jot nor one tittle hath not passed away from the law, but in me it hath all been fulfilled. And behold, I have given you the law and the commandments of my Father, that ye shall believe in me, and that ye shall repent of your sins, and come unto me with a broken heart and a contrite spirit. Behold, ye have the commandments before you, and the law is fulfilled. Therefore come unto me and be ye saved; for verily I say unto you, that except ye shall keep my commandments, which I have commanded you at this time, ye shall in no case enter into the kingdom of heaven.

Ye have heard that it hath been said by them of old time, and it is also written before you, that thou shalt not kill; and whosoever shall kill shall be in danger of the judgment of God. But I say unto you, that whosoever is angry with his brother, shall be in danger of His judgment. And whosoever shall say to his brother, Raca, shall be in danger of the council; and whosoever shall say, Thou fool, shall be in danger of hell fire.

Therefore, if ye shall come unto me, or shall desire to come unto me, and rememberest that thy brother hath aught against thee, go thy way unto thy brother, and first be reconciled to thy brother, and then come unto me with full purpose of heart, and I will receive you.

Agree with thine adversary quickly while thou art in the way with him, lest at any time he shall get thee, and thou shalt be cast into prison. Verily, verily, I say unto thee, thou shalt by no means come out thence, until thou hast paid the uttermost senine. And while ye are in prison can ye pay even one senine? Verily, verily, I say unto you, Nay.

Behold, it is written by them of old time, that thou shalt not commit adultery; but I say unto you, that whosoever looketh on a woman, to lust after her, hath committed adultery already in his heart. Behold, I give unto you a commandment, that ye suffer none of these things to enter into your heart; for it is better that ye should deny yourselves of these things, wherein ye will take up your cross, than that ye should be cast into hell.

It hath been written, that whosoever shall put away his wife, let him give her a writing of divorcement. Verily, verily, I say unto you, that whosoever shall put away his wife, saving for the cause of fornication, causeth her to commit adultery; and whoso shall marry her who is divorced committeth adultery.

And again it is written, thou shalt not forswear thyself, but shalt perform unto the Lord thine oaths. But verily, verily, I say unto you, swear not at all; neither by heaven, for it is God's throne; nor by the earth, for it is His footstool; neither shalt thou swear by thy head, because thou canst not make one hair black or white; but let your communication be Yea, yea; Nay, nay; for whatsoever cometh of more than these is evil.

And behold, it is written, an eye for an eye, and a tooth for a tooth; but I say unto you, that ye shall not resist evil, but whosoever shall smite thee on thy right cheek, turn to him the other also; and if any man will sue thee at the law, and take away thy coat, let him have thy cloak also. And whosoever shall compel thee to go a mile, go with him twain.

Give to him that asketh thee, and from him that would borrow of thee turn thou not away. And behold it is written also, that thou shalt love thy neighbor and hate thine enemy; but behold I say unto you, love your enemies, bless them that curse you, do good to them that hate you, and pray for them who despitefully use you and persecute you; that ye may be the children of your Father who is in heaven; for He maketh His sun to rise on the evil and on the good.

Therefore those things which were of old time, which were under the law, in me are all fulfilled. Old things are done away, and all things have become new. Therefore, I would that ye should be perfect even as I, or your Father who is in heaven is perfect.

3 NEPHI 13

Sermon at the Temple—Lord's Prayer

Verily, verily, I say that I would that ye should do alms unto the poor; but take heed that ye do not your alms before men, to be seen of them; otherwise ye have no reward of your Father who is in heaven. Therefore, when ye shall do your alms, do not sound a trumpet before you, as will hypocrites do in the synagogues, and in the streets, that they may have glory of men. Verily I say unto you, they have their reward. But when thou doest alms, let not thy left hand know what thy right hand doeth; that thine alms may be in secret; and thy Father who seeth in secret, Himself shall reward thee openly.

And when thou prayest, thou shalt not do as the hypocrites, for they love to pray, standing in the synagogues, and in the corners of the streets, that they may be seen of men. Verily, I say unto you, they have their reward. But thou, when thou prayest, enter into thy closet, and when thou hast shut thy door, pray to thy Father who is in secret; and thy Father, who seeth in secret, shall reward thee openly. But when ye pray, use not vain repetitions, as the heathen, for they think that they shall be heard for their much speaking. Be not ye therefore like unto them, for your Father knoweth what things ye have need of before ye ask Him.

After this manner therefore pray ye: Our Father who art in heaven, hallowed be Thy name. Thy will be done on earth as it is in heaven. And forgive us our debts, as we forgive our debtors. And lead us not into temptation, but deliver us from evil. For Thine is the kingdom, and the power, and the glory, forever. Amen. For, if ye forgive men their trespasses, your Heavenly Father will also forgive you; but if ye forgive not men their trespasses, neither will your Father forgive your trespasses.

Moreover, when ye fast, be not as the hypocrites, of a sad countenance, for they disfigure their faces, that they may appear unto men to fast. Verily, I say unto you, they have their reward. But thou, when thou fastest, anoint thy head, and wash thy face; that thou appear not unto men to fast, but unto thy Father, who is in secret; and thy Father, who seeth in secret, shall reward thee openly.

Lay not up for yourselves treasures upon earth, where moth and rust doth corrupt, and thieves break through and steal; but lay up for yourselves treasures in heaven, where neither moth nor rust doth corrupt, and where thieves do not break through nor steal. For where your treasure is, there will your heart be also.

The light of the body is the eye; if, therefore, thine eye be single, thy whole body shall be full of light. But if thine eye be evil, thy whole body shall be full of darkness. If, therefore, the light that is in thee be darkness, how great is that darkness!

No man can serve two masters; for either he will hate the one, and love the other; or else he will hold to the one and despise the other. Ye cannot serve God and Mammon.

When Jesus had spoken these words, He looked upon the Twelve whom He had chosen, and said unto them,

Remember the words which I have spoken. For behold, ye are they whom I have chosen to minister unto this people. Therefore I say unto you, take no thought for your life, what ye shall eat, or what ye shall drink; nor yet for your body, what ye shall put on. Is not the life more than meat, and the body than raiment?

Behold the fowls of the air, for they sow not, neither do they reap nor gather into barns; yet your Heavenly Father feedeth them. Are ye not much better than they? Which of you by taking thought can add one cubit unto his stature? And why take ye thought for raiment? Consider the lilies of the field how they grow; they toil not, neither do they spin; and yet I say unto you, that even Solomon, in all his glory, was not arrayed like one of these.

Wherefore, if God so clothe the grass of the field, which today is, and tomorrow is cast into the oven, even so will He clothe you, if ye are not of little faith. Therefore take no thought, saying, What shall we eat? or, What shall we drink? or, Wherewithal shall we be clothed? For your Heavenly Father knoweth that ye have need of all these things. But seek ye first the kingdom of God and His righteousness, and all these things shall be added unto you. Take therefore no thought for the morrow, for the morrow shall take thought for the things of itself. Sufficient is the day unto the evil thereof.

3 NEPHI 14

Sermon at the Temple

When Jesus had spoken these words, He turned again to the multitude, and did open His mouth unto them again, saying,

Verily, verily, I say unto you, Judge not, that ye be not judged. For with what judgment ye judge, ye shall be judged; and with what measure ye mete, it shall be measured to you again.

And why beholdest thou the mote that is in thy brother's eye, but considerest not the beam that is in thine own eye? Or how wilt thou say to thy brother, Let me pull the mote out of thine eye; and behold, a beam is in thine own eye? Thou hypocrite, first cast the beam out of thine own eye; and then shalt thou see clearly to cast the mote out of thy brother's eye.

Give not that which is holy unto the dogs, neither cast ye your pearls before swine, lest they trample them under their feet, and turn again and rend you.

Ask, and it shall be given unto you; seek, and ye shall find; knock, and it shall be opened unto you. For everyone that asketh, receiveth; and he that seeketh, findeth; and to him that knocketh, it shall be opened.

Or what man is there of you, who,[*] if his son ask bread, will give him a stone? Or if he ask a fish, will he give him a serpent? If ye then, being evil, know how to give good gifts unto your children, how much more shall your Father who is in heaven give good things to them that ask Him? Therefore, all things whatsoever ye would that men should do to you, do ye even so to them, for this is the law and the prophets.

Enter ye in at the strait[*] gate; for wide is the gate, and broad is the way, which leadeth to destruction, and many there be who go in thereat; because strait[*] is the gate, and narrow is the way, which leadeth unto life, and few there be that find it.

Beware of false prophets, who come to you in sheep's clothing, but inwardly they are ravening wolves. Ye shall know them by their fruits. Do men gather grapes of thorns, or figs of thistles? Even so every good tree bringeth forth good fruit; but a corrupt tree bringeth forth evil fruit. A good tree cannot bring forth evil fruit, neither a corrupt tree bring forth good fruit. Every tree that bringeth not forth good fruit is hewn down, and cast into the fire. Wherefore, by their fruits ye shall know them.

Not everyone that saith unto me, Lord, Lord, shall enter into the kingdom of heaven; but he that doeth the will of my Father who is in heaven. Many will say to me in that day, Lord, Lord, have we not prophesied in Thy name, and in Thy name have cast out devils, and in Thy name done many wonderful works? And then will I profess unto them, I never knew you; depart from me, ye that work iniquity.

Therefore, whoso heareth these sayings of mine and doeth them, I will liken him unto a wise man, who built his house upon a rock. And the rain descended, and the floods came, and the winds blew, and beat upon that house; and it fell not; for it was founded upon a rock. And everyone that heareth these sayings of mine, and doeth them not, shall be likened unto a foolish man, who built his house upon the sand. And the rain descended, and the floods came, and the winds blew, and beat upon that house; and it fell, and great was the fall of it.

3 NEPHI 15

Law of Moses fulfilled—other sheep

When Jesus had ended these sayings, He cast His eyes on the multitude, and said,

Behold, ye have heard the things which I* taught before I ascended to my Father; therefore, whoso remembereth these sayings of mine, and doeth them, him will I raise up at the last day.

When Jesus had said these words, He perceived that there were some among them who marveled, and wondered what He would concerning the law of Moses; for they understood not the saying that old things had passed away, and that all things had become new. And He said unto them,

Marvel not that I said unto you that old things had passed away, and that all things had become new. Behold, I say unto you that the law is fulfilled that was given unto Moses. Behold, I am He that gave the law, and I am He who covenanted with my people Israel; therefore, the law in me is fulfilled, for I have come to fulfil the law; therefore it hath an end.

Behold, I do not destroy the prophets, for as many as have not been fulfilled in me, verily I say unto you, shall all be fulfilled. And because I said unto you that old things have passed away, I do not destroy that which hath been spoken concerning things which are to come. For behold, the covenant which I have made with my people is not all fulfilled; but the law which was given unto Moses hath an end in me.

Behold, I am the Law, and the Light. Look unto me, and endure to the end, and ye shall live; for unto him that endureth to the end will I give eternal life. Behold, I have given unto you the commandments; therefore keep my commandments. And this is the law and the prophets, for they truly testified of me.

When Jesus had spoken these words, He said unto those twelve whom he had chosen,

Ye are my disciples; and ye are a light unto this people, who are a remnant of the house of Joseph. And behold, this is the land of your inheritance; and the Father hath given it unto you. And not at any time hath the Father given me commandment that I should tell it unto your brethren at Jerusalem. Neither at any time hath the Father given me commandment that I should tell unto them concerning the other tribes of the house of Israel, whom the Father hath led away out of the land. This much did the Father command me, that I should tell unto them, That other sheep I have, which are not of this fold; them also I must bring, and they shall hear my voice; and there shall be one fold, and one shepherd.

And now, because of stiffneckedness and unbelief they understood not my word; therefore, I was commanded to say no more of the Father concerning this thing unto them. But, verily, I say unto you that the Father hath commanded me, and I tell it unto you, that ye were separated from among them because of their iniquity; therefore, it is because of their iniquity that they know not of you.

And verily, I say unto you again that the other tribes hath the Father separated from them; and it is because of their iniquity that they know not of them. And verily, I say unto you, that ye are they of whom I said, Other sheep I have which are not of this fold; them also I must bring, and they shall hear my voice; and there shall be one fold, and one shepherd.

And they understood me not, for they supposed it had been the Gentiles; for they understood not that the Gentiles should be converted through their preaching. And they understood me not that I said they shall hear my voice; and they understood me not that the Gentiles should not at any time hear my voice; that I should not manifest myself unto them, save it were by the Holy Ghost. But behold, ye have both heard my voice, and seen me; and ye are my sheep, and ye are numbered among those whom the Father hath given me.

3 NEPHI 16

Other sheep—gospel to Gentiles and house of Israel

And verily, verily, I say unto you that I have other sheep, which are not of this land; neither of the land of Jerusalem; neither in any parts of that land round about, whither I have been to minister. For they of whom I speak, are they who have not as yet heard my voice; neither have I at any time manifested myself unto them. But I have received a commandment of the Father, that I shall go unto them, and that they shall hear my voice, and shall be numbered among my sheep, that there may be one fold, and one shepherd; therefore I go to show myself unto them.

And I command you that ye shall write these sayings after I am gone, that if it so be that my people at Jerusalem, they who have seen me, and been with me in my ministry, do not ask the Father in my name, that they may receive a knowledge of you by the Holy Ghost, and also of the other tribes whom they know not of, that these sayings which ye shall write, shall be kept and shall be manifested unto the Gentiles, that through the fulness of the Gentiles, the remnant of their seed, who shall be scattered forth upon the face of the earth because of their unbelief, may be brought in, or may be brought to a knowledge of me, their Redeemer.

And then will I gather them in from the four quarters of the earth; and then will I fulfil the covenant which the Father hath made unto all the people of the house of Israel. And blessed are the Gentiles, because of their belief in me, in and of the Holy Ghost, which witnesses* unto them, of me and of the Father. Behold, because of their belief in me, saith the Father, and because of the unbelief of you, O house of Israel, in the latter day shall the truth come unto the Gentiles, that the fulness of these things shall be made known unto them.

But woe, saith the Father, unto the unbelieving of the Gentiles, for notwithstanding they have come forth upon the face of this land, and have scattered my people, who are of the house of Israel; and my people who are of the house of Israel have been cast out from among them, and have been trodden under feet by them; and because of the mercies of the Father unto the Gentiles, and also the judgments of the Father upon my people, who are of the house of Israel, verily, verily, I say unto you, that after all this, and I have caused my people who are of the house of Israel, to be smitten, and to be afflicted, and to be slain, and to be cast out from among them, and to become hated by them, and to become a hiss and a byword among them. And thus commandeth the Father that I should say unto you:

At that day when the Gentiles shall sin against my gospel, and shall reject the fulness of my gospel,* and shall be lifted up in the pride of their hearts above all nations, and above all the people of the whole earth, and shall be filled with all manner of lyings, and of deceits, and of mischiefs, and all manner of hypocrisy, and murders, and priestcrafts, and whoredoms, and of secret abominations; and if they shall do all those things, and shall reject the fulness of my gospel, behold, saith the Father, I will bring the fulness of my gospel from among them.

And then will I remember my covenant which I have made unto my people, O house of Israel, and I will bring my gospel unto them. And I will show unto thee, O house of Israel, that the Gentiles shall not have power over you; but I will remember my covenant unto you, O house of Israel, and ye shall come unto the knowledge of the fulness of my gospel.

But if the Gentiles will repent and return unto me, saith the Father, behold they shall be numbered among my people, O house of Israel. And I will not suffer my people, who are of the house of Israel, to go through among them, and tread them down, saith the Father. But if they will not turn unto me, and hearken unto my voice, I will suffer them, yea, I will suffer my people, O house of Israel, that they shall go through among them, and shall tread them down, and they shall be as salt that hath lost its savor, which is thenceforth good for nothing, but to be cast out, and to be trodden under foot of my people, O house of Israel.

Verily, verily, I say unto you, thus hath the Father commanded me, that I should give unto this people this land for their inheritance. And then the words of the prophet Isaiah shall be fulfilled, which say, Thy watchmen shall lift up the voice; with the voice together shall they sing, for they shall see eye to eye, when the Lord shall bring again Zion.

Break forth into joy, sing together, ye waste places of Jerusalem; for the Lord hath comforted His people, He hath redeemed Jerusalem. The Lord hath made bare His holy arm in the eyes of all the nations; and all the ends of the earth shall see the salvation of God.

3 NEPHI 17

Asks people to ponder His words—heals afflicted—
prays words that cannot be written—blesses little children

When Jesus had spoken these words He looked round about again on the multitude, and He said unto them,

Behold, my time is at hand. I perceive that ye are weak, that ye cannot understand all my words which I am commanded of the Father to speak unto you at this time. Therefore, go ye unto your homes, and ponder upon the things which I have said, and ask of the Father, in my name, that ye may understand, and prepare your minds for the morrow, and I come unto you again. But now I go unto the Father, and also to show myself unto the lost tribes of Israel, for they are not lost unto the Father, for He knoweth whither He hath taken them.

When Jesus had thus spoken, He cast His eyes round about again on the multitude, and beheld they were in tears, and did look steadfastly upon Him, as if they would ask Him to tarry a little longer with them. And He said unto them,

Behold, my bowels are filled with compassion towards you. Have ye any that are sick among you? Bring them hither. Have ye any that are lame, or blind, or halt, or maimed, or leprous, or that are withered, or that are deaf, or that are afflicted in any manner? Bring them hither and I will heal them, for I have compassion upon you; my bowels are filled with mercy. For I perceive that ye desire that I should show unto you what I have done unto your brethren at Jerusalem, for I see that your faith is sufficient that I should heal you.

When He had thus spoken, all the multitude, with one accord, did go forth with their sick and their afflicted, and their lame, and with their blind, and with their dumb, and with all them that were afflicted in any manner; and He did heal them every one as they were brought forth unto Him. And they did all, both they who had been healed and they who were whole, bow down at His feet, and did worship Him; and as many as could come for the multitude did kiss His feet, insomuch that they did bathe His feet with their tears.

He commanded that their little children should be brought. So they brought their little children and set them down upon the ground round about Him, and Jesus stood in the midst; and the multitude gave way till they had all been brought unto Him. And when they had all been brought, and Jesus stood in the midst, He commanded the multitude that they should kneel down upon the ground. When they had knelt upon the ground, Jesus groaned within Himself, and said,

Father, I am troubled because of the wickedness of the people of the house of Israel.

When He had said these words, He Himself also knelt upon the earth; and behold He prayed unto the Father, and the things which He prayed cannot be written, and the multitude did bear record who heard Him. And after this manner do they bear record: The eye hath never seen, neither hath the ear heard, before, so great and marvelous things as we saw and heard Jesus speak unto the Father; and no tongue can speak, neither can there be written by any man, neither can the hearts of men conceive so great and marvelous things as we both saw and heard Jesus speak; and no one can conceive of the joy which filled our souls at the time we heard Him pray for us unto the Father.

When Jesus had made an end of praying unto the Father, He arose; but so great was the joy of the multitude that they were overcome. Jesus spake unto them, and bade them arise. And they arose from the earth, and He said unto them,

Blessed are ye because of your faith. And now behold, my joy is full.

And when He had said these words, He wept, and the multitude bare record of it, and He took their little children, one by one, and blessed them, and prayed unto the Father for them.

And when He had done this He wept again; and He spake unto the multitude, and said unto them,

Behold your little ones.

And as they looked to behold, they cast their eyes towards heaven, and they saw the heavens open, and they saw angels descending out of heaven as it were in the midst of fire; and they came down and encircled those little ones about; and they were encircled about with fire; and the angels did minister unto them. The multitude did see and hear and bear record; and they know that their record is true, for they all of them did see and hear, every man for himself; and they were in number about two thousand and five hundred souls; and they did consist of men, women, and children.

3 NEPHI 18

Sacrament—pray always—meet often—forbid unworthy—
gives power to give Holy Ghost—ascends into heaven

Jesus commanded His disciples that they should bring forth some bread and wine unto Him. And while they were gone for bread and wine, He commanded the multitude that they should sit themselves down upon the earth. And when the disciples had come with bread and wine, He took of the bread, and brake and blessed it; and He gave unto the disciples and commanded that they should eat. And when they had eaten and were filled, He commanded that they should give unto the multitude.*

When the multitude had eaten, He said unto the disciples,

Behold, there shall one be ordained among you, and to him will I give power that he shall break bread, and bless it, and give it unto the people of my church, unto all those who shall believe and be baptized in my name. And this shall ye always observe to do, even as I have done, even as I have broken bread, and blessed it, and given* it unto you. And this shall ye do in remembrance of my body, which I have shown unto you. And it shall be a testimony unto the Father, that ye do always remember me. And if ye do always remember me, ye shall have my Spirit to be with you.

When He said these words, He commanded His disciples that they should take of the wine of the cup, and drink of it, and that they should also give unto the multitude, that they might drink of it. They did so, and did drink of it, and were filled; and they gave unto the multitude, and they did drink, and they were filled. And when the disciples had done this, Jesus said,

Blessed are ye for this thing which ye have done, for this is fulfilling my commandments, and this doth witness unto the Father that ye are willing to do that which I have commanded you. And this shall ye always do to those who repent and are baptized in my name; and ye shall do it in remembrance of my blood, which I have shed for you, that ye may witness unto the Father that ye do always remember me. And if ye do always remember me, ye shall have my Spirit to be with you.

And I give unto you a commandment that ye shall do these things. And if ye shall always do these things, blessed are ye, for ye are built upon my rock. But whoso among you shall do more or less than these are not built upon my rock, but are built upon a sandy foundation; and when the rain descends, and the floods come, and the winds blow, and beat upon them, they shall fall, and the gates of hell are ready open to receive them.

Therefore, blessed are ye if ye shall keep my commandments, which the Father hath commanded me that I should give unto you. Verily, verily, I say unto you, ye must watch and pray always, lest ye be tempted by the devil, and ye be* led away captive by him. And as I have prayed among you, even so shall ye pray in my church, among my people who do repent and are baptized in my name. Behold, I am the Light; I have set an example for you.

When Jesus had spoken these words unto His disciples, He turned again unto the multitude and said unto them,

Behold, verily, verily, I say unto you, ye must watch and pray always, lest ye enter into temptation; for Satan desireth to have you; that he may sift you as wheat. Therefore, ye must always pray unto the Father in my name; and whatsoever ye shall ask the Father in my name, which is right, believing that ye shall receive, behold it shall be given unto you. Pray in your families unto the Father, always in my name, that your wives and your children may be blessed.

And behold, ye shall meet together oft; and ye shall not forbid any man from coming unto you when ye shall meet together, but suffer them that they may come unto you and forbid them not; but ye shall pray for them, and shall not cast them out; and if it so be that they come unto you oft, ye shall pray for them unto the Father, in my name.

Therefore, hold up your light that it may shine unto the world. Behold I am the Light which ye shall hold up—that which ye have seen me do. Behold, ye see that I have prayed unto the Father, and ye all have witnessed; and ye see that I have commanded that none of you should go away, but rather have commanded that ye should come unto me, that ye might feel and see; even so shall ye do unto the world; and whosoever breaketh this commandment, suffereth himself to be led into temptation.

When Jesus had spoken these words, He turned His eyes again upon the disciples whom He had chosen, and said unto them,

Behold verily, verily, I say unto you, I give unto you another commandment, and then I must go unto my Father, that I may fulfil other commandments which He hath given me. And now behold, this is the commandment which I give unto you, that ye shall not suffer anyone knowingly, to partake of my flesh and blood unworthily, when ye shall minister it; for whoso eateth and drinketh my flesh and blood unworthily, eateth and drinketh damnation to his soul; therefore if ye know that a man is unworthy to eat and drink of my flesh and blood ye shall forbid him.

Nevertheless, ye shall not cast him out from among you, but ye shall minister unto him, and shall pray for him unto the Father, in my name; and if it so be that he repenteth, and is baptized in my name, then shall ye receive him, and shall minister unto him of my flesh and blood. But if he repent not, he shall not be numbered among my people, that he may not destroy my people, for behold I know my sheep, and they are numbered. Nevertheless, ye shall not cast him out of your synagogues, or your places of worship, for unto such shall ye continue to minister; for ye know not but what they will return and repent, and come unto me with full purpose of heart, and I shall heal them, and ye shall be the means of bringing salvation unto them.

Therefore, keep these sayings which I have commanded you that ye come not under condemnation; for woe unto him whom the Father condemneth. And I give you these commandments because of the disputations which have been among you. And blessed are ye if ye have no disputations among you. And now I go unto the Father, because it is expedient that I should go unto the Father, for your sakes.

When Jesus had made an end of these sayings, He touched with His hand the disciples whom He had chosen, one by one, even until He had touched them all, and spake unto them as He touched them. And the multitude heard not the words which He spake, therefore they did not bear record; but the disciples bare record that He gave them power to give the Holy Ghost. And I will show unto you hereafter that this record is true.*

When Jesus had touched them all, there came a cloud and overshadowed the multitude, that they could not see Jesus. And while they were overshadowed, He departed from them, and ascended into heaven. And the disciples saw and did bear record that He ascended again into heaven.

3 NEPHI 19

Twelve teaches multitude, are baptized and receive Holy Ghost—Jesus returns—disciples pray—Jesus prays unspeakable words

When Jesus had ascended into heaven, the multitude did disperse, and every man did take his wife and his children and did return to his own home. And it was noised abroad among the people immediately, before it was yet dark, that the multitude had seen Jesus, and that He had ministered unto them, and that He would also show Himself on the morrow unto the multitude. Yea, and even all the night it was noised abroad concerning Jesus; and insomuch did they send forth unto the people, that there were many, yea, an exceedingly great number did labor exceedingly all that night, that they might be on the morrow in the place where Jesus should show Himself unto the multitude.

On the morrow, when the multitude was gathered together, behold, Nephi and his brother whom He had raised from the dead, whose name was Timothy, and also his son, whose name was Jonas, and also Mathoni, and Mathonihah, his brother, and Kumen, and Kumenonhi, and Jeremiah, and Shemnon, and Jonas, and Zedekiah, and Isaiah (these were the names of the disciples whom Jesus had chosen) went forth and stood in the midst of the multitude.

And behold, the multitude was so great that they did cause that they should be separated into twelve bodies. The Twelve did teach the multitude; and behold, they did cause that the multitude should kneel down upon the face of the earth, and should pray unto the Father in the name of Jesus. The disciples did pray unto the Father also in the name of Jesus. And they arose and ministered unto the people.

And when they had ministered those same words which Jesus had spoken—nothing varying from the words which Jesus had spoken—behold, they knelt again and prayed to the Father in the name of Jesus. They did pray for that which they most desired; and they desired that the Holy Ghost should be given unto them. And when they had thus prayed, they went down unto the water's edge, and the multitude followed them. Nephi went down into the water and was baptized. And he came up out of the water and began to baptize. And he baptized all those whom Jesus had chosen.

When they were all baptized and had come up out of the water, the Holy Ghost did fall upon them, and they were filled with the Holy Ghost and with fire. And behold, they were encircled about as if it were by fire; and it came down from heaven, and the multitude did witness it, and did[*] bear record; and angels did come down out of heaven, and did minister unto them. While the angels were ministering unto the disciples, behold, Jesus came and stood in the midst and ministered unto them.

He spake unto the multitude, and commanded them that they should kneel down again upon the earth, and also that His disciples should kneel down upon the earth. When they had all knelt down upon the earth, He commanded His disciples that they should pray. And behold, they began to pray; and they did pray unto Jesus, calling Him their Lord and their God.

Jesus departed out of the midst of them, and went a little way off from them and bowed Himself to the earth, and said,

Father, I thank Thee that Thou hast given the Holy Ghost unto these whom I have chosen; and it is because of their belief in me that I have chosen them out of the world. Father, I pray Thee that Thou wilt give the Holy Ghost unto all them that shall believe in their words. Father, Thou hast given them the Holy Ghost because they believe in me; and Thou seest that they believe in me because Thou hearest them, and they pray unto me; and they pray unto me because I am with them. And now Father, I pray unto Thee for them, and also for all those who shall believe on their words, that they may believe in me, that I may be in them as Thou, Father, art in me, that we may be one.

When Jesus had thus prayed unto the Father, He came unto His disciples, and behold, they did still continue, without ceasing, to pray unto Him; and they did not multiply many words, for it was given unto them what they should pray, and they were filled with desire. Jesus blessed them as they did pray unto Him, and His countenance did smile upon them, and the light of His countenance did shine upon them, and behold they were as white as the countenance and also the garments of Jesus; and behold the whiteness thereof did exceed all the whiteness, yea, even there could be nothing upon earth so white as the whiteness thereof. And Jesus said unto them,

Pray on.

Nevertheless, they did not cease to pray. And He turned from them again, and went a little way off and bowed Himself to the earth; and He prayed again unto the Father, saying,

Father, I thank Thee that Thou hast purified those whom I have chosen, because of their faith, and I pray for them, and also for them who shall believe on their words, that they may be purified in me, through faith on their words, even as they are purified in me. Father, I pray not for the world, but for those whom Thou hast given me out of the world, because of their faith, that they may be purified in me, that I may be in them as Thou, Father, art in me, that we may be one, that I may be glorified in them.

And when Jesus had spoken these words, He came again unto His disciples; and behold, they did pray steadfastly, without ceasing, unto Him: and He did smile upon them again; and behold, they were white, even as Jesus.

And He went again a little way off and prayed unto the Father; and tongue cannot speak the words which He prayed, neither can be written by man the words which He prayed. And the multitude did hear, and do bear record; and their hearts were open, and they did understand in their hearts the words which He prayed. Nevertheless, so great and marvelous were the words which He prayed that they cannot be written, neither can they be uttered by man.

When Jesus had made an end of praying He came again to the disciples, and said unto them,

So great faith have I never seen among all the Jews; wherefore I could not show unto them so great miracles, because of their unbelief. Verily I say unto you, there are none of them that have seen so great things as ye have seen; neither have they heard so great things as ye have heard.

3 NEPHI 20

Jesus provides bread and wine—sacrament—
Jesus is prophet of whom Moses spake—His people know His name

He commanded the multitude that they should cease to pray, and also His disciples. And He commanded them that they should not cease to pray in their hearts. And He commanded them that they should arise and stand up upon their feet. And they arose up and stood upon their feet.

He brake bread again, and blessed it, and gave to the disciples to eat. And when they had eaten He commanded them that they should break bread, and give unto the multitude. And when they had given unto the multitude, He also gave them wine to drink, and commanded them that they should give unto the multitude. Now, there had been no bread, neither wine, brought by the disciples, neither by the multitude; but He truly gave unto them bread to eat, and also wine to drink. And He said unto them,

He that eateth this bread, eateth of my body to his soul; and he that drinketh of this wine, drinketh of my blood to his soul; and his soul shall never hunger nor thirst, but shall be filled.

Now, when the multitude had all eaten and drunk, behold, they were filled with the Spirit; and they did cry out with one voice, and gave glory to Jesus, whom they both saw and heard.

When they had all given glory unto Jesus, He said,[*]

Behold, now I finish the commandment which the Father hath commanded me concerning this people, who are a remnant of the house of Israel. Ye remember that I spake unto you, and said that when the words of Isaiah should be fulfilled (behold they are written, ye have them before you, therefore search them); and verily, verily, I say unto you, that when they shall be fulfilled, then is the fulfilling of the covenant which the Father hath made unto His people, O house of Israel. And then shall the remnants, which shall be scattered abroad upon the face of the earth, be gathered in from the East, and from the West, and from the South, and from the North; and they shall be brought to the knowledge of the Lord their God, who hath redeemed them.

And the Father hath commanded me that I should give unto you this land, for your inheritance. And I say unto you, that if the Gentiles do not repent after the blessing which they shall receive, after they have scattered my people, then shall ye, who are a remnant of the house of Jacob, go forth among them; and ye shall be in the midst of them, who shall be many; and ye shall be among them as a lion among the beasts of the forest, and as a young lion among the flocks of sheep, who, if he goeth through, both treadeth down and teareth in pieces, and none can deliver.

Thy hand shall be lifted up upon thine adversaries, and all thine enemies shall be cut off. And I will gather my people together, as a man gathereth his sheaves into the floor. For I will make my people with whom the Father hath covenanted, yea, I will make thy horn iron, and I will make thy hoofs brass. And thou shalt beat in pieces many people; and I will consecrate their gain unto the Lord, and their substance unto the Lord of the Whole Earth. And behold, I am He who doeth it.

And it shall come to pass, saith the Father, that the sword of my justice shall hang over them at that day; and except they repent, it shall fall upon them, saith the Father, yea, even upon all the nations of the Gentiles. And it shall come to pass that I will establish my people, O house of Israel. And behold, this people will I establish in this land, unto the fulfilling of the covenant which I made with your father Jacob; and it shall be a New Jerusalem. And the powers of heaven shall be in the midst of this people; yea, even I will be in the midst of you.

Behold, I am He of whom Moses spake, saying, A prophet shall the Lord your God raise up unto you of your brethren, like unto me; Him shall ye hear in all things whatsoever He shall say unto you. And it shall come to pass that every soul who will not hear that prophet shall be cut off from among the people. Verily, I say unto you, yea, and all the prophets from Samuel, and those that follow after, as many as have spoken, have testified of me.

And behold, ye are the children of the prophets; and ye are of the house of Israel; and ye are of the covenant which the Father made with your fathers, saying unto Abraham, And in thy seed shall all the kindreds of the earth be blessed. The Father having raised me up unto you first, and sent me to bless you, in turning away every one of you from his iniquities; and this because ye are the children of the covenant. And after that ye were blessed, then fulfilleth the Father the covenant which He made with Abraham, saying, In thy seed shall all the kindreds of the earth be blessed, unto the pouring out of the Holy Ghost through me upon the Gentiles, which blessing upon the Gentiles shall make them mighty above all, unto the scattering of my people, O house of Israel.

And they shall be a scourge unto the people of this land. Nevertheless, when they shall have received the fulness of my gospel, then if they shall harden their hearts against me, I will return their iniquities upon their own heads, saith the Father. And I will remember the covenant which I have made with my people; and I have covenanted with them that I would gather them together in mine own due time; that I would give unto them again the land of their fathers, for their inheritance, which is the land of Jerusalem, which is the promised land unto them forever, saith the Father.

And it shall come to pass that the time cometh, when the fulness of my gospel shall be preached unto them; and they shall believe in me, that I am Jesus Christ, the Son of God, and shall pray unto the Father in my name. Then shall their watchmen lift up their voice, and with the voice together shall they sing; for they shall see eye to eye. Then will the Father gather them together again, and give unto them Jerusalem for the land of their inheritance. Then shall they break forth into joy—Sing together, ye waste places of Jerusalem; for the Father hath comforted His people, He hath redeemed Jerusalem.

The Father hath made bare His holy arm in the eyes of all the nations; and all the ends of the earth shall see the salvation of the Father; and the Father and I are one. And then shall be brought to pass that which is written: Awake, awake again, and put on thy strength, O Zion; put on thy beautiful garments, O Jerusalem, the holy city, for henceforth there shall no more come into thee the uncircumcised and the unclean. Shake thyself from the dust; arise, sit down, O Jerusalem; loose thyself from the bands of thy neck, O captive daughter of Zion. For thus saith the Lord, Ye have sold yourselves for naught; and ye shall be redeemed without money.

Verily, verily, I say unto you, that my people shall know my name; yea, in that day they shall know that I am He that doth speak. And then shall they say, How beautiful upon the mountains are the feet of Him that bringeth good tidings unto them that publisheth peace; that bringeth good tidings unto them of good, that publisheth salvation; that saith unto Zion, Thy God reigneth! And then shall a cry go forth, Depart ye, depart ye, go ye out from thence, touch not that which is unclean; go ye out of the midst of her; be ye clean that bear the vessels of the Lord. For ye shall not go out with haste, nor go by flight; for the Lord will go before you, and the God of Israel shall be your rearward.

Behold, my servant shall deal prudently; he shall be exalted and extolled, and be very high. As many were astonished at thee (his visage was so marred, more than any man, and his form more than the sons of men); so shall he sprinkle many nations: the kings shall shut their mouths at him, for that which had not been told them shall they see; and that which they had not heard shall they consider.

Verily, verily, I say unto you, all these things shall surely come, even as the Father hath commanded me. Then shall this covenant which the Father hath covenanted with His people be fulfilled; and then shall Jerusalem be inhabited again with my people, and it shall be the land of their inheritance.

3 NEPHI 21

Free people established—unrepentant Gentiles cut off—
New Jerusalem—dispersed people gathered

And, verily, I say unto you, I give unto you a sign, that ye may know the time when these things shall be about to take place, that I shall gather in, from their long dispersion, my people, O house of Israel, and shall establish again among them my Zion. And behold, this is the thing which I will give unto you for a sign, for verily I say unto you, that when these things which I declare unto you, and which I shall declare unto you hereafter of myself, and by the power of the Holy Ghost which shall be given unto you of the Father, shall be made known unto the Gentiles, that they may know concerning this people who are a remnant of the house of Jacob, and concerning this my people who shall be scattered by them;

Verily, verily, I say unto you, when these things shall be made known unto them of the Father, and shall come forth of the Father, from them unto you; for it is wisdom in the Father that they should be established in this land, and be set up as a free people by the power of the Father, that these things might come forth from them unto a remnant of your seed, that the covenant of the Father may be fulfilled which He hath covenanted with His people, O house of Israel;

Therefore, when these works, and the works which shall be wrought among you hereafter, shall come forth from the Gentiles, unto your seed, which shall dwindle in unbelief because of iniquity; for thus it behooveth the Father that it should come forth from the Gentiles, that He may show forth His power unto the Gentiles, for this cause, that the Gentiles, if they will not harden their hearts, that they may repent and come unto me, and be baptized in my name, and know of the true points of my doctrine, that they may be numbered among my people, O house of Israel; and when these things come to pass, that thy seed shall begin to know these things, it shall be a sign unto them, that they may know that the work of the Father hath already commenced unto the fulfilling of the covenant which He hath made unto the people who are of the house of Israel.

And when that day shall come, it shall come to pass that kings shall shut their mouths; for that which had not been told them shall they see; and that which they had not heard shall they consider. For in that day, for my sake shall the Father work a work, which shall be a great and a marvelous work among them; and there shall be among them those[*] who will not believe it, although a man shall declare it unto them.

But behold, the life of my servant shall be in my hand; therefore they shall not hurt him, although he shall be marred because of them. Yet I will heal him, for I will show unto them that my wisdom is greater than the cunning of the devil. Therefore it shall come to pass, that whosoever will not believe in my words, who am Jesus Christ, which[*] the Father shall cause him to bring forth unto the Gentiles, and shall give unto him power that he shall bring them forth unto the Gentiles (it shall be done even as Moses said), they shall be cut off from among my people who are of the covenant.

And my people who are a remnant of Jacob, shall be among the Gentiles, yea, in the midst of them as a lion among the beasts of the forest, as a young lion among the flocks of sheep, who, if he go through both treadeth down and teareth in pieces, and none can deliver. Their hand shall be lifted up upon their adversaries, and all their enemies shall be cut off.

Yea, woe be unto the Gentiles, except they repent; for it shall come to pass in that day, saith the Father, that I will cut off thy horses out of the midst of thee, and I will destroy thy chariots; and I will cut off the cities of thy land, and throw down all thy strongholds; and I will cut off witchcrafts out of thy land,[*] and thou shalt have no more soothsayers; thy graven images I will also cut off, and thy standing images out of the midst of thee, and thou shalt no more worship the works of thy hands; and I will pluck up thy groves out of the midst of thee; so will I destroy thy cities.

And it shall come to pass that all lyings, and deceivings, and envyings, and strifes, and priestcrafts, and whoredoms, shall be done away. For it shall come to pass, saith the Father, that at that day whosoever will not repent and come unto my Beloved Son, them will I cut off from among my people, O house of Israel; and I will execute vengeance and fury upon them, even as upon the heathen, such as they have not heard. But if they will repent and hearken unto my words, and harden not their hearts, I will establish my church among them, and they shall come in unto the covenant and be numbered among this the remnant of Jacob, unto whom I have given this land for their inheritance; and they shall assist my people, the remnant of Jacob, and also as many of the house of Israel as shall come, that they may build a city, which shall be called the New Jerusalem.

And then shall they assist my people that they may be gathered in, who are scattered upon all the face of the land, in unto the New Jerusalem. And then shall the power of heaven come down among them; and I also will be in the midst. And then shall the work of the Father commence at that day, even when this gospel shall be preached among the remnant of this people.

Verily I say unto you, at that day shall the work of the Father commence among all the dispersed of my people, yea, even the tribes which have been lost, which the Father hath led away out of Jerusalem. Yea, the work shall commence among all the dispersed of my people, with the Father, to prepare the way whereby they may come unto me, that they may call on the Father in my name. Yea, and then shall the work commence, with the Father, among all nations in preparing the way whereby His people may be gathered home to the land of their inheritance. And they shall go out from all nations; and they shall not go out in haste, nor go by flight, for I will go before them, saith the Father, and I will be their rearward.

3 NEPHI 22

Strengthen stakes—no weapon shall prosper (See Isaiah 54)

And then shall that which is written come to pass, Sing, O barren, thou that didst not bear; break forth into singing, and cry aloud, thou that didst not travail with child; for more are the children of the desolate than the children of the married wife, saith the Lord. Enlarge the place of thy tent, and let them stretch forth the curtains of thy habitations; spare not, lengthen thy cords and strengthen thy stakes; for thou shalt break forth on the right hand and on the left, and thy seed shall inherit the Gentiles, and make the desolate cities to be inhabited.

Fear not, for thou shalt not be ashamed; neither be thou confounded, for thou shalt not be put to shame; for thou shalt forget the shame of thy youth, and shalt not remember the reproach of thy youth, and shalt not remember the reproach of thy widowhood any more. For thy Maker, thy Husband, the Lord of Hosts is His name; and thy Redeemer, the Holy One of Israel; the God of the Whole Earth shall He be called.

For the Lord hath called thee as a woman forsaken and grieved in spirit, and a wife of youth, when thou wast refused, saith thy God. For a small moment have I forsaken thee, but with great mercies will I gather thee. In a little wrath I hid my face from thee for a moment, but with everlasting kindness will I have mercy on thee, saith the Lord thy Redeemer.

For this, the waters of Noah unto me, for as I have sworn that the waters of Noah should no more go over the earth, so have I sworn that I would not be wroth with thee. For the mountains shall depart and the hills be removed, but my kindness shall not depart from thee, neither shall the covenant of my peace be removed, saith the Lord that hath mercy on thee.

O thou afflicted, tossed with tempest, and not comforted! Behold, I will lay thy stones with fair colors, and lay thy foundations with sapphires. And I will make thy windows of agates, and thy gates of carbuncles, and all thy borders of pleasant stones. And all thy children shall be taught of the Lord; and great shall be the peace of thy children. In righteousness shalt thou be established; thou shalt be far from oppression for thou shalt not fear, and from terror for it shall not come near thee. Behold, they shall surely gather together against thee, not by me; whosoever shall gather together against thee shall fall for thy sake.

Behold, I have created the smith that bloweth the coals in the fire, and that bringeth forth an instrument for his work; and I have created the waster to destroy. No weapon that is formed against thee shall prosper; and every tongue that shall revile* against thee in judgment thou shalt condemn. This is the heritage of the servants of the Lord, and their righteousness is of me, saith the Lord.

3 NEPHI 23

Search prophets and words of Isaiah—
fulfillment of Samuel the Lamanite prophecies recorded

And now, behold, I say unto you, that ye ought to search these things. Yea, a commandment I give unto you, that ye search these things diligently; for great are the words of Isaiah. For surely he spake as touching all things concerning my people which are of the house of Israel; therefore, it must needs be that he must speak also to the Gentiles. And all things that he spake have been and shall be, even according to the words which he spake.

Therefore give heed to my words; write the things which I have told you; and according to the time and the will of the Father they shall go forth unto the Gentiles. And whosoever will hearken unto my words and repenteth, and is baptized, the same shall be saved. Search the prophets, for many there be that testify of these things.

When Jesus had said these words, He said again, after He had expounded all the scriptures unto them which they had received,

Behold, other scriptures I would that ye should write, that ye have not.

He said unto Nephi,

Bring forth the record which ye have kept.

And when Nephi had brought forth the records, and laid them before Him, He cast His eyes upon them and said,

Verily I say unto you, I commanded my servant Samuel, the Lamanite, that he should testify unto this people, that at the day that the Father should glorify His name in me that there were many saints who should arise from the dead, and should appear unto many, and should minister unto them. Was* it not so?

And His disciples answered Him, Yea, Lord, Samuel did prophesy according to Thy words, and they were all fulfilled. Jesus said,

How be it that ye have not written this thing, that many saints did arise and appear unto many, and did minister unto them?

Nephi remembered that this thing had not been written. Jesus commanded that it should be written; therefore it was written according as He commanded. When Jesus had expounded all the scriptures in one, which they had written, He commanded them that they should teach the things which He had expounded unto them.

3 NEPHI 24

Words of Malachi are written—tithes and offerings (See Malachi 3)

He commanded them that they should write the words which the Father had given unto Malachi, which He should tell unto them. After they were written, He expounded them. These are the words which He did tell unto them, saying,

Thus said the Father unto Malachi, Behold, I will send my messenger, and he shall prepare the way before me, and the Lord whom ye seek shall suddenly come to His temple, even the Messenger of the Covenant, whom ye delight in; behold, He shall come, saith the Lord of Hosts.

But who may abide the day of His coming? And who shall stand when He appeareth? For He is like a refiner's fire, and like fuller's soap. And He shall sit as a refiner and purifier of silver; and He shall purify the sons of Levi, and purge them as gold and silver, that they may offer unto the Lord an offering in righteousness. Then shall the offering of Judah and Jerusalem be pleasant unto the Lord, as in the days of old, and as in former years.

And I will come near to you to judgment; and I will be a swift witness against the sorcerers, and against the adulterers, and against false swearers, and against those that oppress the hireling in his wages, the widow and the fatherless, and that turn aside the stranger, and fear not me, saith the Lord of Hosts. For I am the Lord, I change not; therefore ye sons of Jacob are not consumed.

Even from the days of your fathers ye are gone away from mine ordinances, and have not kept them. Return unto me and I will return unto you, saith the Lord of Hosts. But ye said,* Wherein shall we return? Will a man rob God? Yet ye have robbed me. But ye say, Wherein have we robbed Thee? In tithes and offerings. Ye are cursed with a curse, for ye have robbed me, even this whole nation.

Bring ye all the tithes into the storehouse, that there may be meat in my house; and prove me now herewith, saith the Lord of Hosts, if I will not open you the windows of heaven, and pour you out a blessing, that there shall not be room enough to receive it. And I will rebuke the devourer for your sakes, and he shall not destroy the fruits of your ground; neither shall your vine cast her fruit before the time in the fields, saith the Lord of Hosts. And all nations shall call you blessed, for ye shall be a delightsome land, saith the Lord of Hosts.

Your words have been stout against me, saith the Lord. Yet ye say, What have we spoken against Thee? Ye have said, It is vain to serve God, and what doth it profit that we have kept His ordinances,* and that we have walked mournfully before the Lord of Hosts? And now we call the proud happy; yea, they that work wickedness are set up; yea, they that tempt God are even delivered.

Then they that feared the Lord spake often one to another, and the Lord hearkened and heard; and a book of remembrance was written before Him for them that feared the Lord, and that thought upon His name. And they shall be mine, saith the Lord of Hosts, in that day when I make up my jewels; and I will spare them, as a man spareth his own son that serveth him. Then shall ye return and discern between the righteous and the wicked, between him that serveth God, and him that serveth Him not.

3 NEPHI 25

Proud and wicked burned—Elijah binds hearts (See Malachi 4)

For behold, the day cometh that shall burn as an oven; and all the proud, yea, and all that do wickedly, shall be stubble; and the day that cometh shall burn them up, saith the Lord of Hosts, that it shall leave them neither root nor branch. But unto you that fear my name, shall the Son of Righteousness arise with healing in His wings; and ye shall go forth and grow up as calves in the stall. And ye shall tread down the wicked; for they shall be ashes under the soles of your feet in the day that I shall do this, saith the Lord of Hosts.

Remember ye the law of Moses, my servant, which I commanded unto him in Horeb for all Israel, with the statutes and judgments. Behold, I will send you Elijah the prophet before the coming of the great and dreadful day of the Lord; and he shall turn the heart of the fathers to the children, and the heart of the children to their fathers, lest I come and smite the earth with a curse.

3 NEPHI 26

Expounds beginning to the end—people's faith tried—children utter marvelous things

When Jesus had told these things, He expounded them unto the multitude; and He did expound all things unto them, both great and small. And He saith,

These scriptures, which ye had not with you, the Father commanded that I should give unto you; for it was wisdom in Him that they should be given unto future generations.

And He did expound all things, even from the beginning until the time that He should come in His glory; yea, even all things which should come upon the face of the earth, even until the elements should melt with fervent heat, and the earth should be wrapped together as a scroll, and the heavens and the earth should pass away; and even unto the great and last day, when all people, and all kindreds, and all nations and tongues shall stand before God, to be judged of their works, whether they be good or whether they be evil; if they be good, to the Resurrection of everlasting life; and if they be evil, to the Resurrection of damnation, being on a parallel, the one on the one hand and the other on the other hand, according to the mercy, and the justice, and the holiness which is in Christ, who was before the world began.*

And now there cannot be written in this book even a hundredth part of the things which Jesus did truly teach unto the people; but behold the plates of Nephi do contain the more part of the things which He taught the people. And these things have I written, which are a lesser part of the things which He taught the people; and I have written them to the intent that they may be brought again unto this people, from the Gentiles, according to the words which Jesus hath spoken.

And when they shall have received this, which is expedient that they should have first, to try their faith, and if it shall so be that they shall believe these things then shall the greater things be made manifest unto them. And if it so be that they will not believe these things, then shall the greater things be withheld from them, unto their condemnation.

Behold, I was about to write them all which were engraven upon the plates of Nephi, but the Lord forbade it, saying,*

I will try the faith of my people.

Therefore I, Mormon, do write the things which have been commanded me of the Lord. And now I, Mormon, make an end of my sayings, and proceed to write the things which have been commanded me.

Therefore, I would that ye should behold that the Lord truly did teach the people, for the space of three days; and after that, He did show Himself unto them oft, and did break bread oft, and bless it, and give it unto them. He did teach and minister unto the children of the multitude of whom hath been spoken, and He did loose their tongues, and they did speak unto their fathers great and marvelous things, even greater than He had revealed unto the people; and He loosed their tongues that they could utter.

After He ascended into heaven the second time that He showed Himself unto them, and had gone unto the Father, after having healed all their sick, and their lame, and opened the eyes of their blind and unstopped the ears of the deaf, and even had done all manner of cures among them, and raised a man from the dead, and had shown forth His power unto them, and had ascended unto the Father, behold, it came to pass on the morrow that the multitude gathered themselves together, and they both saw and heard these children; yea, even babes did open their mouths and utter marvelous things; and the things which they did utter were forbidden, that there should not any man write them.

The disciples whom Jesus had chosen, began from that time forth to baptize and to teach as many as did come unto them; and as many as were baptized in the name of Jesus, were filled with the Holy Ghost. And many of them saw and heard unspeakable things, which are not lawful to be written. And they taught, and did minister one to another; and they had all things common among them, every man dealing justly, one with another. They did all things, even as Jesus had commanded them. And they who were baptized in the name of Jesus were called the Church of Christ.

3 NEPHI 27

*Church named—gospel defined—judged out of books—
repent and be baptized—enter strait gate*

As the disciples of Jesus were journeying and were preaching the things which they had both heard and seen, and were baptizing in the name of Jesus, it came to pass that the disciples were gathered together and were united in mighty prayer and fasting. And Jesus again showed Himself unto them, for they were praying unto the Father, in His name; and Jesus came and stood in the midst of them, and said unto them,

What will ye that I shall give unto you?

And they said unto Him, Lord, we will that Thou wouldst tell us the name whereby we shall call this church; for there are disputations among the people concerning this matter. And the Lord said unto them,

Verily, verily, I say unto you, why is it that the people should murmur and dispute because of this thing? Have they not read the scriptures, which say ye must take upon you the name of Christ, which is my name? For by this name shall ye be called at the last day; and whoso taketh upon him my name, and endureth to the end, the same shall be saved at the last day.

Therefore, whatsoever ye shall do, ye shall do it in my name; therefore ye shall call the Church in my name; and ye shall call upon the Father in my name, that He will bless the Church for my sake. And how be it my church save it be called in my name? For if a church be called in Moses' name, then it be Moses' church; or if it be called in the name of a man, then it be the church of a man; but if it be called in my name, then it is my church, if it so be that they are built upon my gospel.

Verily I say unto you, that ye are built upon my gospel; therefore ye shall call whatsoever things ye do call, in my name; therefore if ye call upon the Father, for the Church, if it be in my name, the Father will hear you; and if it so be that the Church is built upon my gospel, then will the Father show forth His own works in it. But if it be not built upon my gospel, and is built upon the works of men, or upon the works of the devil, verily I say unto you, they have joy in their works for a season, and by and by the end cometh, and they are hewn down and cast into the fire, from whence there is no return. For their works do follow them, for it is because of their works that they are hewn down; therefore remember the things that I have told you.

Behold I have given unto you my gospel, and this is the gospel which I have given unto you, that I came into the world to do the will of my Father, because my Father sent me. And my Father sent me that I might be lifted up upon the cross; and after that I had been lifted up upon the cross, that I might draw all men unto me; that as I have been lifted up by men, even so should men be lifted up by the Father, to stand before me, to be judged of their works, whether they be good or whether they be evil; and for this cause have I been lifted up; therefore, according to the power of the Father, I will draw all men unto me, that they may be judged according to their works.

And it shall come to pass, that whoso repenteth and is baptized in my name, shall be filled; and if he endureth to the end, behold, him will I hold guiltless before my Father, at that day when I shall stand to judge the world. And he that endureth not unto the end, the same is he that is also hewn down and cast into the fire, from whence they can no more return, because of the justice of the Father. And this is the word which He hath given unto the children of men. And for this cause He fulfilleth the words which He hath given, and He lieth not, but fulfilleth all His words.

And no unclean thing can enter into His kingdom; therefore nothing entereth into His rest, save it be those who have washed their garments in my blood, because of their faith, and the repentance of all their sins, and their faithfulness unto the end.

Now this is the commandment: Repent, all ye ends of the earth, and come unto me and be baptized in my name, that ye may be sanctified by the reception of the Holy Ghost, that ye may stand spotless before me at the last day. Verily, verily, I say unto you, this is my gospel; and ye know the things that ye must do in my church; for the works which ye have seen me do that shall ye also do; for that which ye have seen me do even that shall ye do; therefore, if ye do these things, blessed are ye, for ye shall be lifted up at the last day.

Write the things which ye have seen and heard, save it be those which are forbidden. Write the works of this people, which shall be, even as hath been written, of that which hath been. For behold, out of the books which have been written, and which shall be written, shall this people be judged, for by them shall their works be known unto men. And behold, all things are written by the Father; therefore out of the books which shall be written, shall the world be judged.

And know ye that ye shall be judges of this people, according to the judgment which I shall give unto you, which shall be just. Therefore, what manner of men ought ye to be? Verily I say unto you, even as I am.

And now I go unto the Father. And verily I say unto you, whatsoever things ye shall ask the Father, in my name, shall be given unto you. Therefore, ask, and ye shall receive; knock, and it shall be opened unto you; for he that asketh, receiveth; and unto him that knocketh, it shall be opened.

And now, behold, my joy is great, even unto fulness, because of you, and also this generation; yea, and even the Father rejoiceth, and also all the holy angels, because of you and this generation; for none of them are lost. Behold, I would that ye should understand; for I mean them who are now alive of this generation; and none of them are lost; and in them I have fulness of joy.

But behold, it sorroweth me because of the fourth generation from this generation, for they are led away captive by him, even as was the son of perdition; for they will sell me for silver, and for gold, and for that which moth doth corrupt and which thieves can break through and steal. And in that day will I visit them, even in turning their works upon their own heads.

When Jesus had ended these sayings, He said unto His disciples,*

Enter ye in at the strait gate; for strait is the gate, and narrow is the way that leads to life, and few there be that find it; but wide is the gate, and broad the way which leads to death, and many there be that travel therein, until the night cometh, wherein no man can work.

3 NEPHI 28

Christ departs—Three disciples changed to minister until Judgment Day

When Jesus had said these words, He spake unto His disciples, one by one, saying unto them,

What is it that ye desire of me, after that I am gone to the Father?

And they all spake, save it were three, saying, We desire that after we have lived unto the age of man, that our ministry, wherein thou hast called us, may have an end, that we may speedily come unto Thee in Thy kingdom. And He said unto them,*

Blessed are ye because ye desired this thing of me; therefore, after that ye are seventy and two years old, ye shall come unto me in my kingdom; and with me ye shall find rest.

And when He had spoken unto them, He turned Himself unto the three, and said unto them,

What will ye that I should do unto you, when I am gone unto the Father?

And they sorrowed in their hearts, for they durst not speak unto Him the thing which they desired. And He said unto them,

Behold, I know your thoughts, and ye have desired the thing which John, my beloved, who was with me in my ministry, before that I was lifted up by the Jews, desired of me. Therefore, more blessed are ye, for ye shall never taste of death; but ye shall live to behold all the doings of the Father, unto the children of men, even until all things shall be fulfilled, according to the will of the Father, when I shall come in my glory, with the powers of heaven.

And ye shall never endure the pains of death; but when I shall come in my glory, ye shall be changed in the twinkling of an eye from mortality to immortality; and then shall ye be blessed in the kingdom of my Father. And again, ye shall not have pain while ye shall dwell in the flesh, neither sorrow save it be for the sins of the world; and all this will I do because of the thing which ye have desired of me, for ye have desired that ye might bring the souls of men unto me, while the world shall stand.

And for this cause ye shall have fulness of joy; and ye shall sit down in the kingdom of my Father; yea, your joy shall be full, even as the Father hath given me fulness of joy; and ye shall be even as I am, and I am even as the Father; and the Father and I are one; and the Holy Ghost beareth record of the Father and me; and the Father giveth the Holy Ghost unto the children of men, because of me.

When Jesus had spoken these words, He touched every one of them with His finger, save it were the three who were to tarry, and then He departed. And behold, the heavens were opened, and they were caught up into heaven, and saw and heard unspeakable things. And it was forbidden them that they should utter; neither was it given unto them power that they could utter the things which they saw and heard; and whether they were in the body or out of the body, they could not tell; for it did seem unto them like a transfiguration of them, that they were changed from this body of flesh into an immortal state, that they could behold the things of God.

But it came to pass that they did again minister upon the face of the earth; nevertheless, they did not minister of the things which they had heard and seen, because of the commandment which was given them in heaven. And now, whether they were mortal or immortal, from the day of their transfiguration, I know not; but this much I know, according to the record which hath been given; they did go forth upon the face of the land, and did minister unto all the people, uniting as many to the Church as would believe in their preaching; baptizing them, and as many as were baptized did receive the Holy Ghost.

About the Compilers

KENNETH O. LUTES was born in Illinois, about two hours from the city Joseph Smith called Nauvoo the Beautiful. More than thirty years passed before he learned the significance of Nauvoo and about the Prophet Joseph. While living in the San Francisco Bay area, Ken was introduced to the missionaries. They left a Book of Mormon with him. While reading it, he gained a testimony of The Church of Jesus Christ of Latter-day Saints and of Joseph Smith, and was baptized a few months later. From that time until today, the restored gospel has been a constant source of excitement and joy to him.

Prior to joining the Church, Ken graduated from West Point and completed a master's degree in electrical engineering at Texas A&M University. During his careers, he has worked for several well-known corporations, owned his own businesses, and lent his talents to the Church as he worked in the Temple, Family History, and Information Systems Departments.

Of his many callings, Ken treasures most the many years of working and serving in the temples of the Lord. He also especially enjoyed the ten years he spent as the director of the Jordan River Temple Grounds Tours, the three years he served on the high council of a Brigham Young University (BYU) married student stake, and serving in several bishoprics.

LYNDELL JOHNSON LUTES was born and raised in the San Francisco Bay area, but did not meet Ken until she was working for the Family History Department of the Church. She earned a bachelor's degree from the University of California at Santa Barbara and a master's degree in education from BYU, where she is currently working and completing her doctorate in instructional pyschology and technology.

Lyndell enjoys reading, singing, playing the piano, skiing, and travel. Her favorite callings have been teaching the Gospel Doctrine class and Relief Society, and serving in the stake Young Women presidency.